# Danny Daniels' Autobiography

## "THE BRIDGE TO THE BIBLE"

## Danny Daniels

# Danny Daniels' Autobiography

## "THE BRIDGE TO THE BIBLE"

## Danny Daniels

MILLIGAN BOOKS, INC.        BOOKS        CALIFORNIA

Printed and Bound in the United States of America
Published and Distributed by:
Milligan Books

Cover Design/Photography: Kevin Allen
Formatting: Milligan Books

Second Printing, September 2009
2 3 4 5 6 7 8 9 10


ISBN 978-0-9792016-1-5


The text book is composed in 12 pt. inch Franklin Gothic

Library of Congress Cataloging-in-Publication Data
Daniels, Danny
 Danny Daniels' Autobiography: The Bridge To The Bible, Danny Daniels
 p. cm.


1. Autobiography

---

Milligan Books, Inc.
1425 W. Manchester Ave., Suite C
Los Angeles, California 90047
www.milliganbooks.com
drrosie@aol.com
(323) 750-3592

# Special Message From The Author

It GIVES ME THE GREATEST pleasure to announce the release of my most recent contribution to the arts. After having spent years of my life in the film industry, and having now retired, I consider it my duty and of paramount importance to leave behind evidence of my achievements and contributions.

The accompanying manuscript, which has been crafted over the years, is presented in a unique way, which, unlike other artistic biographical works, unfolds my life's story in the first half and then encapsulates the inspirations I have received during my more recent spiritual encounters.

I have been advised that a manuscript of this contemporary art will make provocative reading for millions of literary connoisseurs around the world and as such, ought to be put in print. Therefore, at the encouragement of my friends and publisher, may I present to you *Danny Daniels' Autobiography: The Bridge to the Bible.*

# About the Author

DANNY DANIELS WAS BORN IN the city of Georgetown, British Guiana (renamed Guyana after independence). He now resides in Guyana, South America, where he designed and built the home which he promised God that he would build.

Danny, an author/actor, trained at the London School of Dramatic Arts. He has a host of credits attesting to his works.

## Screen Credits

*Flame in the Streets* • *Sapphire* • *Passionate Summer* • *Call Me Bwana* • *Woman of Straw* • *On the Fiddle* • *Prehistoric Women* • *The Oblong Box* • *The Mercenaries* • *One Plus One* • *Imperial Venus* • *Our Man in Havana* • *Thunder Run* • *Retribution* • *The Lamp* • *Ace Ventura, When Nature Calls* • *Naked Gun 33S! The Final Insult*

## Television Credits

*Man in a Suitcase* • *Crime Buster* • *Power Game* • *No Hiding Place* • *Emperor Jones* • *The Galloping Major* • *The Murder Club* • *Trouble Shooters* • *Diamond Crack Diamond* • *Washington Behind Closed Doors* • *The Fall Guy* • *The Favorite Son*

# Stage Credits

*Benito Serino * Jack of Spades * The Black Macbeth*

Danny has had the privilege to work with world-renown actors such as:

Sir Alex Guinness • Sir Ralph Richardson • Sean Connery • Roger Moore • Burl Ives • Cornel Wilde • Syver Sims • Charleston Heston • Richard Burton • Elizabeth Taylor • Jean Simmons • Victor Mature • Barbara Murray • Patrick Wymark • Rhodes Reason • Forrest Tucker • and many more

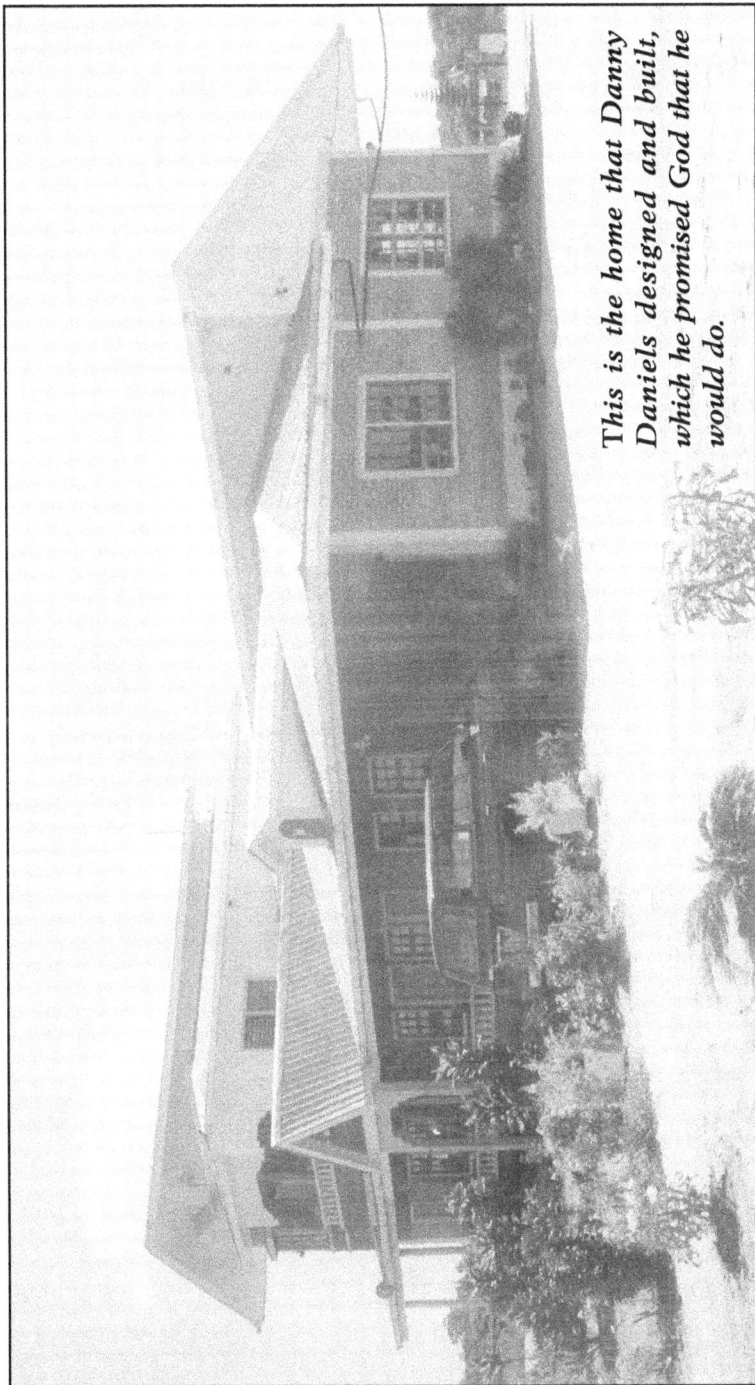

*This is the home that Danny Daniels designed and built, which he promised God that he would do.*

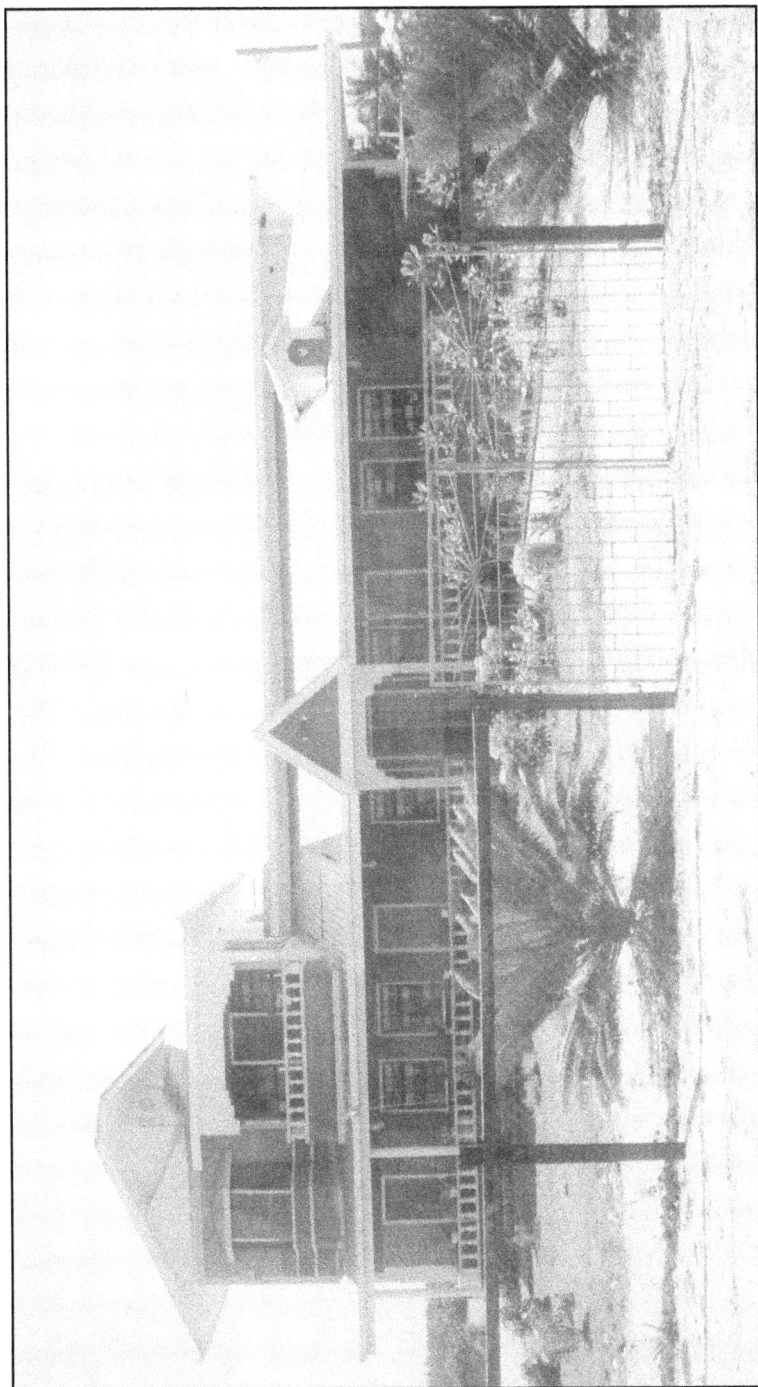

# Table of Contents

# Preface

THIS IS AN OUTSPOKEN BOOK. What it reveals is true, and will therefore arouse controversy.

The reader should approach the contents with a philosophic mind.

We live in a nuclear age, or one might call it. "The Atomic Age," "the age of Automation,' "The second Industrial Revolution," "The First Step Towards Third World," or "The Terrorist Intervention Against the World." Whatever the phase, the essential fact is that we are living in a time when one must be prepared to face reality and changes. Nothing stays the same forever. We are at a time when new scientific knowledge and techniques are profoundly changing the basis of our social lives, of relationships between man and man, between nation and nation. These changes coincide with vast political changes.

During my own lifetime, I have seen many forms of social aggression all over the world. Ever since I was a small boy, my mother used to say to me, "When one fails to face reality, one stands to be hurt by it." I have grown to realize that this is a fact!

What is human? God only knows. Human beings are mankind. Mankind is animal, as opposed to plants and mineral. Man is superior to the rest of the animal species due to his mental and physical capabilities. Yet man acts unmercifully, irrationally, and selfishly towards his fellow men.

Man does not have any general sense of purpose, regard, or respect in relationship to himself. Isn't that a shame? We are, at present, exploring other planets. Should we find life forms similar to our own on one of these planets, will we be able to unfastened their way of life, their point of view towards themselves, and at the same time, not try to change it? That will not be possible because, on our planet, we do not even try to understand ourselves. So how can we begin to extend ourselves?

We should first tidy up this planet. We should try to remedy all the human problems that we create, and nature's problems that have been created by nature, and are known to be against man.

Ever since the world began other animals were known to be man's, enemy, but man has, in fact, been his own worst enemy and quite often, the cause of his own destruction.

# My Parents in Brief

M Y PARENTS WERE BORN AFTER the main seed had been stolen from Nigeria, Africa. This I learned from my research. I found out that in 1736, a slave ship by the name of "Devil's Paradise" like other similar ships, brought my ancestors to British Guiana. On that occasion, the ship had sailed along the Nigerian Coastline heading towards Lagos, Nigeria. The ship was low on food and water. It was also low on the quantity of slaves needed for the shipment.

It was afternoon when the Devil's captain decided to drop the ship's anchor in the Bay of Lagos Island, which is now know as the capital of Lagos. The captain and crew of the Devil's Paradise rowed their boats ashore in order to get food and water. They also had to get more slaves to complete the full load.

When the captain and crew arrived in the village, they spoke to the chief requesting supplies of food and water. They also requested the assistance of some of the villagers to transport their items aboard.

The captain and chief of the village had established a barter system. An open invitation was also extended for members of the village to feast and celebrate aboard the ship. That of course, was a trap. Quite a lot of the villagers accepted the invitation, and went aboard in friendly spirits.

But as soon as everyone was aboard and the feast had started, the villagers became captives. The fighting began, shouts and screams followed as some of the villagers tried to escape by jumping over the side of the ship. However, in their bid to escape captivity, they landed in the sea and drowned because they were unable to swim or fight the tide in the sea. After a while, the captain and crew took control of the situation, and the unfortunate villagers were caught and put in bondage. They were chained and shackled to each other.

There was a little African boy by the name of Padan onboard. He was twelve years old, well built, and tall for his age. Padan was dark-complexioned and very good-looking with a charming personality. The boy's father and older brother were among those who jumped over the side of the ship and had died. Padan was now on his own at the tender age of twelve.

The "Devil's Paradise" lifted its anchor and raised its sails, and was bound on its long, slow voyage through the Atlantic to the West Indies, South America, and finally to British Guiana.

During the weeks that followed while the ship was heading towards the West Indies, the slaves endured a long and bitter ordeal with the sea and storms. The slaves were living in squalor, eating in the presence of their own filth and urine. The conditions were sordid indeed. Then God laid his hands on the vessel.

Plague hit the Devil's Paradise! The slaves started to die, one after the other. The sickness spread daily among the slaves in the ship's hatch. It became an epidemic that took the lives of a quarter of the slaves. Hundreds of them were lost. The ship's owners lost a lot of money as well because the epidemic was killing off their "black gold'. Now, this calamity, I believe, was sent by the Almighty as a divine punishment to those who were making money off the slave trade. It was a gross loss of human lives.

Finally, the ship dropped anchor in Essequibo Port and the unloading and counting of slaves was in progress. The slaves who survived the epidemic were inspected, given a clean bill of health, and a full count was made. Padan was among the lot.

An Englishman by the name of Daniels made the count. Danielstown, Essequibo was named after him- it was he who saw Padan among the other slaves during the count.

Mr. Daniels took an immediate liking for the twelve year old, Padan. This little Africa boy was to become Daniels' prized possession. The boy was taken away by Mr. Daniels and was brought up in Danielstown in the Daniels' household.

The relationship between Padan and Mr. Daniels started off with great contempt, because Padan resented his captivity from the moment he was captured as a slave. So when Daniels decided to change Padan's name to Alfred Daniels, Padan showed even more resentment and refused to obey or comply with this new name. Padan and Mr. Daniels' relationship was not an easy one. Daniels had his work cut out for him. Padan become more and more stubborn, refusing to yield, obey or comply. Mr. Daniels would say to Padan, "Your name is no longer Padan. From now on, your name is Alfred Daniels." Padan would shout with rage, " No! My name is Padan."

However, this kind of resentment went on for a short time only. Daniels was not the kind of man to be beaten easily. He decided to whip Padan each time he refused to respond to his new name, Alfred Daniels. He did so gradually. Mr. Daniels eventually began to educate Padan. He made it his duty to train him in the art of broiler maker on the sugar estate, which he became an expert, in no time. Padan, or rather Alfred, was a quick learner in whatever Mr. Daniels taught him. He no longer used the name Padan, but took the name Alfred Daniels.

By this time he had reached the age of twenty, Alfred Daniels fathered a son, whose name was Henry Daniels, out- of-wedlock (not married). He later left the child's mother and started a new relationship with another woman. They later married and had eight children-five boys and three girls. One of the boys was named after him, Henry Daniels Jr., who later had a son by the name of Manson Daniels.

Manson Daniels was my grandfather and his son, Eric Daniels, was my father

# 2

# *My Grandmother*

I HAVE WRITTEN OF MY parents in brief in two sections, one on my father and the other on my mother. I will commence this chapter by describing my maternal grandmother. My grandmother's maiden name was Martha Morris. She was from a poor family who were farmers. Martha was born in the early nineteenth century in Danielstown, Essequibo. Martha Morris became pregnant while attending school at the age of fifteen. In those days, a girl was looked down upon when she became pregnant while attending school. It was a disgrace for both the child and the parents. The fact that she was young and pregnant, not being married also added to the disgrace. As a result, she was rushed into marriage to soften the impact of the embarrassment. The boy, Jeremiah Ramsey, was attending the same school as well. Both parents, Jeremiah's and Martha's, had agreed on a small family marriage. His parents were farmers and were also very poor. Jeremiah was one year older than Martha. As one can well see, these two children lives were more or less doomed to poverty and deprivation. You will see this as I go along in this chapter.

Jeremiah and Martha ended up with five children in their marriage, all were girls - my mother was the eldest of the five, her name was Margaret. The other sisters were

Clarista, Ruby, Matilda, and Verna. Martha was 5 feet 7 inches tall, medium built, and bow-legged. She was very strict and serious with her children and grandchildren as well, regardless of their age. At times, her stern attitude was interpreted as cruelty. Martha's so-called cruelty was legacy handed down to her by the Dutch and British slave masters. These methods all became a way of life during Martha and Margaret's lifetime. Moreover, as time went by, these methods began to change. To Martha, this was a way of punishment to be executed upon her children or grandchildren also. Most of the slaves of African race experienced this type of treatment here in British Guiana at the time.

During the years of having to rear her children, life was a struggle for Martha. Her husband Jeremiah Ramsey, became sick and was confined to his bed. His working days were over. Martha had to carry the burden of raising her five girls. She became both father and mother to her children. Jeremiah had a habit of gambling, and one day he bet their house in a gamble and lost. A few days later, a gentleman came to Martha and claimed the house. She had no particular money of her own, and so was unable to purchase the house. They lost their home and ended up living in monthly rented property. Of course, that was quite difficult for her since she had a sick husband as well.

Other problems began to follow as well. Martha had a small farm of about two acres where she planted cash crops and vegetables. She also had a little stall in the market where she sold her crops to earn a living and support her family. She would sell in the market until her two eldest girls relieve her at the end of their school session.

Each day while they took turns, the other would accompany her to the farm to tend to the crops. They had to plant and reap to satisfy the demand of the market. However, on weekends, all the girls would go to the farm. On some occasions, one of the elder girls would go home after school to take care of the home, the smaller children, their sick father, and also to start the day's meal. This was a daily routine for the Ramsey Family. The younger children were given special duties in and around the house. Martha was a great taskmaster.

By this time Martha sensed that Jeremiah would not recover from his illness, she extended her production from farming to baking pastries, and making gravy browning, also called "cassava casreep". This was a preservative and a meat tenderizer, and was made from the root of the cassava plant.

Life was virtually a struggle, but more trouble was yet to come. Margaret Ramsey was having a secret affair with a boy by the name of Sergeant. He was a year older than she was. Margaret was fifteen at that time and had become pregnant. No one knew or sensed an affair between the two of them, not even friends, schoolmates, or her sisters. When she was about three months pregnant, it started to become evident, since her clothes were all becoming smaller. As the weeks went by, Martha noticed the changes in Margaret and began to pay close attention to her. After a few weeks, Martha decided to question Margaret, who quickly denied that she was pregnant.

When Margaret, my mother, described my grandmother's behavior to me, she was near tears as I sat listening to her. When Margaret said to her mother, "No, I am not pregnant." Martha flew into a rage, was wild and berserk, and she began to interrogate Margaret. "So you are calling me a fool and a liar! Girl, I can see your belly rising with a child, and you are telling me that you are not pregnant! All right, so you are not. We will see!"

A week later, she confronted Margaret again, but Margaret still refused to speak. Martha decided to put the Dutch and British slave masters' method of punishment into effect. Margaret was put to kneel on a grater as punishment. Martha stood nearby with a belt and continued to question her. She said, "You are playing a big woman, I will treat you like a big woman." Margaret started to scream when the first stroke from her father's belt landed on her. She continued to scream and fell off the grater as one stroke followed the other. She got on and promptly fell again as she felt the belt. As she lay on the floor, Martha raise the belt in mid-air and asked again, "Who is the father of this child you are carrying?" But Margaret would not say that she was pregnant, much less to say whom the father was. Martha stopped the whipping and continued talking.

"You are bringing disgrace upon me and this family, getting a child and only fifteen years old and in school as well." No matter how much I flog you, you will not tell me! This is called dumb insolence, impertinence, and impudence! Go and have a bath right now!"

Margaret rushed into the bathroom, and the household became quiet and peaceful.

Another week ended, and Martha decided to confront Margaret again. By this time, one could see that Margaret was bearing a child. It could no longer be kept a secret. She was about four-and-a-half months pregnant, and her stomach was well risen. She had reached the stage of being expelled from school. So Martha was summoned, and the sad news was given to her. She was upset and got into yet another rage with Margaret's attitude. Later that day, she went into the market to close the stall, and Margaret and Clarista were busy attending a customer. Martha reached under the stall and took out a large walking stick. She asked quietly, "Margaret, I keep asking you the same question day after day for the past month. I can't get head or tail out of you. Do you want me to go to jail for you?" By this time tears has begun to settle in Margaret's eyes. Martha continued, "Margaret, I am not going to keep asking, and I will kill you." Martha raised the stick, but Margaret quickly blocked the blow with both hands and started to scream.

It was a Friday afternoon, and the marketplace was very busy. As soon as the girls finished serving the customers, Martha closed the stall. The three of them headed towards home in silence. They were walking through some fields that led to their house. These fields were once a jungle, but over the years it was cleared in sections by small tracks and dirt roads. The distance home was about two miles and they were heading speedily and silently. It began to rain. It was one of those heavy tropical rainstorms. The thunder and lightning was awful. After the first mile, Martha dropped back behind the two girls. The girls were now walking ahead, Clarista in front of Margaret. Martha had dropped back purposefully, she had designed a new wave of attack on Margaret. By this time, Martha had caught up with Margaret by taking a short cut across the field. Martha jumped out on her from among the bushes and wielded the stick across Margaret's body. Margaret fell to the ground from the blow. She quickly tried to get up, but she slipped again into the mud. On her second attempt, she scrambled up and started to run, but her mother was just as fast even though their ages were seventeen years apart. Martha kept running closer to her daughter for the remaining part of the journey home, beating her all along the way. Clarista running behind them, shouting, "Stop Mamoo! Stop! You'll kill her."

Martha's children also called her Mamoo, everyone of them were slipping and sliding in the muddy fields now as the thunderstorm continued. The rain and lightning became unbearable as Margaret sped up the short hill ahead of them. Clarista followed and then behind her was Martha. All of the women looked greatly stressed and their bodies showed the exertion. The final stage of the journey had come to an end. Margaret ran to the back of the house and disappeared between the nearby fruit trees, and finally stopped under a mango tree-she sat and whispered quietly so as not be heard. In her mind the world seemed totally against her. She thought over the humiliating event at the market place in front of the shoppers, the weeks of interrogation, and the long journey home in the rain under the stick. As she thought of her new move, it is fair to say that the stick made little changes on her body, but no changes on her mind. She decided not ever to tell the boy's name and family. She wanted this to be her secret. She knew if she told her mother the boy's name, there would be a confrontation between the families. After that, a date for a marriage would be fixed and that thought presented great horrors for her. Margaret was not in love with the boy Sergeant. She further thought that all she had wanted was an early sample of the fruit of nature. Margaret was hoping to escape bearing the fruit of sex. The rain and wind were shaking the mango tree and the other surrounding trees.

Meanwhile, Clarista and Martha had reached up the hill and into the house. They stopped on the verandah, remove their muddy shoes and then disappeared into the house. My grandfather was catching up on his late afternoon sleep when the pair walked into the living room. He was awakened by the furious tone of Martha's move as she shouted to Clarista, " Go and find your sister, Clar, and tell her to come in here, otherwise, she will catch pneumonia, and I have no money to bury her."

Clar, as we called my aunt Clarista, went to find Margaret. Meanwhile, Martha enquired of her sick husband if he wanted anything to eat. My grandfather replied, "Woman, go and remove those wet clothes from your back before I have to bury you instead. Stop fussing about Margaret. What is done is done. The horse is already out of the stables."

By this time, Martha had walked into their bedroom to remove the wet clothes. She listened to Jeremiah as he talked and found her husband's statement very out of place. So she quickly replied, "This horse is not out the stable; this horse is in my barn! It looks as if she's in there for keeps and I will have to feed her. So, don't be talking like a mad man. I have to think like a woman." A short while later, Clar and Margaret came into the house. Martha decided not to persist in her manner towards Margaret in trying to learn the name of the baby's father. Martha conceived a new approach to the problem.

She decided to extract information from Clar instead. However, she failed to recognize the closeness between Clar and Margaret. Clar wouldn't betray her sister to no one. They were like peas in a pod, never to be separated. In any case, Martha had planned to play the game of criminal and detective. Martha said, "Clar, you come with me young woman, I will teach you not to keep secrets from me, you go and fetch those graters."

Clar knew the old slave master's punishment that was oftend executed on them so she burst into tears as she went to get the graters. Martha took Clar to the bedroom and instructed her to kneel on the graters. She then placed two glasses filled to the rim with drinking water in Clar's hands. Clar knelt on the graters and held the glasses. Her mother instructed her not to spill a drop and to stay there for half an hour. She then returned to Margaret and told her to remove her wet clothes and go to bed without supper.

Now, the Dutch slave masters introduced this grater punishment. Martha had been the recipient of such punishment and so had my mother and her sisters. If one drop of water was spilled, then the punishment would then be extended to whipping while still kneeling on the grater. Clar was very aware of this second punishment so she was taking full care not to spill a single drop from either of the glasses. Certainly the second part was very painful on the knees and the body. The half-hour had come to an end, and Mamoo returned to check for spillage. Fortunately, Clar did not spill any, she was told to go have her bath. Martha then went to Clarista and asked her, "Are you ready to tell me who Margaret's boyfriend is?" Clar replied, "Mamoo, I don't have any idea who he

11

is." Mamoo stood and watched Clar with a stern look and wondered what else to do. While Clar went away from the scene of the punishment, Verna and Matilda returned from school. There was no further questioning that night, only peace and quiet.

Mamoo by this time felt that she was losing the battle, so she decided to drop the issue for a while and deal with the immediate issues in the house and family affairs. Christmas was only "around the corner" as Mamoo saw it and she decided that she wanted her sick husband and the rest of the family to enjoy it.

Several months passed and the baby of Margaret and Sergeant was born on December 15th, 1923. Margaret had stopped seeing him many months before the birth of the child. She saw no need to continue the relationship. Her mother and her mother's friends had closely watched her. Also, she took no chances with her younger sisters in case they found out the boy's identity. They might tell her mother and that was the last thing she wanted. Further, Margaret had no desire to prolong the relationship since she had no intention of marrying Sergeant. She was not in love with him.

On the day of the baby's birth, Clar approached the father, Sergeant, while they were in school- this was unknown to Margaret. Clar told him of the bouncing baby and most importantly that if he, Sergeant, didn't come forward and disclose this to his mother, then she would do it. The boy Sergeant became flabbergasted. He stood with his mouth open for few seconds and stared at Clarista- he was speechless. Then after a while he said, "Alright, there is no need for you to do that, I will tell my parents."

Clar quickly butted in and said, "Today - not later." He simply nodded his head and walked away. The boy Sergeant did not take the chance of not telling his parents about Margaret and the child. He collected his wits as soon as he got home. Clar was with him as he told his

12

mother about Margaret and the child. She in turn told his father.

After that, Sergeant cursed the day he was born. His parents gave him a good hiding that he would long remember. They later showed up at Mamoo's house. Everything was discussed and settled between the parents. Everything including marriage in the future and the name of the child before the marriage. Margaret had been beaten again and again by her mother for being stubborn and not revealing Sergeant's identity herself. At last she was forced to tell Mamoo that she was not in love with the boy, so she was not going to marry him. But unfortunately, this decision only led to more beatings. It became so overbearing, that it drove Margaret and Clarista closer and closer together. They both ran away from home to the big city, Georgetown.

Martha was frantic and agitated and turned her wrath on her three remaining daughters. She questioned each of them, but in the end, she was convinced that they were not in the plot. So she rearranged all the household duties among all the remaining children and told herself that life must go on. She could not help wondering about her girls, Margaret and Claista - where they were and if they were being taken care of, were they getting proper meals and did they have a place to sleep. She blamed herself in part for their actions.

Meanwhile, Margaret and Clarista had started a new life in Georgetown. They did not have much money to start with, but a friend helped them by getting Clarista a job in a restaurant. Margaret learnt all about looking after her son, Donald Mc Kewan Sergeant. She did the housekeeping, cooking, sewing, and baking. Margaret finally decided to try her hand in making pastries and homemade bread, and buying and selling fruits and vegetables. She got a vending stall at the gateway where she was living on Leopold Street, so as to try and feed herself and son.

Most of the times under the moonlight we gather together for my mother to tell use her life story; we all ended up in tears.

# 3

## My Birth and Birthplace

I, DANNY DANIELS, WAS BORN on the 1st day of November in the year 1927. It was a Tuesday. The week begins on a Sunday. Therefore, from Sunday to Tuesday it is three days into that week. I have mentioned that little bit so you may get accustomed to the figure "3." I will deal with the "3" later in the book. It will be one of the great proofs of my genius-ship.

I was born in the public hospital in the city of Georgetown, British Guiana, renamed Guyana after Independence; it is located on the north eastern shoulder of South America. It is eighty three thousand square miles in area and the Atlantic sea coast stretches for two hundred and seventy miles, from the ocean, the land extend into the interior for about four hundred and fifty miles. Its boundaries meet those of Venezuela's in the west, Brazil's in the south, and Suriname's in the east. The country has four distinct geographical areas, or more recently known as natural regions - the low coastal plains, the forested area, the hilly sand and clay region, and the interior savannahs.

During the time when my mother Margaret gave birth to me in the Public Hospital, she was living at Lot 66 Leopold Street, Werk-en-Rust, Georgetown, Guyana, South America. Margaret was not married to Eric Daniels my father. So under British law, Margaret could not use my father's name to register my birth. So she named me Neville Ramsey. I was the third of my mother's children. Donald Mc Kewan Sargent and Reginald Aaron preceded me in the respective order. Margaret took me home from the hospital to 66 Leopold Street. My father, who was a seaman during that period, was away at sea.

An important bit I must mention here and now, so as to keep you the reader on track, is this. As I started to write this chapter about myself, the Almighty God gave me an inspiration to numbers. God inspired me to remove the 19 from 1927 and to total the two remaining numbers, which are 2 and 7. Now see what total you came up with, 2 and 7 equals 9. I was further inspired to keep doing that. The number 9 has 3 threes. It was as if I was being guided to pay attention to the number 3 or the numbers that produce 3s. My inspiration continued. I was guided to check what day of the week I was born. It was a Tuesday and that is the third day of the week, if one was to accept Sunday as the first day of the week. Furthermore, my mother's address was 66 Leopold Street. Now 6 has two 3s each and that is 12. Two and one is three. Well, God taught me by way of inspiration to use the various numbers and to add one number against the other, and I will come up with the three or threes.' When the Almighty gave me the inspiration to deal with the above numbers, I became terrified, because other numbers were given to me as well.

I was told by my aunt that Eric, my father, was a little perturbed because he was not at home during the time of my birth. On his return he said to Margaret, "You named him Neville Ramsey? Okay, I will name him, and we will christen him at the Trinity Methodist Church at the corner of High and Leopold Streets. I will name him Sylbert Vincent Daniels.

At the end of my direction; by the Almighty for me to examine the name, which Eric had given me. I was directed through divine inspiration to count the letters of the three names given to me by my father, and total the letters in each name. I did as I was directed and the number of letters in each name is 7. I came up with three sevens and three sevens are twenty-one and the digit 2 and 1 in the number twenty-one also total three.

# 4

## *Leopold Street*

**M**Y HOME AT LOT 66 Leopold Street was the first place, which was foremost in my mind, all the years I was growing up. I can recall events that took place as far back as two years old. Not that I could not remember living at other places. The fact was, Leopold Street and my childhood experiences at that address left me with events indelibly printed on my mind. The memories kept coming back from the subconscious mind, and at times are very impressionable on the conscious mind. I have tried many times to think of a place before living at Leopold Street and I just could not think of another. There was no other place before I was two years old.

I can clearly remember the location and the property. They were a set of one-room range houses, three rooms facing the east and three rooms adjoining the three on the east. The other three rooms were facing the west. Above the six rooming houses were large upper apartments. I cannot remember who lived in that large house above our home. But I do remember at the end of our room was a small walkway and along the walkway was a broken fence, built with small openings. That fence separated our property from the property next door. The property next door, or I should say, 'the yard' next door, had a white painted cottage standing on four stilts. Therefore, one can see straight under the cottage.

The house I was living in was three feet off the ground, also on stilts. Most houses in Guyana were constructed on wooden or concrete stilts because of flooding, the coastline is low and under sea level. My house had three treaders of steps. So every evening as the sun went down and darkness fell, at about 6 p.m., I would come out of the house and sit near the entrance of the door and steps. I would then sneak down the three treaders by pulling my butt slowly down each treader. I was very caution during my escape out of the house. I would sit quietly, looking between the boards of the fence and through the bottom of the white cottage to the opposite side of the cottage. I would then see a man walking up and down from east to west. I could only see him from the waist down. He had a wooden leg, his trousers over one leg was long, and over the wooden leg was short. (The wooden leg was like 'Peg Leg' in the movie The Pirate.) I could see the lower section of his shirt sleeves and hands as he walked from one end of the cottage to the other end, without stopping. He just kept turning around, and off he went to each end of the house. It looked like a game to me. I was only two years old. I thought the man was playing with me. I would sit for a few minutes and looked at him. A few minutes later, I would turn my head to the right side towards the gate at the entrance of the property, and across Leopold Street, to the roof of a set of range houses on the opposite side of Leopold Street. I would then see a man sitting on top of the roof looking towards where I was sitting. I would quickly turn my head back to the white cottage in silence and see the man with the wooden leg. I would then start to shout loudly, "Look! Look at the 'halfer foot' man!" I would quickly turn my attention to the man on the roof top, "Look! Look at the man on the roof top!" I would point to him as well. I would keep on repeating myself while turning and looking at the two people. By this time, who ever was in the house would hear me shouting and then I would hear a voice saying from behind me inside the house, "I've told you girls to watch that boy- when it turns six o'clock, keep your eyes on him."

I never knew who it was that used to be telling the girls to keep an eye on me, and to prevent me from going out of the house at 6 o'clock. I must have known that it was forbidden for me to go out of the house when it became dark, had I had known I would not have sneaked out of the house while no one was watching me. What was I seeing? The man with the wooden leg and the other one on the Rooftop- exactly who were they?

Well, it's simple, I was apparently seeing two ghosts at six p.m., each time I came out of the house, Yes, a dead person conceived of as appearing to the living as a shadowy apparitions.

# 5

## My Godparents

I WAS THREE YEARS OLD when I understood that a man and woman who were living around the west side of the same tenants building where my relatives were living as well, were my godparents. I would often leave my home on the east side and go to the back of the building, which is on the west side to visit the home of the man and woman. They were Mr. and Mrs. Moore, my godparents. The Moores were living in a large room, which was separated by a room divider made of fabric. One section was their bedroom and the other was their living room. The front door was quite often left open, so I would go there and walk into the house unannounced in search of my godmother, who was quite often alone at home. Mr. Moore would be at work six days a week. It was like living in two homes, I was a frequent visitor at the Moore's home. They had no children living with them.

Mrs. Moore had a light complexion and she was about 5 feet 6 inches tall, and weighed about one hundred and thirty- five pounds. Mabel Moore was a very quiet woman and quite striking in appearance as well. Mr. Stephen Moore was 5 feet 8 inches and dark in complexion. He was also soft- spoken and highly spiritual. Both husband and wife were of African decent. Mr. Moore was also the

Grand Master of the White Blossom Flower Lodge, which was formed in British Guiana in the year 1897 and exists to this day. The signboard still stands on the front of the building at 134 Fourth Street, Alberttown, Georgetown. God rest their souls; yes, they are both dead now.

All the years I have known both of them, I have never heard either of them being abusive or utter a foul language to each other or to anyone else.

It is during those early years of my life, being around my godparents, that I had my fist encounter with the sex act, or my first sexual experience, so to speak.

It happened one day while I was about three and a half years old. As usual, I wandered over to my godparents' home and found that the front door was open, like it usually was most of the time. So I went into the house and I looked around the living room to see if my godmother was home, like she normally was most of the time. Not seeing her, I ventured further into the house to the opening that was the entrance to the bedroom. Pushing the curtain to one side, I stepped into the bedroom. It is here that my sexual experience began.

As I stopped at the foot of the bed, my attention was suddenly drawn to the bed where I saw Mrs. Moore with both legs in the air, and she was shaking her body. Both she and Mr. Moore were naked and Mr. Moore was lying between both of Mrs. Moore legs while she kept jerking up and down, she was also moaning and groaning. I stood at the foot of the bed watching quietly. I was quite stunned by what I saw, especially seeing Mr. Moore genitals which strangely resembled mine, though a lot larger, entering into a hole on Mrs. Moore's body, and worst of all it kept going up and down in the very hole. They continued to make noises, which also sounded like crying to my three-years-old ears, they seem as though they were fighting with each other. Of course, I had no knowledge of what I was really seeing. So I turned and walked quietly away from the foot of the bed and through the door. I kept thinking that Mr. Moore was fighting with Mrs. Moore.

I was only three years old, what else could I have thought of at that age? My godparents should never have left the door open and retire to bed, knowing that I would probably wander into the house unannounced. The image and memory stayed with me until my own hormones took over and I had a full understanding of what it was that I really saw that day when I was just three years old.

# 6

## The Moores' # 1

THE MOORES' DECIDED TO TAKE up new residence away from Leopold Street. The new resident was just around the corner in Breda Street. Their new home had two bedrooms, a living room, and a kitchen. It was a cottage. They also decided to let Mrs. Moore's mother, who was living alone, come and live with them.

Mrs. Moore's mother was called Titee. I have never heard Mr. or Mrs. Moore call Titee by any other name, so I do not know Titee by any other name. She was around fifty years of age, 5 feet, 7 inches tall, and weighed around one hundred and forty pounds. She was of African decent and light in complexion. The Moores had asked my mother for me, for the sole purpose of bringing me up as their own child, not just as my godparents, but as my parents and guardians. My mother had agreed to their request.

Margaret was still young and was expecting her fourth child. Basil Daniels was born on February 6th, 1929. The Moores felt sympathetic towards Margaret since she had so many children at such tender age. I was three years old when the Moores finally moved to Leopold Street, taking me along with them. My father Eric Daniels, had gone into the interior of Guyana to prospect for gold and diamonds. Eric was gone while Margaret was eight months pregnant with Basil, no wonder the Moores felt sympathy for her. She was cornered- she had no man by her side. The fathers of her children had all deserted her and gone their different ways. All this must have led to the Moore's decision to take me with them.

I was now three and a half years old, my mother was facing financial difficulties and could hardly feed herself, let alone four children. She was living in a one room flat with a curtain divider, which separated the room into a bedroom and living room.

Margaret's mother was living in a room next door to her with her own daughters, and she had a child who was just three years older that I was.

I was now taken to the new home on Breda Street. By this time, we had all settled down. Titee was the one who took full charge of me. She did not have an easy task, because by the time I was three years old, I started to get sickly. I called it, "born weak and grow strong." I can remember that period of my life clearly. Yes, I was a handful to look after. I was almost near death. The memory is as if it was only yesterday. I started to suffer with bronchitis and eczema; quite often those two go with each other. Bronchitis is inflammation of the mucous lining of the bronchial tubes. This could be very dangerous indeed because of the blockage to one's breathing. This blockage could cause one to choke and stifle to death. That would come about because of the lack of air supply to the lungs. I had it so bad, I had to be propped up with two or three pillows under my head. Titee would have to rush over to me and replace my head on the pillows if they should slip. She would try to make sure that my head did not slip off those pillows, and my head was always high on those pillows. That was an every night occurrence.

That eczema gave me sores all over my legs, and between my fingers. Titee is greatly responsible for me being alive this day- I really owe my life to her, she taught me the meaning of true love. Titee was of African decent and had a very patient manner, God rest her soul. I loved that woman so deeply, I could cry when I have visited death's door quite a few times because of my sickness and she always rescued me with the help of God.

Titee used to bathe me in the mornings and evenings. She would scrub my skin with sulfur and carbolic soap. Afterwards, she would dry my skin and get a fowl feather and paint my sores with iodoform. In the mornings, I would then be prepared for school, and she would see me off to school each morning.

Titee was a hard working woman. She would go the various homes of policemen who were on duty that wanted lunches to be brought from their homes to them at various police stations or locations all over the city of Georgetown.

Mrs. Moore did not work, her husband did. He was a Custom's Clerk and worked for the Colonial Master. Mr. Moore was responsible for everything that was shipped to Guyana from the English Government and the crates or boxes were marked: O.H.M.S., that meant, On Her Majesty Service.

Let me give you an idea of Mr. Moore's responsibilities. When the various merchandise came into the country, the merchandise were for the Public Hospital department and many other government institutions. All this Mr. Moore was in charge of- The Courts, the Governor, the Lord Chief Justice, not to mention he also worked for most of the large importing merchants in the city of Georgetown as well. Mr. Moore would clear the merchandise and pay the duties and then transport the items with his dray carts, which he had owned, he also had a small cart. Now one can see that Mr. Moore was a person who was making a lot of money, but he very seldom would buy me the clothing I needed to go to school. Instead, I was  sent to school without shoes and my shirt or trousers would be torn and patched. Frankly speaking, I had never worn a pair of leather shoes until I reached the age of fifteen. I had never been bought a child's toy. I had to wait until

I was old enough to work to buy my first pair of leather shoes.

Mr. Moore was a very mean man. It was his mother-in-law, Titee, who was the one that used to work and spend some of her wages on the clothing I needed to wear. I never had a toy as a child while growing up. I had to learn to build my own toys to entertain myself.

I can remember at times when one of Mr. Moore's donkey cart driver would get sick and did not show up for work, my godfather would take me out of school so that I could drive his donkey cart.

Mr. Moore's workload was very heavy because of the British Government contracts, especially when a Governor or a Lord Chief Justice was being exchanged in the country. Mr. Moore would have to see to their luggage as they came and went to and from England. He made a lot of money, but the money was never spent in his home. It was spent elsewhere. I do not know where, but I do know that he never liked to pay rent for the homes he lived in. We were always on the move from place to place.

When England shipped British Guiana currency, the money that was used in British Guiana. Mr. Moore would take me out of school for the day to accompany the driver of the cart to the docks when the shipment of money had arrived. I had to help in the loading and guarding of the wooden pitch pine boxes.

The boxes could be as much as two dozen of various sizes, with coins and notes. I would sit on top of the boxes, facing the back of the cart and close to the driver's back as the cart rolled along the street, followed by a Customs officer riding a bicycle close to the back of the donkey cart. We would travel from La Penitence Dock, down Lombard Street, and to the Public Buildings.

Transporting money on a donkey cart would be impossible these days, mainly because of the crime situation, the rate of hijacking and stealing in Guyana today is very high. That consignment would never arrive at the Public Buildings, it would never sit on the donkey cart in these times in Guyana- times have changed.

School was closed for the holidays, and I was home alone at Breda Street. My grandmother had moved from Leopold Street and was now living in Ketley with her daughters. I asked Titee's permission to go and visit Mamoo. She told me it was okay to go. So I waited until she went to work and then left home in Breda Street and went to see Mamoo on Ketley Street.

It was a beautiful day and the sun was shining brightly. I was nine years of age at that time. I finally arrived at Mamoo's and spent a few hours with her and my aunts. The time was getting late, though, it was around 3 p.m. Mrs. Moore and her mother should be home by now as well.

On my way home , heading towards  the corner of Ketley and Princess Streets,  intending to make a left turn, I saw a sudden change in atmosphere. The clouds became black and the rain started to drizzle. It was raining even as the sun was shining. The sun eventually disappeared, and a heavy downpour of rain started. I was then walking along Ketley Street going north heading towards Princess Street.

Thunder and lightning started to create havoc. I had never seen anything like it. The blanket of black clouds became worst and it started to rain even heavier, with the thunder rumbling continuously between short stops. By this time, I was almost halfway to the head of Ketley Street, which ends at the junction of Princess Street. Suddenly, there was an extremely loud clap of thunder, much louder than those that went before. My attention was immediately drawn to the sky, intending to see what was going on above my head. As I looked up, I saw a bright flash of lightening, which discharged what appeared to be a 'shooting star'. This 'shooting star' was speeding towards the earth.

I became afraid, which was compounded by the fact that I was soaked right through and very cold. Focusing my attention on reaching the junction in front of me, I saw a man of African decent, who appeared to be in his fifties or sixties, tall and slim, walking from the direction of Smyth Street which is east of High Street.

The man could not see what was going on behind him in the sky. I heard another rumbling even as the lightening flashed once more. The 'shooting star' was still ranging downwards. By this time, I had arrived at the junction and was about to walk passed the man. I took my last glimpsed at the sky. I was not comfortable with what I was seeing. The 'shooting star' was not burning out or disappearing. It came to me then that it was not a 'shooting star' but a lighting bolt, and it was falling about six lamp posts away from the man and me. I had joined the man in the center of Princess Street. There was a shop with a bridge, which runs across a gutter leading from the road to the door of the shop. As I was about to pass the man, a voice said to me loudly, "Take cover!". The voice was a baritone, very deep and impressive.

I quickly turned around and leaped into the air, throwing myself on the opposite side of the road and the verge, which sloped down to the gutter and the shop bridge. The glare from the lightning bolt lit up the area as it came closer to the earth. The bright light, which emanated from it, was penetrating my eyelids although I had my eyes tightly closed. I crawled beneath the shop bridge, placing my face onto the hard ground.

Seconds later, I opened my eyes and looked around me. It had become a bit dark, but things seemed more normal. I quickly stood up, getting out from under the bridge, walked up the verge and stopped. I looked for the man who had been on the street, but he was nowhere in sight. The lightning bolt had struck him, and he was burnt up and turned into ashes. That's right, he was nowhere in sight. I realized then what had happened, the lightning bolt had hit him and he was burnt to ashes. There was nowhere for him to hide in the area. To tell you the honest truth, I took off running like a jet into the church yard and across Durban Street into Breda Street.

When I arrived home, Mr. and Mrs. Moore were at home. I was really scared as I explained to them both, "I seen a man burnt up after he was hit by a lightning bolt on Princess Street." Mr. Moore said to me, "Boy, shut up, you see what lightning bolt kill what man?" I said, "Yes, it's true, Papee."

They then decided to go to the area to find out. When we arrived at the shop, they went into the shop and inquired. They were told of the incident. They did not mentioned to the Moores' that they saw me coming from beneath the shop bridge, ran across the bridge and through the church yard. It was then the Moores' believed me.

# 7

# The Moores #2

L IFE WITH THE MOORES WAS not easy. Mr. Moore gave me an early responsibility. He said to me, "Now, your job before you go to school is to take the spare donkey out of the stable every morning, and put him out to graze. Make sure he grazes in a pasture where there is growing grass, and tie him properly. You are to clean the stable as well. When you come home from school, you are to cut three bags of grass to feed the donkeys." These duties were given to me at just ten years of age. Over the years, Mr. and Mrs. Moore moved to five different places in the city of Georgetown.

After World War 11 started in 1939, Mr. Moore became scared of the Germans invading Guiana (now known as Guyana) and dropping bombs on the city of Georgetown. He decided to move out of the city and take up residence on the east bank of the Demerara River. We then moved to Meadow Bank, we lived there a while, after which we moved to Mc Doom Village, where we lived for a year and six months before moving to Agricola, and then later on to Eccles. It seemed that Mr. Moore was always in the process of moving from place to place.

While living in Mc Doom Village, I was given the task of looking after the donkeys. There I discovered that Mr.

Moore did not like to pay the house rent after moving in and paying the first month's rent. He always would say to me, "Do not go to sleep tonight because we will be moving." I would then reply, "OK, Papee," but I would be very annoyed at having to be uprooted. Having to change schools one after the other, not to mention all the friends I would have to leave behind, it was very frustrating, not to mention all my duties of looking after the animals. I would have to cut grass in the sugar fields, in trenches, and cemeteries before I could play with my friends.

After school each day, my East Indian friends and I would congregate at the canal with two or three canoes, grass knives (sickles) and cutlasses. Then off we will go, and I would be the one to lead us on our journey. We would start off on our journey at approximately 3:30 in the afternoon and return home at about 8 or 9 o'clock in the evening. After returning, we would separate and go home in various directions with our grass to feed the animals.

After this, we would return to our stables and attend to our animals. We had to perform those duties seven days a week. We had no time to play during the day from Monday to Friday. It was only on Saturdays and Sundays that we were given a little playing time, and that only came about if we doubled up and helped each other quickly cut the grass. Sometimes we spent all day on Saturday cutting enough grass for Sunday so we could have a day to ourselves.

It was not an easy task for us. It was a laborious, tiresome duty which I had to endure at an early age. It was now 1943, and it had been four years of hard work, through sun and rain, day and night.

A separation came in my life. Mrs. Moore's mother was no longer in my life. As I pointed out before, Titee did not move to the east bank with us. She remained in Georgetown. A year later after living in Eccles and then moving to Agricola Village, an addition was made to the home. Mr. Moore brought his granddaughter, who was then four years of age, to live with us. Her name was Patricia Moore.

She had been living with her father. Eugene Moore, who was her uncle, had murdered his sister, who was her mother. However, he was not convicted for the killing of his sister. Instead, he was found not guilty and set free. In my opinion, Eugene should not have escaped the death penalty. It was a clear-cut case.

This is what took place between Eugene and his sister in Barr Street, Albouystown. I was about ten years of age at the time of the incident. Eugene and Patricia's father was working for Mr. Moore, driving his donkey carts. Eugene was living with his mother and sister at that time and supporting them. He would go home each day to have his lunch between 11 a.m. and 12 p.m. His sister was the one who was charge of running the home. However, she was always late when it came to cooking lunch, so Eugene could not get his meals on time. Quite often, Eugene and his sister would argue fiercely. His sister's tongue was very sharp so Eugene, on the day of the murder, said to her, "Why can't you ever get my food on time? You are a big waste, and you go from house to house involving yourself in other people's business."

Patricia's mother then started to shout, "Who the hell you think you are? You are not my father! You kiss my ass!"

Eugene then got into a rage and rushed towards her saying, "So, I must kiss your ass? I will kiss it!" Eugene tried to slap her face, but she ducked. She then kicked him in the groin and ran out of the house.

There was a bakery shop next to where they lived. His sister ran into the bakery shop and hid from him. But he was too fast for her. He ran quickly behind her, picked up a wooden window bar which was lying in a corner, and struck her on the head. She died later in hospital and the case was brought to court for a year or so.

So Patricia came to live with us after being taken care of by her father for four years or so. Mr. Moore also had a daughter whose name was Dorothy, she was 4 feet in height and of average built, but she looked like she was fifty years of old.

Dorothy had a severe birth defect that not only caused her to be a midget, but also to look like a man, and to appear far older than she really was. In short, she was a very unusual looking person. From the time she came to join her father and saw her niece Patricia and me, she instant dislike us both. Dorothy totally resented everything we did in the home. Mr. Moore was very protective of her and she became sheltered under her father. I felt a bit sympathetic towards her because of the way she looked and because the children would call her names all the time.

Dorothy had a secret unknown to Patricia and me; however, her father was aware of it. I guess Mrs. Moore knew of it as well. Dorothy was a medium; a person through whom communications are supposedly sent to the living from spirits of the dead. The first time I saw Dorothy possessed with a spirit, that of an Englishman, I became shocked and terrified. I had never seen anything of that sort before. Dorothy started to shiver and tremble and at the same time, she started to make grunting sounds.

We were sitting at the dining table one evening when the spirit entered her body. I was fifteen years of age at the time. Dorothy fell on the floor, and Mr. Moore strolled over to her and asked, "Who are you, and what is your purpose?"

Dorothy said to Mr. Moore, "I was sent." She spoke with the voice of an Englishman. The accent and the English were perfect.

Mr. Moore then questioned her once again, "Okay, who sent you?" The spirit replied, "Do not rush me and

I will tell you." Mr. Moore said, "I have no time to play games with you."

Dorothy by this time in her possession state, started to crawl on her back with her legs stretched out flat. She wriggles her body like a snake as she traveled to the locked front door and crawled backwards, headfirst. When she arrived at the door, she raised one hand into the air above her head and turned the key. Unlocking the door, she then opened the door, moving her body back into the house as the door was being opened. Dorothy then traveled head first through the door, still on her back, and down the steps, she then wriggled herself all the way down until she reached the bottom. Dorothy took Mr. Moore to the back of the property and then the spirit, who was in control of her, said to Mr. Moore, "Dig here, and you will find a vial. This place is haunted. It needs to be cleared." Mr. Moore then dug up the spot and he found the vial.

At other times, Dorothy would sit in a chair or in other sections of the house when she would become possessed by evil spirits. Sometimes the spirit which enters her was a woman, and sometimes it is a man. The spirit would be a person who was once alive, but had died and became weary, restless, and controlled by the devil. Some of these spirits would enter Dorothy and they were hostile, cunning, and evasive. The spirit would tell

Mr. Moore that it was sent to kill Dorothy or one of the house members. Mr. Moore would then speak in Latin or Spanish, and would get a Manicole broom, which is kept hanging across the front door. He would then start to whip Dorothy as he questioned the spirit. The spirit would start to cry while saying, "Please, Do not beat me. I can't tell you who sent me. I have a job to do."

Mr. Moore would then snap his finger at his wife, who was standing nearby. She would then give Mr. Moore a piece of black thread and a needle while he continues to beat the spirit with the broom, speaking in tongues and Latin. He would take the thread and needle, and start to tangle it in the center of Dorothy's head, while he continues to speak. Then quickly, he would snap his finger once again and Mrs. Moore would then pass a vial to him. He would place the vial close to her knotted hair and pulled some of the hair with the needle, then drop it into the vial and quickly cork it.

Mr. Moore would lecture to me as he gave me the vial to dispose of. He would say, "Now do not forget, don't stop and play with your friends on the way, take care of this vial. Do you understand?"

I would respond saying, "Yes, Papee." That was the name I called him Papee.

Then he gave me the vial to dispose of into the sea or salt water, by throwing it over my head while backing into the sea. I would walk away as I tossed the vial over head.

At the age of fifteen, I came to realize that my life with my godfather was not what I had planned it to be. So one day I said to him, "Papee, I would like to go and learn a trade at Central Garage on High Street. I would like to be a machinist." Mr. Moore said to me, "You have more ambition than I thought." I thought of what he had said to me. Mr. Moore saw me as having ideas different from those of his own. He wanted me to grow up and attend to his stables, cut his grass and drive his donkey carts barefoot with little or no education.

I realized that my godfather and godmother only saw me as a cart boy. This, in my mind, was my harness, such as the harness of the donkeys he wanted me to shepherd around the city of Georgetown.

Mr. Moore had given his daughter, Dorothy, the duty of cutting grass as well as feeding the donkeys. I felt sorry for her because I knew she would not be able to. She was too fragile. Therefore, she would be unable to go into the places to find the grass and fill the big bag, let alone to carry it back, especially if it rained or if the bag got wet. Dorothy was quite short and not strong. She use to struggle when I saw her coming home with the bag on her head.

Then one day, we got news that she went by the Demerara riverbank cutting grass and someone raped her there. This was very sad. I wondered how one human being could do something like that to another, especially to someone like Dorothy. I could not understand it. That individual had to be sick mentally. How could anyone do such a thing to a woman, especially when the woman was resisting, and physically handicapped?

Then came the biggest upset of my life at that time. It all started one evening, as I was sitting reading a book in a corner of our home. Mr. and Mrs. Moore were discussing the death of Titee. They were in their bedroom. I was in the corner near the bedroom door. Mrs. Moore said to her husband, "It's a shame, Steven, that boy can't go to the old lady's funeral."

Mr. Moore said, "Mabel, Titee's death came upon us so sudden, I wish I had the money to buy him some clothing."

I became stunned as I listened to their conversation and overheard them saying that Titee had died and that they were keeping it a secret from me. They were in their bedroom discussing the final details of the funeral. Mrs. Moore said to her husband, "Steven, you know how close Sylbert and Titee were. How can we keep her death from him? He will not be going to Trinity Church to see her for the last time tomorrow afternoon. He will be very upset, Steven." Mr. Moore said, "Well, it just can't be helped. It's just one of those things."

I cried myself to sleep after listening to them speak. I lay in my bed crying and thinking, wondering why Titee had to die and leave me. Her death was a great loss to me, not to mention the fact that I had already suffered a great loss when she did not come to live with us on the east bank. The following morning I got up bright and early and attended to my daily duties. I had decided not to be left behind but instead, I would go and see Titee for the last time. While attending to my duties, I kept a close eye on the clock and also on Mr. and Mrs. Moore.

Finally, time had come for the Moores to leave home to go to the funeral. They left home and I kept out of sight, so that they could not give me a last minute order to do any other chores. I let them leave home and give them half an hour's head start. Then I left home after taking a bath and putting on the best clothing I could find. I had no shoes for my feet, but I didn't worry about that. I set off for Georgetown, running all the way to the Trinity Church on High and Durban Streets.

When I arrived at the church, I saw the hearse and cars standing in front of the church along with a few people milling around. I rushed into the church, crying and screaming. I pushed pass the people who were walking slowly in a line and looking into the coffin, viewing the body. As I got to the coffin, I held it as I continued crying and speaking to Titee as she lay so peacefully, with a slight smile on her face.

"Titee, what am I going to do? What am I going to do without you? Who is going to sew the buttons on my shirt?" I then flew into a rage and started screaming, while I held the coffin and began shaking it. The coffin slipped off the trestle and out rolled Titee's body onto the floor. By the time, the congregation had moved away from Titee and me. No sooner had her body fallen out of the coffin and hit the ground, then I rushed over and hugged it. The body felt as stiff as a piece of board and I continued wailing, "You can't leave me."

Then I felt a hand on my shoulder and then another and I was picked up and put into a corner. Others picked up Titee's body and laid it back in the coffin. Mr. Moore came to me and said, "Go on home. You should not be here in your condition."

I walked out of the church as the funeral service was about to commence. I thought Mr. Moore was very unreasonable. I did not want to go back home. So when I left the church, I waited at the corner of Leopold and High streets. The service lasted for two hours while I stood in hiding and wondering what could be taking them so long in the church. I have never attended a funeral service before, so I had no idea what went on inside.

Finally, the service ended and everyone came out of the church. The funeral procession started to line up. Mr. Moore's Lodge members were dressed in their fine regalia and armed with swords in their hands. Mr. and Mrs. Moore got into a car immediately behind the hearse and carriage and the procession moved down Durban Street. I then came out of my hiding place and started running as I held on to the back of the carriage, trying to stop the two horses from pulling the carriage with Titee's coffin inside. I was crying and saying, "Don't leave me, Titee, please don't leave me." Of course, it was impossible to hold back the horse and carriage, but I was determined to hold on.

When that did not worked, I took off and ran to the front of the procession and stopped it just before they reached Smyth Street. Everything came to a halt. Then someone came out of one of the cars and carried me into it, and they then continued to the cemetery. Now and forever, may God rest Titee's soul.

I finally came to my true senses and decided to run away from the Moores. I just could not take anymore of my godfather's ill treatments. It became overbearing for me. I was now fifteen years of age, and had been taken out of school at third grade because I became too big for a third grade.

Each year I had to be left behind in my class or else be moved into a class grade above what I was in. I was very tall and lanky, not to mention the fact that I also stuttered very badly. My stuttering became so bad that when I was called upon to get up from my seat in class and to read a section of a book, it would take me forever to walk from the back to the front of the class out of fear and embarrassment of the other children, who would often laugh at me while I tried to read. They would also make faces at me as I kept stammering. I can tell you that was no fun. It was humiliation to the highest degree. Children can be very cruel to each other. One needs to be strong in such cases.

My fear and stuttering was caused by Mr. Moore. At nights, he would burn the mosquitoes around the room off the wall. He would take a small bottle with a wick that was filled with kerosene. His lamp is called a "spiceasy". It would be lit, and he would travel slowly as he sighted a mosquito on the wall. The dining table was in the center of the room. Mr. Moore would call me, "Sylbert, go and get your book and come to the table." Whenever he said that to me, I would wish to die.

I would bring a book that he managed to get secondhand from parents whose children had already used it. He rarely bought me any schoolbooks. So I would come with my book and sit at the table and Mr. Moore would say, "Read to me about the old woman who had so many children she did not know what to do." I would start to read but would not be able to pronounce some of the words. Then he would say to me, "Go and bring me the wild cane." I would go and get the cane and then return to my reading as he commanded. "Start from the top." He would have the cane in one hand and the lamp in the other.

As he continued to burn the mosquitoes, I would be reading and then I would get to a word that I could not pronounce and he would say, "Spell it." I would then spell the word and he would come over to me and whip me as he spelled and then pronounced the word, striking me as he repeated each letter.

I finally had enough of this abuse and left. I went to my mother, who was then living at 63 Cross Street, Georgetown. To this day, the Moores have never inquired where I was. When I left their home, all I left with was the clothing on my back.

# 8

# 63 *Cross Street*

T HE YEAR WAS 1943, THE month was June, and 63 Cross Street was now to be my new home. In fact it was my mother's home.

Margaret, my mother, was a bit surprised when she saw me walked up the steps. She said, "Boy, what a surprise, what brings you here? I haven't seen you since the past, how long?" I said "Over a year." Margaret said, as she gestured to a chair, "Come and sit down." I then sat down and said to her, "I ran away from home, I couldn't stand the way Mr. Moore wanted to bring me up." Margaret said, "Sylbert, I did not approve of the way I saw he had you growing up, but Mr. Moore took you from me as a baby. I did not want to act ungrateful by taking you away from him. After Moore moved from Georgetown, I saw the life and the clothing he had you wearing and living."

I then said to my mother, "I am not going back." She reassured me that she was not sending me back. As I sat down facing my mother, I could see that she was pregnant. I wondered when is my mother going to stop having children. She already had five of us. She had a girl after having Basil Daniels, after him she had Eileen Joseph, God rest her soul. Eileen was living with my mother's sister, Clarista. Donald was also living with my Aunt Clarista. After Donald grew up, he was working on a ship as a seaman under Clarista husband, who was the captain of the ship. Donald was living at home with Margaret, when he was not at sea. Reginald was also living with Margaret at the time I went back home. Basil was living with an adopted aunt and her husband- Papa and Aunt Sarah.

My mother introduced me to a boy who was about four years older that I. Margaret had taken care of him while I was living with the Moores'. She brought up Henry Griffith as one of her own sons. We all lived as a family.

While thinking about my brothers and sisters, I wondered what my mother was doing with her life. She was still living in a one-room house, which was separated with a room divider. On arriving there I saw how crowded the house already was. I quickly came to the conclusion that I will have to sleep on the floor, which was nothing new to me.

I settled in with my mother and the next day, I went in search of a job at one of the waterfront. I was hired at one dollar and twenty cents per day. It was not a lot of money, but it was a job, and that job and money will help to get me on my feet. My duties were to transport goods from the ship to the bond on a hand truck.

Margaret was with the father of the child she was expecting, Mr. Leon. He was working at the Bauxite Company in McKenzie. My mother would go to McKenzie and stay there for a while away from home. So it would be Reginald and me most of the time if Donald were not at home. The two of us would be in the house, so in actual fact, the house was never really crowded.

I left the wharf pushing trucks for I was offered a job by my uncle-in-law Captain Timmers. I started work on the S.S. Ethel Rill with Captain Timmers and my brother Donald. I worked as a Cabin Boy, the ship was an oil tanker, which sometimes transport molasses as well.

It was now 1944, and we were in Port of Spain, Trinidad. When we arrived in Trinidad, we were given shore leave, so I went ashore and did some shopping. I was in need of clothes, so I bought myself some. When I returned aboard ship, Captain Timmers saw me with a few shopping bags. He called me to his cabin and he said, "When you get your pay you should take your envelope to Sister Margaret and give it to her." I then said to him, "I usually give my mother an allowance out of my pay. I cannot give her my entire paycheck, what would I have out of it." Mr. Timmers just looked at me for a while before he said, "You can go,"

I then went to my cabin and put my shopping and returned to my duties. I could sense that Mr. Timmers did not like what I told him. How can I surrender my pay to Margaret with the children she continues to have, one after the other? Especially, considering I was almost naked when I left the Moores'.

On our way to Guiana with a load of oil, I was in the pantry washing up the dishes, I had some rice on a plate, which I threw through the porthole. The tanker was a small ship, so when I threw the rice out of porthole, some of the rice landed on the fender of the ship. The ship was entering the Demerara River and the water of the river is much calmer than the sea. On sea, the waves would wash the rice off the ship's fender. The Captain was on the bridge as we were sailing into port up the river. So when the Captain saw the rice flying into the air while sitting on the port side of the ship, he then looked down from the bridge onto the fender- he then saw the bundle of rice sitting on the fender. Captain Timmers quickly sent a message with Donald to tell me to report to the Captain on the bridge.

I went to the captain after receiving the message from Donald, and the Captain gave me a warning not to throw food out of the ship's porthole. I went and got a bucket and a rope to tie the bucket so that when I threw the bucket overboard to dip water I would not lose the bucket. I then washed the food away. We finally arrived at the American Air Base at Timehri, and we pumped out the shipment of oil. After a while, we moored the ship at the company's wharf and shore leave was given.

By this time, I had become a popular dancer and singer. I was improving my dancing skills every day. I would improvise various steps and styles. The types of dance at that time was the jitterbug and the bebop. They were also my favorites. I had also learned the foxtrot and waltz, among other dances.

Being talented as a singer and dancer, I started to become popular. Therefore, I had to choose my friends. Most of the young men my age and younger were being drawn to me because of the popularity. The beautiful girls also would become attracted to me. Not just because of my friends were a select few. One was Hector Barrow; he was Donald's girlfriend brother. There were also two of Hector's friends and three boys from the trade school who came from respectable families. The four of us were a pack, "The Rat Pack." We were always well dressed. We knew our fabrics, and we had the best tailor to make our suits.

My working on the ship became an asset to the boys. I would shop for "The Rat Pack." Therefore, most of our clothing was foreign; we stood out when we went to functions. It was all fun, but I did not let it get to my head. I was quiet and reserved by nature. So as the designated "shopper" so to speak, I would buy clothing for the boys and myself whenever I went abroad with the ship.

I worked on the ship for one year and four months. I lost the job when my forgetfulness caused me to repeat the act of throwing food through the porthole. The captain saw it and became angry. So he decided to pay me off. That was the last of me working with my uncle-in-law, the Captain.

I was now out of a job, finding jobs in those days was not easy for early school leavers. I must say, while I worked whatever job I did, I would always give my mother half of my wages. So whenever I was short of pocket money, I would borrow it from her and give her interest whenever I repaid her.

Margaret and Mr. Leon had come down from McKenzie, because he was given two weeks leave from his job at the Bauxite Company. I hated being about the house and not working. I told myself it was a sin, having to depend on others for their support after growing up and being capable of working. A person has to work in order to survive and to provide for himself and his family if he or she has one. Such provisions have to be sustained until his or her children reached the age where they are capable of supporting themselves. Many people today refuse to work and support themselves. Instead, they depend on their parents. They also tell themselves that their parents are responsible for giving birth to them therefore; it is their parents who should maintain them at age twenty-five or thirty, quite often even older. The realization that I should fend for myself and not depend on others came to me at an early age, that is why I ran away from my godparents and took an early start towards supporting myself.

A few days after losing the job on the ship, I went job hunting. I was successful in obtaining a job at Sanitary Dry Cleaners and Laundry on High and Princess Streets. The wage was very small and my duties were as a deliveryman, but it was a bit of money in my pocket.

I was now working four weeks at the sanitary laundry. One day I was walking home from work when suddenly two guys who looked about in their twenties, both riding bicycles flanked me on both sides. As I was now sandwiched between the two bicycles, one of them said, "My name is John, and Robert, he is my brother. Do you still work at the laundry?"

I replied, "Yes, Why?" Robert took over the conversation. "We have a job for you in a dry cleaner we are opening. We would like you to run it. The pay will be good." I asked, "Where is your place?" John replied, "Smyth and Leopold Streets, two corners from here. Come after work tomorrow and we will discuss business." I said, "OK. I have to turn at this corner." We made arrangements to meet at 5 p.m. the following day, and then they rode off quickly.

While I was living with Mr. Moore my godfather, a young man whose name was Henry Griffith, was taken care of by my mother Margaret. On my return to live with my mother, he was already in the Volunteer Force as a Infantryman. "Griff", as everyone called him loved to party.

My brother Reginald was very seldom at home, instead, he stayed at his girlfriend's. Reginald loved older women, who were quite often twice his age, and women who already had quite a few children. I often wondered why his taste for women ran in that particular direction. The women would come to the gate at 63 Cross Street and whistle, calling him. Margaret would become very annoyed and would shout to the women if Reginald was not at home, "Can't you see my son is as old as your son? You are not ashamed? Go and find a man your own age. Stop coming at my gate."

The woman would then walk away quietly, because by that time, she would realize that Reginald was not at home. This was just one woman; I have seen at least three women on various occasions. When Reginald was finished with one, he goes for another one. I came to realize that these women provided Reginald with boarding and lodging and other basic amenities. He could not have a bed at Margaret's or enough food, since he was a big eater. Reginald and I used to sleep on the floor, on old clothing. We were poor, but had a strict upbringing. Margaret was a very serious woman. We were never too old to receive a slap about the ears.

.One day on my way back to work after making a de-livery, I decided to do a quick visit home. Henry and

Margaret were at home. Henry was very jovial, and he was singing ballads of the '40s such as, 'My Funny Valentine' and 'Summertime.' I sat down for a short time listening to him. I said to him, "Griff, like you hit the jackpot?" He replied, "Sylbert, my boy, I will be leaving soon." I said, "Where will you be going, my boy?" Henry replied, "The South Caribbean Forces will be shipping out to Virginia, U.S.A." I said, "That's great."

"Here I am, going to face a lot of Germans and you think I am going to the U.S.A. to dance the jitterbug and the bebop. Sylbert, when we are gone, they will be picking people, so you can try your luck."

Margaret asked, "Sylbert, you want something to eat?" I replied, "No, I have to rush back to work, Griff, I'll see you later." I then left the house and went back to work.

There was a house next to us which was much more spacious than ours. When I got home, I saw a beautiful young lady coming out of the house next door. A large vat which supplied the yard with drinking water stood between my home and the house where this beauty strolled out from. She went to the vat and filled a bucket with water, then went back into her house. I never saw her before so I assumed that she was not living there. I later inquired about her. It so happened that her father and stepmother, also her brother and sister, were the ones who were living in that home. She used to live with her mother, but was now sent to live with her father. Well, I became attracted to her from the time I set eyes on her.

The following day, I went to Imperial Dry Cleaners, which was situated on the corner of Smyth and Leopold Streets. It was here the two Portuguese boys on the bicycle who spoke to me about running the dry cleaner, had their business. I saw John and Robert De Freitas and we discussed the nature of the job and wages among other things.

I started to work a week later. John and Robert were familiar with me by my delivering clothes to them in the Kingston area of Georgetown. They knew that I was working at Sanitary Dry Cleaners. They told me that after I enquired how come they knew me, and where I was working. They also knew where I lived as well. So, apparently I was no stranger to them.

The time had come for Henry to be shipped out overseas. Henry also saw the new girl who had moved in next door. Henry said to me one day, "Have you seen the new girl who moved into the yard?" I replied, "Yes. She's a hit, isn't she Henry?" "It's a pity the army shipping me out, otherwise I could move my best foot forward," Henry said. I then said, "Well, you can't be any competition, because you will be off from the scene." "Well, you and the boys in the yard can try to tackle her," said Henry. I asked, "How long will you be staying in America- your final stop is where?" Henry replied, "We will be heading for North Africa, I'll be leaving in three days." I said, "Well, I wish you a safe return and bring me something from the Germans."

Henry said, "Well, Sister Margaret, you're sitting quietly without a word." Margaret said to him, as she got up from her chair to go to the kitchen, "I am letting you boys have your chat. I am going to miss you, try and come back." Henry replied, "I will be back."

I started my new job running the cleaners. Henry had been gone two months already when I heard that the army would be picking a new batch of recruits in a week or so. I went and registered and was selected. I then joined the army in early 1944. I was given a date on which to report to the barracks. So by that time I was sure that I would be in the army, I then gave in my notice to John at the dry cleaners. The boys were a bit peeved when I give them notice of leaving the job, but that was life, one has to move on in life. I was in search of betterment.

I was now in the army having my basic training, and that was tough. I never thought that a human being could stand so much stress and harassment. Being in the army have taught me so many things about others and myself as well. It taught me to get along with people that I dislike. I learned to tolerate people's differences. I also learned of the vast personalities among us all. It also taught obedience, which has been a great asset in my life. The army taught me self-control and how to endure hunger and how to do without. The army is one of the greatest places to learn all the things I have just mentioned.

At seventeen years of age, I was ready for life. I had forged my age in order to be eligible for the army. I was tall and well built, so it was difficult for them to know that I had forged my age without a birth certificate to prove. I had forged my age because my living conditions at home with my mother, which was not very good. I saw it as living in great poverty. I knew that there were other people in the world who were living in worst poverty, but I saw my state and condition as being poverty-stricken.

So the army gave me a bed, good food, clothing, money and medical treatment as well. My six weeks basic training was completed, and I was enjoying a bit of life at that time. I was now doing a lot of dancing almost every night, once I was not on duty, and if I was on duty and had a few hours to escape from camp. I would be absent from barracks for two or three hours. I remembered that every two months, I would be put on C.B. (confine to barracks). Even though I was on C.B. for seven days or fourteen days, I would still break C.B. to go sporting and dancing. I was not a heavy drinker. I would take two or so drinks whenever we were out.

# 9

# My Return from Thakama
## My Strange Experience with My Grandmother

URING THE YEAR 1945, AND 1946 one year to the day my grandmother had took in sick at her home, and my mother brought her home to live with us at 63 Cross Street. Her illness was very serious and therefore she needed close attention. During the first six months while my grandmother was living with us she became bedridden, and being attended by my mother Margaret. I was coming and going into the jungle of Thakama. She had to be attended to by my mother all through her sickness at that period of time which was one year as stated. During the second six months to complete a year she became worst and lost her voice. My grandmother became a shock to me, to see her fading away each six months. She simply could not get out of the bed or utter a sound- she was in a bad shape. She was suffering from a small 'Gout' on her neck. When I say a small Gout on the neck, I really should say a small lump at the side of her neck. The feet and hands. It also causes swelling and severe pain as well.

Martha, as you may remember, was my grandmother. I've also mentioned that we all called her Mamoo. So I will refer to her as Mamoo, since I was coming to the end, and a great moment in her life. At the end of a year, she became so thin, all that was left were skin and bones - she became a skeleton. By this time, I had made my two trips to Takama in that year of Mamoo being sick and with us. I came down from Takama with my entire company. The company was confined to camp on our arrival in the city. The following day, most of us were given an evening pass to go out of camp, we all had to report back to camp that same night at 23.59 p.m, which is one minute to midnight.

So I went home to 63 Cross Street on the mid evening after making my rounds seeing a few friends. When I got home, I found Mamoo alone in the house. After entering through the opened front door and walked into Mamoo bedroom, she was in a slight doze. As I stood looking at her for a few seconds wondering if she was asleep or not, she turned her head towards me. Because I would have hated to wake her up, since it was known that she did not get enough sleep at times.

She opened her eyes as I was about to walk away from her. I said to her, "Hello, Mamoo. We came from Takama yesterday, where is Sister Margaret?" Mamoo raised her hands slightly and move it back and forth to signal to me that Margaret had gone out, and not at home. I walked out of the room and made myself at home. I sat by the window, facing Tina's home, (the new kid in town) I would avoid looking across her way. My grandmother was not much company, not being able to speak, so I sat alone waiting to see my mother. But time was running out, so I went into the kitchen and got me some food out of the pot, Margaret always had cooked food in the house. I then ate the meal and half an hour later, I decided to go to the back of the yard, about 50 yards away from our house. Like I said, it was getting late, the time was 10 p.m. and I also wanted to go to one of the clubs before going back to camp.

I went to the toilet at the back of the yard. The toilet is called a Out House. The Out house consisted of three cubicles and was built out of galvanized sheets and stands about twelve inches above ground level. I used the toilet, and then pulled the chain of the cistern which flushes the water. I then opened the door while fitting my shirt into my trousers and stood at the opened door while trying to buckle the belt of my trousers. I was standing in the center cubicle when suddenly a face shot out from around the corner of the separating wall, and pass closely into my face, at a speed of around a hundred and fifty miles an hour. It just came so close to a distance of one inch from touching my face, and then quickly disappeared. I, by that time started to feel as though my head was expanding, as I was calling out the names of three of the boys my age, who could have been outside using the Out-house (Toilet) that time of the night. Normally, small children are not allowed to be out of their homes alone at the age of ten years old and below. If a child needs to use the Out-house, then a member of the family would accompany that child. So after calling each name as I stepped down from the cement floor onto the ground, making a right turn, I raised my feet, and quickly kicked the galvanized door open. It was the first cubicle on my right. As I stood in the middle entrance of my cubicle, no one could have slipped by me. When the galvanize door slammed wide open to show its emptiness. The expansion of my head by that time was expanded to its final expansion. Facing the Out-house was the side, and the end of a set of two long range set of houses. My home was on the other end of the range houses on the left side.

As I walked towards my house, my heart finally stopped, my head and body became light, as though I was floating on thin air, as I walked briskly to my house. I reached the steps which leads to our door, the steps which bears five treaders. I quickly made two leaps up the set of steps onto the floor of the house. As I walked slowly and became very cool and calm, entering the large room which was separated by a long folding screen which had an entrance in the middle and extended from one end to the other end of the room, a second separate the inner section of the long screen into two bedrooms. My grandmother lying in her bedroom at the far end away from me, as I shouted while walking to go into her bedroom. I said, "Mamoo, do you know what happened just now?"

By this time I had taken two to three steps along the screen on my left at the end of my question, Mamoo started to laugh a ghostlike laugh and chuckles, at the said time (suppressed sound), then she began to speak at the end of the chuckling without taking a breath, as she spoke. She said, 'Ah, Ah, Ah, you where just scared by a ghost!" I quickly and excitedly began to question her, asking, 'How do you know that?' She replied, "Boy! When you are lying where I am lying, and going where I'm going there are things you can see, but you cannot speak."

I stopped walking towards my grandmother. It was as if I had been under some form of control for a period of time, while she spoke to me. With the end of her sentence I can assure you whatever was controlling me, it did a job to be remembered.

Because at the end of my grandmother speech to me, I came out of a semi-trance and bewilderment, and was further guided not to ask her anymore questions.

# 10

## Henry Griffith and I

THE NEW GIRL MENTIONED WAS named Christina, but was called Tina's skeptism was long lasting amongst us boys- she was not an easy catch. I like that, she was very reserved, no fooling about the place. I was drawn to her, and she was drawn to me. But I was concentrating on my career as a soldier career at that time, Henry and his crew was now at sea, sailing on the S.S. State of Virginia.

I recalled my time of joining the Army. Conscription started from the letter 'A to M'. Because of this system of conscription, strange things were happening. For example, I knew a young man who was standing in line next to me, as we were being asked our names and ages. This young man next to me, when asked, "what is your name?" He said, "Winston Branch, Sir." His name was not "Branch". He decided quickly not to take any chances by giving his real name. After we all were lectured to, the officer had told us, "Those of you men who are not selected today, those men will be called back at a later date."

So getting back to Mr. Branch, he decided not to take any chances on a re-call. Because the crowd of young men standing and waiting with blood in their eyes, as the saying goes. Branch wanted to be in the early bunch of men. His real name was Pilgrim. "P" in the alphabet did not give Branch much choice; it was way down in the alphabet.

So, Branch was chosen before me. He had placed himself in the second choice as the letters run alphabetically. Therefore because of extreme poverty, saw the army as a better life, poverty and colonialism breeds.

Those ways of sharp thinking in trying to beat the system, or should I say, to stay ahead of the system. "Now in my eyes or ways of thinking. I looked upon Branch as being a clever young man, because he did not know the amount of men which were to be chosen. So that was one of the reasons Branch pushed himself forward. Not to mentioned he came from a large poor family, and needed a job badly and a suitable roof above his head, and a proper bed to sleep in, and four square meals each day.

The greatest amount of men who had join the army in various colonies, were attracted by those fulfillment. Because of their social life which had confronted them at a young age. 'B' company had a great set of men. 'B' became the leader of companies, which was 'A', 'B', 'C' and 'Ships Guard Unit', etc. 'B' company was always put to the front of things. Six months later the task of building an army battle school was being planned in the jungle of Guiana, a 'Platoon' of men was chosen out of 'B' company. The Platoon of soldiers had consisted of twenty-eight men, I was one of them. In short it was my squad, a Military unit composed of three sections in the squad, and our Commanding Officer , a Lieutenant, a Sergeant and Corporal. We were all sent to a location in the Colonial's jungle to build a battle school by the name of 'Takama' this battle school area was selected specially because of its dense jungle and rainforest, not to mention, its infested wild life as well. This area was similar to the jungle in Burma, so it was the British intention to train a Caribbean Fighting Force along with American Troops as well, to go and fight in Burma- so the battle school was all scaled and mapped out and we the twenty-eight men started to construct.

We spent three months constructing the camp. It was hard work in the hot sun and in rain storms. The place was infested with rattlesnakes, there were also snakes in the camp area, along with the wild foxes and hungry tiger. We all survived the torment in the thick jungle and swamps here and there; also, early in the morning- the sand flies, and during the nights- mosquitos' infestation.

Finally, our three months ended. It was now 1945, and we were relieved by 'A' Company Unit, for three months to continue the construction. After this, they would be relieved by 'C' Company for another three months. During that six -month period of being in Georgetown. I wrote home to Tina's parents asking permission to become engage and later be married. They gave me their permission, and we started to see each other more and more. By this time, it was time for my return to Takama Battle School. So off I went to the land of torture, as I thought it was at the time. But on this trip, it was the entire 'B' Company, and it was battle training. What construction remained to be completed was our assignment. We started out training, which was very hard indeed.

We had built one of the hardest assault units in the history of the British Army. We also set a battle ground with barbwire running over the distance of one mile long, and the entire battle ground was two miles long. So we were also put under "Baptism of Fire,' which is a combat test for a soldier. It was the first time that new troops were under gunfire or in combat. An experience to test one's courage, strength, etc. our training was near the end of our three months.

My Platoon Officer who's name was Lt. David Rose, was young, tall and very good looking. He was trained at Sand Hurst, England. He had requested my services as his batman. I was working as Lt. David Rose, Batman, when one day while alone in his hut cleaning it out, I saw a revolver which was placed in a holster and hanging on a wall. I became very inquisitive. I went to the holster and removed Rose's pistol and started to investigate the pistol. I started to touch here and there, not knowing what I was touching and moving on the pistol. I then read the inscription on the pistol, which had this name on it, "A German Luger Semi-Automatic Pistol." It was the first time I had seen such a gun- it was a beautiful piece of weaponry. The German's were great at that period in building weapons that I knew of by using the copy of the British version of the "Bren Gun," which was named after the man who was a German, and he had designed the gun 'Breno' for the German Army.

The British got a hold of one of the guns and redesigned it, and put it in production for the British Army. I was a Bren-Gunner at that time, so I knew the ability of that gun. It was one of the most outstanding guns in the entire world at that time. It was light-weight, accurate, and had a terrific cooling system, because of the amount of bullets which can pass through the chamber any given minute. Anyway, getting back to the topic of the luger, after examining the gun, I raised it and put the muzzle against my temple and bend down and put the muzzle of the pistol between the open cracks in the floor, which were boards. I then pulled the trigger, the pistol went off, and scared the daylight out of me. I quickly replaced the pistol into its holster, then hurried up my work and rushed out of the hut. I did not clean the pistol before replacing it. I just didn't want to mess with the pistol anymore. So, I guess Lt. Rose must have smelled the carbon in his hut when he returned, but he never approached me about it. Instead, two days after, he summoned me and said, "I will not need you to work as my batman any longer." I said, "Okay, sir," and that was that. Weeks later, we were on our way to Georgetown, we had returned and stationed in the city for another six months in the year 1945.

So, while being at home, myself and Tina became so close, that we started to sneak off to the back of the yard when her parents retired to their bed early in the evening around 9:30p.m., which I supposed was late for them - but, early for us young folks. So, as I was saying, we would sneak off in the dark at the back of the yard and make love while we stand. A month later, we both found out that she was pregnant.

My mother used to spend most of her time with her boyfriend Mr. Leon, in the city of McKenzie, which was where he worked at the Bauxite Company. Margaret would spend three or four months up there, and one or two months at home with Leon, and they both would returned back to McKenzie. Well, I was starting to plan a wedding. Also, time was drawing near for me to make another trip to Takama while Tina was in her first month of pregnancy.

By this time, we were away training to leave in six months' time for the front line of Burma. But while we were in the middle of training, news came over our radio station of VE Day. "Victory over Europe." Everyone in the camp began to jump up into the air with joy. A few weeks later, we heard rumors of our boy, Henry, was returning home. It was great news to us all. Five or six weeks later after hearing the gossip, the boys did return safely- Army and Air Force Boys. By this time, World War 11 was coming to a close. The sinking of ships by the Germans was over; starvation around the world was at its' end. Women, children, and men were about to become meaningful. During the war, a human life meant nothing, one was living from day to day. The men we picked up out of the sea while I was working on our ship in 1942 were becoming a nightmare, so to speak. People had begun to see great changes taking place in their lives. Some people saw the changes coming about over night, including myself. But that was not so, I had that experience ahead, to see and to learn. But I did know that Christina Reece by this time was three and half months with our first child. My mother, whom we often called "Sister Margaret," by her sisters and her own children, because she was young when she gave birth to her first child, she was in her fourteenth year, going towards fifteen at the time. So she was practically growing up with her children as she kept getting them one after the other. So, Sister Margaret came down from McKenzie before Henry Griffith returned home from overseas. Margaret was confined to her bed while being sick, and Tina would go across to her, about twenty yards away between both houses, to assist Margaret during her time of sickness. Tina was very helpful to her, as I later assumed.

Henry came home weeks after Margaret arrived at home. So from time to time as Tina would go to Margaret bedroom to attend to her, as Tina would walk past the other nearby bedroom where Henry would placed himself so as to see Tina when she walked by. Henry decided to sweet talk Tina after he took her into the bedroom and they both struck a sexual relationship. The sex acts took place on three different occasions. During all that time I was still in Takama, playing with the pistol if you remember, I did not know that my mother was sick. I knew my foster brother, Henry had returned, but I knew nothing my girlfriend and him. Now getting back to my return to barracks from Takama.

On the second day of my arrival into town, we were given one day passes to go home to our families. I went home and my close friend Branch, you remember him - Winston Pilgrim, he went home to his family, and we had made arrangements to meet at my home. When I got home, I saw my sick mother and Tina, we were all glad to see each other. Griffith was not at home right at that time. So I sat and talk about one thing to another, after which, Tina and I went to our hideout and made love.

It was getting late by this time, as I was about to leave to go to the "Grand America." This was a night spot where most of the young men would go to listen to music and have a dance with the beautiful prostitutes- no sex. Those women strictly went with the American Soldiers. Guys such as, Branch, and myself were only entertained by those women on the dance floor, after that the women would return to their money guys. Myself and a few more were great dancers, Branch and I enjoyed ourselves and then raced back to barracks. That evening was well spent, after being away for three long months.

The following day was a Friday. On Fridays, the weekend sport begins, so on this Friday there was a ding-dong Garden Fete in Middle Street Gardens, such a fete was a great occasion. It was like a big open air gala dance between small, beautiful roads with seashells and bright, colorful flowers lining both sides of the road. Also, strings of lights nicely placed on the large trees, and a colonial bandstand sits in the center. Not to mention the various vendors as well selling food, soft drinks, ice creams, etc.

Branch and I planned our entire evening on that Friday. I followed him home and then he came with me to my home. When we arrived, Griffith was home, along with Reginald and Margaret. I greeted Griffith because this was the first time in two and a half years I had seen him. So, our greeting was full of hugs and kisses and with loud laughter. Henry said to me, "I am going to the Garden tonight, what you guys planning?" Branch replied, "You don't think we are going to miss that, do you?" Griffith said, "Good, the treat is on the old soldier. We will go to D.I.H. and get a room by ourselves." Griffith then started to sing as always. He loves to sing and did have a wonderful voice. I was changing into civilian clothes while Griffith was dressing and singing. My mother was feeling much better and started to move around in the house.

We finally got ready and headed to D.I.H. Bar. The letters D.I.H. stands for Demerara Ice House. We finally arrived at the bar and was given a cubicle and the large bottle of rum and coke, and commence our drinking. Then Griffith said, to Branch and me, "we heard about the battle school at Takama, how tough it is, and so on."

Pilgrim, said, 'Yes, it is, the training is very tough, it makes you feel as if you should not be born." Henry said, 'Yes, I know what you saying. I can tell you some stories as well from the trip I returned from. Life outside is tough my boys. We were in Naples for a while and the situation was so bad- no food, clothing, toilet paper, soap to bathe with, and the women, young and old, were selling their bodies for a bar of chocolate…. also, those things I've mentioned. We use to get a woman for a bed blanket as well. The Germans had cut off parts of Italy, so many things did not pass beyond the Germans."

Henry had begun to show signs of the liquor rocking the brain -getting drunk. I said, so you boys had a nice time? Lots of women, sex?"

Henry quickly said, "What else was there to do? Other that kill or be killed."

I said, "that's war I guess."Henry said, "Sylbert, I am going to tell you a story. But I don't know if I should, while your friend Branch is here."

I said, "Of course you can. We keep no secrets from each other."

Henry said, "Good, I am going to put you on the right road. I want you to imagine that there is a long road, and at the end of that road, there is a fork road. The road forks into two directions, one is the right road and the other is the wrong road." He continues sipping his drink more often than myself and Branch. The two of us sat looking quietly at Henry. Then Henry starts to sing. "Ava Mria," and a verse or two, and then he stopped and said, "Sylbert, you know I was away. I did not know Tina, or know that you were going with her. If you remember, when she moved into the yard, I was about to leave for overseas, so I really did not know much of the girl." I said, 'Yes, I remember, you left around three weeks after she came to stay with her father."

Henry said, "Okay, well this is what happened. Tina uses to come over to the house to help Sister Margaret when she was sick. So I got chatting with her a few times as she would walk pass my bedroom. So, one day I held her and took her into the bedroom and we started to have sex. That continued three or four times. After which she decide to tell me that you two were engaged to be married-also, she was three months pregnant. She did not tell me those things before the affair. I am sorry it did happen." I said, "Stop blaming yourself, she should have told you before, and not waited until after three incidents."

Henry finally closed the conversation by saying, "Now it's up to you to choose the right path of the forked road. Don't let her know that I've told you. You will have to find a way to put it to her." I said to him while being shocked and a bit stunned, "I will know how to put it, I'll find a way."

By this time the drinks had finished, and Henry was high as a kite, but not drunk. So I said to both Henry and Branch, "come on, let's go." We all raised, and Henry paid for the drinks and we left. We finally ended up at the Fair in the Garden and had a nice time until the Fair ended. At that point we parted company. Henry said, to us he was going home. Also, Branch and I took off back to the Army Barracks.

The following day I was off duty, so I went home to 63 Cross Street. Even though I was not prepared to face Christina Reece and her parents, and break the news as well to them. I come to the conclusion that I needed to break off my engagement and not marry Tina, because of what Henry Griffith had told me. But, my first decision before breaking such news, is that I will first have to get confirmation from Tina herself about the affair between her and Henry. So I kept thinking about my approach to her, in order to get her to confirm what I have been told. As I continued to walk from the barracks in Eve Leary to Leopold and Cross Streets, which is a couple of miles, my brain was busy trying to workout the best approach to her. An approach which will not implicate Henry as being the one who told me of the affair. Do not forget, Henry had kindly asked me to find a way so as not to implicate him as being the person who told me. Such a request was not easy to achieve. Various ideas and approaches came to the brain, one after the other, when finally the best of all entered the brain, and became the best of solutions.

By this time I had arrived home and settled myself down in the house. Luckily enough as I was sitting by the window, which overlooked across to where Tina home was, I saw her father and mother stepping out of the house. Both of them were all dressed up as if they were going to some sort of function. My mother was not at home, I was alone in the house, as I sat by the window waiting to confront Tina. Mr. and Mrs. Reece walked out of the house and disappeared out of sight. I got up from the window and went across to Tina's home. She was waiting for my arrival as always- Tina knew this, when she saw me by the window looking across her way. It was an opportune moment I would be waiting for to get together with her. It was a sort of code between us both. Because I can see the movements in her living room and the kitchen in her house, if and when she is going to the back of the yard, I can see all of her movements from that window.

As I arrived at the front door of Tina's home, she was standing at the door waiting to greet me with a big smile on her face. I quickly felt sorry for her, her beautiful face and broad smile sent shivers through my entire body. It's the human feeling which goes with first desire... and partly leads to the tree of love. I will explain briefly as I understand it.

My understanding of desire for love, and without desire, there can be no love. The point is, Tina being the first woman which I became attracted to. Attracted to her physique- body and built, her face -the contour of the individual face, which attracts me. The smile, those are all desires, which come to me by having an inner human measurement of my vision and needs. Now that's in the true sense of the word, and meaning of love. I will later explain love as I know it. So, that is the feeling which came over me as Tina stood and smiled, as I arrived close to her. Then she gracefully raised both her hands and placed it around my neck, and pulled me close into her body and said, "My darling." I responded with a closer embrace, as I said, "My love, the light of my life," and kissed her.

I have always called her the light of my life until then. We strolled into the house as we let go of each other. I sat into a chair, and she came and sat with her legs wide open across both my legs. As she approached in that fashion which was quite often, I knew exactly where she was leading me. This was her introduction to sex. I eased her out of her position and separate our close contact. She went and sat into a chair close to me. Then I said to her, 'Tina, listen to me. Have you ever heard, that when a woman not having sex, her parts become tight and close?

She said, "Yes" I said, "Well, I want you to tell me the truth now. Who did you go with while I was in Takama? You were not what I expected you to be when I had sex with you the other night." I suddenly saw tears settled in her eyes, as she was listening to me. She said, " I am very sorry, but it was your brother, Henry, I had sex with". I then asked, "How many times did you become involved in that?" Tina said, "Three or four times."

I then questioned her fully to find out what sort of morals she had away from her looks or beauty. Morals come from within the human mind, not looks or beauty. So I said, "When Henry approached you the first time, why did you not tell him that you were engaged and expecting a child- being three months pregnant?"

She said, "I don't know, I guess I did not want Sister Margaret to know that he had pulled me in the bedroom. Your mother was in the other bedroom lying sick. I use to go over to help her during the time it happened." I said, "But you could have told Henry quietly and refused the first time, also all of the other times. Well, I have to tell your father and mother, I can't go through with a marriage after that." The tears were heavy by this time. I then said to her as I stood up to leave, "I am very sorry, but I must go, I'll be seeing you."

I then walked out of her life at that point. I had decided to take care of the child and the preparation of the things she will need before the birth of the child. I quickly walked out of the house. A couple of days later I when home from camp, Mr. Reece approached me and said, "Christina told me what happened between her and Henry; also, your decision. I

am so sorry to hear about it. I can't blame you for your decision. She should have known better." So as you can see it, I did not have to tell the father and mother, because she had done it for me.

My mother called me on the same evening and said, "What's this I'm hearing about you not going ahead with the marriage to Tina? "Don't be silly, after all Henry is you brother, you can still marry the girl."

I was so shocked to hear what had come out from my mother's mouth to me, her son. I felt so disappointed with my own mother. I began to question her way of thinking in advising her son. With a serious situation such as what I was confronted with, I then asked my mother, "So you think I should go ahead and get married to Tina?" she said, "Why not, of course?" I went into a sudden rage and burst out saying, "I tell you what- you marry to her then!" We did not exchange anymore words at that time or after on the subject. I regret having to say this.

That first experience of what my mother's had said to me and Christina's action, and my mother was condoning it, and wants me to do the same, drove me into believing that women will stick together in thick and thin- women will always see eye to eye. I said to myself, "How can I go ahead with such a marriage, what will or can happen after such a marriage". Well, it's very simple; I would be living in a house with a wife such as Tina. I would leave her at home to go to work or go somewhere, on my return home I find one of my brothers, or hear one of them was in the house while I was out. The first thing would enter my mind, it is possible that my wife and brother were in the bed while I was out; and, is this second or third child truly mine? Those will be the things which will haunt me while living as husband and wife with Tina. That could send me mad or early to my grave or in jail. So after coming up with those fundamental reasoning, I said to myself and to my mother, you marry her. I wanted no part of building my life around such an eye opener. Thank God, I was not a stupid young man. I had a firm brain in my head and a good head sitting on my shoulder.

I was a great thinker, at times I would find myself sitting on the jetty, which was called the Seawall, thinking and day dreaming from the age of ten years old. I would sit alone looking out into the horizon above the far deep blue sea, straining my eyes as I looked out into the far distance. I would day dream about going abroad to one of those far away countries beyond where the sky comes down and touches the water in the sea… the sea kept splashing towards me, and the waves and tides kept rising towards the Jetty, or as one would call it- the Seawall. At times, I would be so deep with my vision. Imagination can be one of the greatest things that can be experienced by a person. I know I've been there and have fulfilled some of those, or most of them.

Well, Tina gave birth to a son, which I took as being my child. The boy was named Sydney and six months later, Tina had begun to date a young man by the name of Patrick Seaward. This young man was an identical copy of me in the sense of height and looks. It was as if we were twins. This is so funny, I have to laugh. But, Laughing is now, but not years ago as things were happening, Seaward affairs started before Tina came into my life.

It all began while working at the Laundry. I would go to my tailor, Premdass, with a suit length or a trousers length in order for him to sew it up. My other three friends would to the same store and purchase the same materials in order for the four of us to dress alike. Three of us will take our materials to the same tailor and the other friend would take his to a different tailor. So, cutting a long story short, the four of us would sit down and plan our new outfits wear on the various holidays, or when we go dancing and enjoying ourselves. Then suddenly, Seaward would appear in our company dressed similar to us, same material, style, or jacket. We began to notice the boy as he tries to rub shoulders with us.

Like I've said before I was a great dancer. So most of the girls would come and flocked amongst myself and three other friends. Which meant we had access to most of the beautiful young ladies in a dance, or where ever we were. We all did not pay much attention to Mr. Seaward. Not until one day, he said to me, "You must come to where I am living. My mother is keeping a little get-together for my birthday."

So I said "okay, I will come."

So I went to his house, he lived at the corner of King and Croal Streets, which were a few corners away from where I was living. On my arrival at Seaward's home, his mother was very surprised when she saw I was identical to her son in looks. She made a big thing out of it. The evening went by, and I had a few drinks and left.

As the years went by, he tried to be friends with me and my friends. We continued to side step him. So when Christina and I had finished, I saw him standing at the entrance of where I was living speaking to Christina. Then months later, Tina became pregnant with his child.

By that time, I was going with another girl named Ruby. Apparently Ruby was very elusive and used to baffle me quite often. She lived with her aunt on Murray Street. The aunt was a ship worker. She would clean out the ship's hatch when all of the ship's cargo was empty. She would work hard to help maintain Ruby, since Ruby did nothing day or night. Ruby never talked about herself or her family or anything, for that matter. Somehow, she seemed to have a lot of problems at her age of nineteen years. Truly speaking, I did not know much about her, other than she was light- complexioned, 5 feet 6inches, lovely-built, and very good looking; also, very sexy to look at- and in bed. I used the word 'bed', but we had never went on a bed. Ruby quite often would wait each week until I went on barracks duty, then come to the barracks and send word through someone at the guard house at the gate to call me. I would go to the gate to answer her call she would say to me, "Come, let's go for a walk on the Seawall."

Then off we would go and end up in the nearby field, and there we would lay on the grass and damp soil and make love. That went on for about six long months. She got pregnant and gave birth to a boy. The boy was named Lennox. Shortly after the birth of the child, which was about three months, I was discharged from the army. No sooner I came out of the army, Ruby's aunt took her to the court house, and make her take out a summons for child support. Now that was two weeks after coming out of the Army. I had never been in a court house or stood in front of a judge before. This was going to be my first time. So Ruby, her aunt, and I showed up in court for the case.

The Judge, or should I say the Magistrate, said to me, "Mr. Daniels, this child Lennox, is it your child?" By this time, I was shaking with fear of being sent to jail. I had no idea of the judicial system or the outcome of such a case. I said in reply to the Magistrate's question, "Yes, my Honor."

Then the Magistrate asked, "Why haven't you supported the child since the child was born, which three months ago?"

I said, "Your Worship, I was stationed at Takama for the past three months and just return to the city. We do not get paid while being in the jungle of Takama."

He then said, "Okay, you are ordered to pay one dollar a week into the court to support the child."

That was the end of the case and we all walked out of the court, after I agreed to pay the dollar a week- what the Magistrate had ordered.

When we came on the street, Ruby came over to me and said, "Please don't blame me for this, it's my aunt who has been pushing me to do this."

I then said, "How could you and your aunt bring me here for a dollar a week to support a child? Do you think a dollar a week can support a child?" That was the end of that. I paid the dollar a week during the period of my stay in Guyana. I started to look around for work and found out it was extremely difficult in order to find work, since many of us came out of the service. I then decided to go abroad.

But during the three weeks or so before coming out of the army, I was riding my bicycle home from the Army camp when I happened to see a lovely young lady strolling by on her way home. I quickly peddle my bike close to her and began to speak to her. I asked her where she was going and what was her name. She replied by saying, "I am going home, and my name is Leila Daly."

I continued to question her as I jumped off of my bike and started to walk along side her. I then asked her, "How far are you living?"

She said, "Charlotte Street, near Orange Walk."

I then asked her, "So what are you doing way down this way?" She said, "I usually attend sewing lessons here," and she pointed to a few houses behind us, as we walked away from that direction.

I then said, "My sister goes to sewing somewhere nearby here as well." She asked, "What is you sister's name?" I said, "Eileen Joseph."

She said, "I know her, she attend the same class." I then made a date to see her a few days later after sewing lessons- she accepted, and we continue to see each other.

I had discussed the meeting of Leila Daly with my sister, and she said that she knew the girl, and that the she was a beautiful girl. Eileen was a bit not too keen of the idea that I had made a date with the girl Leila- Why not, I do not know on to this day? Time was drawing near towards me getting out of the Army and going to Barbados. I told Leila of my plans to stow away in search of a better life. She had agreed with me and my plans. Time had come for me to leave and I said farewell, and promised to write to her. So I took off for Barbados.

# 11

## *Barbados*

T HE YEAR WAS 1947, DURING the month of May. I
was out of the Army, and I had received my army
severance pay. I gave my mother part of the money
and my child's mother, Christina, for the child which she
had for me. I then went and booked my passage from
Guiana to Barbados. I was told at that time, that the
American Farm Labouring Department, was selecting
farm workers in Barbados during that period. Before the
trip was planned, my brother Basil had a friend by the
name of Harris Allen. Harris had relatives who were living
in Barbados. So, Allen's mother had made arrangements
for both Harris Allen and I to stay with them when we
arrived. My closed friend in the army who I mentioned
before had decided to go as well. A place to stay was
arranged for Branch. Better known as 'Winston Pilgrim.'
The three of us finally sailed down to Barbados. Then
we hit the streets and started to make contact in getting
selected for the Farm Labouring work.

When we made contact in Bridgetown, the city capital
of Barbados, we were given sad news. It was a big let down
to the three of us, we were told that the consignment
of Farm workers had sailed to its destination in Florida
three weeks ago. I then asked, "When will it be the next
selection?" The boss name was "Big Sam." He was in his

thirties, seven feet tall, well built, dressed a bit rugged, but clean. Big Sam, told us we would have to wait six more weeks, we would then get word for the time." "So you boys can stick around, just keep checking the office twice a week in case there are changes." Harris said,

"We'll be here, see you around." We continued to keep in touch with Big Sam, and at the said time we also kept a close watch on the Bay area. Harris father was a seaman, sailing on the deep Sea Vessels, Canadian and American. So Harris had learned a lot about ships from his father. Also paying visits with this father on the ship in which the father was on. In short, Harris had never sailed at that time. Winston had no experience about ships. Luckily enough I did- I knew well about ships and the way in which a ship was constructed.

Harris and I were living in Que Road, at Bank Hall. Each day, we would walk from Que Road to Bridgetown and back home- as I were saying, we would sit on the jetty looking out into the Bay, checking on the ships as they come and went, in and out. We had joined the Seaman's Union and checking for jobs whenever a ship sailed into harbour, or bay as it's called. Then at nights, we would frequently visit the various clubs along the shore to enjoy ourselves releasing the human tension which life bears upon us, along with mixing amongst seamen. One could always hear about a job in a nightclub where seamen dwell. This routine became an everyday life, our money was becoming exhausted, and greed had begun to step in. Friends began to hide off around corners while they shop and eat a cake and sweet drink. Solid food was once a day provided by the family who was poor, but willing yet to share the little which was provided.

Two months had passed and like said, our money was almost to an end. I had to move, because the family could not afford to feed me any longer. So I moved into the house where Winston and two other friends of ours were staying with a woman from Guiana, who could have been either of us mother, but yet she was living with one of the boys who was an engineer on a ship, her name was Anita. We all gave her money in order to live at her house. The young man who Anita was sharing her bed with was age 24 years old, and she was forty-six years old. We all knew Anita and her two daughters from Back home. Her daughters were seen going to various dances in Guiana, while we too attend some of them. She did not know us- her two daughters were very, very beautiful and elegant, also well shaped. They were around age twenty-one and twenty-three years old respectively. It was not a comfortable home, but suited the purpose. It provided a roof over our heads and a wooden floor to lie on. I had bought a bed when I was staying with Harris' family, so I was grateful, so was all of us- we shared the same desire. The desire to go abroad and work hard and live above the standard we were living all our lives.

We continued our visits to big Sam's office and still no date was set, and we had already been around for eight weeks. We were becoming a bit jittery because our money was running out. We would also work as standby on some of the ships, but the work was not regular. We began to plan to leave Barbados before our money left us completely. By this time, it was only Winston and myself who still had a bit of money remaining. The two of us were the ones financing the group of five with food and provisions.

We would sit on the jetty examining the pros and cons as to which country we would stow away to. If we went to the U.S.A. and got caught, we will be deported, the same applies to Canada. Most of us would rather go to the U.S.A or Canada, because of a better job opportunity in those two countries. One had to be a Colonial Citizen in order not to be deported from either of the two countries. So the vote amongst us went to England or the British Isles. We were British Colonials; therefore we will stand a better chance if caught. So, England was decided upon to stowaway, we continued to keep a close eye on the ships as they sailed into the harbour for three days.

A Harrison line did enter the harbour to load up with sugar on the third day. As the ship was loading, we made contact with a shore boat to take us out to the ship, at the said time as the ship workers would be going out to the ship to start work.

Everything was nicely arranged and all was set. The Harrison Ship was anchored in the blue sea, being loaded with its cargo of sugar, for the twenty-four hours before sailing. We all went home and had a good night's sleep in order to get up early to board ship- so said, so done. Five of us went aboard, as soon as our feet hit the deck of the ship, we all separated into various directions and head for the coal bunker area. Then we all disappeared into the bunker area near to the ship's engine room and dug holes into the "Smith Coal," which was used as fuel for the ship. After digging out holes in the coal, where we could sit down in the coals and not to be seen, and be comfortable for the entire journey to our next home- abroad. A few hours later the ship lifted its anchor and sailed out of the harbour to its destination. We all, by this time had begun to feel great of our achievement. We then started to listen to the ship's bell striking the shift changes and time of the day.

The heat from the sun beating down on the steel deck of the ship, and the heat flowing out of the engine room was tremendous. We did not take any food or water when we went aboard the ship. So after eight hours, we all began to feel hungry and thirsty. Hours later, we felt the ship and its engine slowing down. This became very alarming to all of us, because we were told that the ship was going to England after leaving Barbados. We were not told of a stop before heading to England. After a short moment, we heard the ship anchor drop into the sea. Then a few hours later, we heard voices and work activity. We came to realized that the ship was stopping for more sugar. We decided to sleep while the ship continued to load sugar. Early the next morning, we heard several voices shouting, "Come on out! Hurry up!"

As we try to see what was happening, we saw a group of the ship's crew standing on top of the coal bunker with water hoses in their hands all to the ready, as they shouted, "Come on hurry. Come on out, otherwise we will turn on the steam hose." All of us crawled out from our hiding place and out we went.

When we were all mustered on deck, the five of us were also joined by seven other stowaways, who had joined the ship after us five went aboard in Barbados. Not only that, but one of the seven guys went upon deck during the night and stole a bottle of coke-a cola from a table in one of the ship's crew's cabin. That what alerted the ship's crew, of the ship having stowaways on board. The seven stowaways were from Dutch Guiana, we saw them when they arrived in Barbados from Dutch Guiana. All of them had stowed on a passenger liner from Dutch Guiana to Barbados- they were all known to us five.

We were all taken off of the ship where it had anchored in the sugar area and port by the name of 'Rouseo' on the island of St. Lucia. The police came and transported us to the capital of St. Lucia, which was Castries, and put us in the police compound next to the prison. The following day, we were taken to court in front of a Magistrate and he recommended that we be deported back to our respective countries- that became a two weeks wait on a ship to take us back home. At the end of two weeks, the French passenger liner, which was called the Dukedamall, took all of the stowaways at the end of the two weeks wait- we who were from British Guiana were sent home.

The others were sent back to Dutch Guiana on the same ship we were on. But we were separated while being on the ship. We all were placed in prison cells on the ship on our way home. The ship sailed back to Barbados. While the ship was in Barbados, two of the shore boat workers came on board the ship, because they had heard that we were on board the ship on our way back home. The two boys came to our cells and said to me, "Hi buddy, we heard of you boys getting caught. Daniels, if you want to see your suits, they're all hanging on the coat hanger swinging like this." The guy spread both of his arms wide apart and starts to swing his body from side to side, as he continued to describe the motion of the suits swinging in the wind.

He continued, describing the wind blowing the jackets, like this, outside of the pawn shop on Baksters Road. To be told that was terrible, but I burst out laughing, because of the way in which he describe the clothing swinging outside of the pawn shop on the walkway. As I saw it all the time, Miss Anita did not waste much time after she heard from her boyfriend that we all had left. I can imagine her rushing around gathering up the clothing that belonged to all of us who had stowed away. Yes, she was a bitch of a woman and so was her boyfriend. They both took all of our clothing to the pawn shop.

Her boyfriend was a young man, the same age as her two daughters, and he was sleeping with the mother because he was working and earning a few dollars. She was a slack big woman. Now, that's the way I interpreted that relationship at the time. I had planned in my mind, that when I had arrived in England and started to work and earned some money, to write to her and send her some money, and at the said time asked her to send me my clothing to England.

The ship lifted its anchor and sailed to Grenada, Dominica, Trinidad and then to British Guiana. When the ship arrived and moored alongside Garnet's Wharf, we all were then taken to the captain's cabin. The captain handed us our passports and papers, and then we were escorted to the entrance of the gangway. As soon as our feet touched the Wharf, we started to run so as not to be seen by the string of workers who was about to report for work in half an hour's time- which would be seven a.m. We were all ashamed of our condition, our clothing was dirty looking, torn in places, because of the coals eating into the material which we were wearing.

I ran all the way from Water Street to 63 Cross Street, which is about a mile. The other boys went to their respective homes. We all had returned home around the end of November, which meant Christmas was around the corner. My brother, Donald and Basil, helped me to buy a couple of pants and shirts.

I then was faced with having to go and look for work once again on the waterfront. Things were not going very well, such as getting enough work to make ends meet. For example, the wages per day was $1.20 cents, in British exchange at that time was five shillings. In space of a week, I would earn three days work in a most given week. My child support which I had to pay to the court was one dollar per week. So, I was then left with chicken feed -a little amount.

On the day of my returned home, I stopped at the entrance of 63 Cross Street, and view the activity in the yard. It was quiet and deserted. I then sneaked into the yard quickly, using the shortest way to my house so as not to be seen. The door was opened, as I swung around the side of the house and ran up the steps. When I enter the house, I first encountered my sister as she walked out of the bedroom.

She became alarmed and shouted, "Oh, my God!" Then she became silent for a few seconds and quickly burst out laughing. She said, "Now, what happened to you?" "Boy, you look terrible."

My mother then came out of her bedroom and look at me with a long silence trying to workout what happened to me, and then said; "Look at your condition. Now what happened?" I sat down looking at both of them, my sister and mother, before answering both their questions.

They both sat down and listen to my adventure. My sister later got herself all dressed up to go to her sewing lessons.

My sister, Eileen, just could not wait to go and break the news to my new girlfriend, Leila Daily, that I had returned home, practically naked, and that I had lost all my clothing; and, that she must avoid having anything to do with me of course. Leila had told me everything that my sister had said to her, when I visited her three days later, at her mother's home. Leila's mother had like me for a son-in-law, and thought the world of me. I had also thought the world of both of them, and brother as well.

# 12

# Georgetown to Mc Kenzie

D URING THE MONTH OF FEBRUARY 1948, I Danny
Daniels had left my home at 63 Cross Street,
Georgetown, Werk-En-Rust, to go in search of a
job at Mc Kenzie Bauxite Company because of the work
situation in the City of Georgetown. I and my brother
Basil Daniels, along with Harris Alleyne, Winston Pilgrim,
and Hector Barrow, who were all friends of Basil and
me. We had planned to go in searched of work at the
Bauxite Company. We went and boarded the riverboat
by the name of R.H. Car, when we arrived at Mc Kenzie,
later renamed Linden, we stayed at the resident of Harris
Alleyne's mother, who fed and boarded us, because we
all were dead broke-so to speak. Mrs. Alleyne was one of
the most kind, and wonderful woman one can find. We
all went in search of work at the Bauxite Company. We
inquired in various section of the Bauxite Company so as
to seek employment.

In the Early part of the second week, we were offered
a job to paint the exterior of the white people's cottages.
The money which was offered to paint one cottage was
five Guiana dollars, which was the equivalent of one
British pound Sterling. We needed the money badly, so we
decided to split ourselves into two working groups. Two
of us worked on one of the cottages, and the other three

worked on another cottage. Then as soon as one cottage was completed, because there were three workers, one would go to join the other two on the next cottage.

At the end of our second cottage, which was given to us by a Black painting contractor, who only paid; us five dollars per cottage, came to an end after the second week- we were back at square one, out of a job. But, all of us had given Mrs. Alleyne some money for our room and board. Approaching our third week, I woke up one morning and looked across the Demerara River from the Wismar River Bank on the Westside of the main city, which is located on the east river bank. As I looked across to the east side towards the city, I noticed an old beat up ship which needed a good chip and paint job. All around one can see the paint scaling off of the ship, I said to the boys, "I am going to that ship to see if I can get a job."

So I did, but when I got to the ship, it was loading up with the Bauxite. I saw one of the sailors; "Excused me Sir, I came in searched of a job. Are there any vacancy?" The sailor said, "No, son, we have a full crew, we are not shorthanded. But, I'll tell you what, the sister ship is coming to load Bauxite as well, its due to arrive in three days' time. You can check that one when it gets here, they might be shorthanded."

I then said, "Thank you very much." I quickly glanced at the name of the ship- the Blair Spree, and it was flying an English Union Jack Flag.

I then returned back across the river, and join the boys, I said to them, "I went aboard the ship to see if there was any opening for a job, but was told by one of the crew, that the ship had a full crew, but its sister ship will be arriving in a few days and maybe that crew will be shorthanded."

Harris said, "That ship looks beat up." I quickly said, "That's why I am planning to go back to Georgetown and wait on this one to come in, because if the looks of this one is like it is, then it's a good ship to stowaway on. So I don't know about you boys, but I will be leaving here in the morning, so as to get myself ready for that ship- it's not leaving without me."

Basil said, "I will be going tomorrow as well." The others agree to travel and get ready to stowaway as well- so said so done. We all went to the city and ended up at my home on Cross Street. We sat down and planned. I told them, "Since I am living closer to the waterfront, I will be keeping a check on the ship to see its movements." Now you boys will have to keep in touched with me." Everyone agreed, and then to their various homes.

I saw the Blair Spree as it sailed down from the Bauxite Company and then dropped its anchor to wait on the tide to sail away. Then a day later I saw the sister ship sailed into the Demerara river and dropped its anchor. It was waiting to head up to the Bauxite Company to load its Bauxite. The boys came to see me, and I informed them all of the ship's movements. We planned to meet at Lombard and Broad Streets at 9 p.m. so that we can make our arrangements to get a river boat to take us out to aboard the ship. They all took off, so as to do their last minute business.

I went to my girlfriend's house, who lived with her mother in Charlotte and Orange Walk, to give them the last minute visit, and to let them know of my departure. I told my girlfriend, Leila Daly, and her mother, "Mrs. Daly, when I arrive in England and settled down, I will be sending some money for Leila to book her passage on a ship by the name of 'Araka' to join me in England.

As I was about to leave, Mrs. Daly, got up from her chair and walked into the bedroom. She returns to Leila and myself and said, "Take this and when you leave here. You're to go the market and buy a bottle of white lavender water, and a cake of indigo blue, and when you are ready to take your bath, mix the white lavender and the indigo blue into the bucket of water, take the calabash and mixed it up. Then, while dipping the water to pour it over your head and body, you are to say the, Psalm 23, of David."

*The Lord is my Shepherd; I shall not want*
*He maketh me to lie down in green pastures;*
*he leadeth me beside the still waters*
*He restoreth my soul, he leadeth me in*
*the paths of righteousness for his name's sake*
*Yea, though I walk through the valley*
*of the shadow of death, I will fear*
*no evil; For thou art with me; thy rod and thy*
*staff they comfort me Thou prepares*
*a table before me in the presence of mine*
*enemies Thou anointest my head with oil, my cup*
*runneth over Surely goodness and mercy shall follow me*
     *all the days*
  *of my life and I will dwell in The house of  the*
*lord for ever.*

As you can well see by the above, I had left Leila and Mrs. Daly, home after saying goodbye to both daughter and mother. I bought the two items and went to the biscuit factory and bought four cents broken biscuits to travel with. Time was drawing near for me to go and meet the boys. Before leaving home, I got two Canadian milk bottles which held two pints of liquid and filled the bottles with water to travel with as well.

The time had arrived. It was now 9:15 p.m., and the boys did not show up to board the ship. But the funny thing about it all was, as I stood waiting for my brother Basil Daniels, Harris Alleyne, Winston Pilgrim and Hector Barrow,  to my surprise three others who I had known, came over to me and said, "Danny what's happening?" I said, "Not much." One of the boys I had known by the name of Reds, it was him that spoke to me first, and asked, "What was happening." One of the other was known as Bumbie and the other was known as Daddy- O.

I was very familiar with Daddy-O, because he was in the army in Trinidad, and would be stationed at our camp, while waiting to return back Trinidad. His correct name was Claude Roberts, which I later found out.

So back to our earlier meeting, Bumbie said, "I heard that a set of you boys planning to stowaway on that ship out there". I said, "Did you hear that?" Bumbie said, "Yes, you know nothing can't hide for long from us." Daddy-O then asked, "What happened to the other boys?" Reds Quickly said, "Like, they chickened out".

By this time, it was 9:30p.m., and time was getting late. Bumbie said, "How do you plan to go on the ship?" I said, "I will have to contact one of the boys who have a riverboat to take us out."

But it doesn't look as if those guys are going to show," Claude Roberts said, "lets make a move, it s getting late."

Bumbie took off down the road towards a young man and stopped to speak to him. A couple of minutes later, I saw the two of them walking towards us. As they join us, Reds said, "George, I haven't seen you in a while." George replied, "I heard you got a job on a ship and was away."

Red responded, "It was a short trip." Bumbie said, "George, this is Basil Daniels brother, and this is Daddy-O."George said, "So you boys want to make a trip out in the harbour, I could take you all, but I don't have a lamp. I know your brother, he's my buddy, and we went to Government School together. Basil and I use to live in the Foundry Yard up the road here, with Mrs. Sarah your mother and Donald's grand mother, almost all the family lived in that yard. But you didn't?"

I said, "No, because I use to live with my godparents. My name is Danny."

George said, "It's nice meeting you boys. Let go down to the wharf, and I'll use one of the other boys' boat, my boat is not working- but, we need a lantern."

By this time we all started to walk towards La Penitence Wharf. When we arrived at the front of the wharf, which was situated at Sussex and Lombard Streets, there was a male black street vendor, who was sitting behind a coconut cart. Sitting on top of the coconut cart was a lantern that was shining very bright. Bumbie said, "I will borrow this Lamp."

Bumbie picked up the Lamp, while the man was asleep, and we went down the wharf. George then got hold of a boat and called us over, and we all sailed towards the ship.

When we reached the ship, a little way from the ship's Gangway. I shouted " A Hoy There", a White Sailor standing at the top of the Gang way answered , "A Hoy There", I further shouted "can we come up and shelter from the rain ? The sailor answered, "Yes, come on up." By the time we reached the top of the Main Gang way, I then said to the sailor. "We're on a fishing trip." The sailor said, "It's Okay what a terrible night, with thunder and lighting, followed by a heavy down pour.

# 13

## *My Voyage to Scotland*

T HE BURLY SAILOR SAID, "YOU guys haven't even started to fish yet, and you are already soaking wet."

I said, "That's the way it goes at times." The man was keeping watch that evening and told us, "I'm going to go and have coffee. If you leave before I get back, take good care on your fishing expedition." Then the sailor strode across the lower deck, passing all of the hatches as he disappeared into the dark river night through the rain, and into the stern of the ship.

There was a fire escape door, two to four yards from where we were standing. I led the way, followed by Claude, Reds, and Bumbie. I went down the steps and in to the stoke coal area. The boiler and furnace, also nearby was the Smith Coal area. I was like Moses leading a group of people out of Colonial bondage, and hungry young men out of a job. I then climbed quietly onto the coals heap and tried not to slide or slip, knocking down the coals on top of each other. I kept signaling the others to be quite and careful. We all crawled on top of the heap of coals all the way to the back wall. The coal was packed three feet below the ship's deck. We had to dig holes into the coal to sit in it, so as to be well away from the hot steel deck above us. I tucked myself into my little hole, and taking large pieces of coals and packing them on top of each other, to barricade ourselves from view. I then unloaded my supplies, two bottles of water and about three pounds of broken biscuits- I then fell asleep.

We were all aboard the sister ship. The name of this sister ship was the "Blairesk". We were awakened by the sound of the ship's bell as the strike of four strokes, which had signaled 4a.m., and minutes later, we heard the sound of the anchor being pulled up from the bottom of the river bed. The engine room started up, and the propeller began to spin, and the ship started to move. Our voyage had started. I went back to sleep while listening to the noise of the engine room and propeller shaft.

We all were awakened by the sound of nine strokes of the bell. The water and biscuits, I shared some to the three boys, as they were crying out for thirst and hunger. I said, "How on earth, all of you came to stowaway with your two long arms, nothing to eat or drink?"

No one uttered a word. I would hold the water bottle as I let each one of them take a couple sips of the water. Cutting a long story short, the ship took two and a half days to sail from Demerara/Georgetown, to Port-of-Spain Trinidad. But after one and a half days, all of the water and biscuits were finished. Bumbie was fifteen years old, I told him he was not old enough to stowaway, but he insisted that we take him along; and if we didn't he would report us, and no one will make the trip. So we had to do as he said, but I can tell you it was not easy picnic trying to make the trip with him. Bumbie cried the entire journey. Neither of us knew that the Blairesk would make a stop at Trinidad- at least not me. When we entered the last day, Bumbie and Reds, began to get overbearing, and disgusting. Not forgetting to mention, the moaning and groaning through the last three hours. Reds would then use Bumbie, by telling Claude and me that Bumbie was dieing from de-hydration, and the boy needs water and biscuits. I said to them, "That's the entire ration we had, it finished one day ago, and you two still asking for more water and biscuits. You two have been asking me for water every time you all wake up, you guys are mad." Normally we were awakened for as long as ten hours, and slept 14 hours, if we were not awake, and sipped a bit of water, and nibble a few biscuits.

Now three hours later after being pestered by Reds and Bumbie, the ship started to dock along the loading area, after two and a half days. We were unaware as to where we were, but we kept hearing voices shouting from the dock area. By nightfall we came to realized that the ship was load up more Bauxite, it is called "toping off its final load." Well most ships with its cargo sailing out from the Demerara river was unable to cross the bar at the mouth of the rive, to enter the Caribbean Sea. So getting back to the loading of the Blairesk in Trinidad, Port-of-Spain.

I came to realize that we were on a slow boat to China, "like the saying goes." Because of the slow two and a half days in traveling no further than Trinidad, and had estimated that we had sailed pass Trinidad. Well by this time the ship started to load all night, and Claude, and I went to sleep. Claude and I were near to each other all of the way. I could not say how close Bumbie and Reds were from each other, because the place was pitch black, day and night. But looking towards the direction where we traveled into the area where we were, we can see day light during the day. Secondly, the bunker hatch was always open. So as to get air below in that area of the furnace, and engine room. I was awakened at 3a.m. by Reds and Bumbie rushing back to our hiding place and coals falling on top of each other. Reds said to me, "Hey, Daniels, we went and get water. Boy, a man saw us pumping water by the ship's kitchen and he shout at us, I had a belly full of water, we are okay now." "Now you listen to me," I told them. "That was a foolish thing to do. That man who shouted and ran after you two, now known that the ship has stowaways. Now in the morning the crew of the ship will be here looking for stowaways. I'll tell you two this, when they come in the morning calling and looking, you two will have to go out. Do not tell them about us, because we haven't move from here. Please tell me, how did you two run away from the man who chased you?" Bumbie said, "We ran through that area, then we came out into the engine room into the stoke coal areas." I said, just pray that they do not find Claude and me in here when they come searching in the morning. If they do, I will beat both of you from Trinidad back to Guiana. You two go out alone."

Hours had passed, and the day begun. At the foot of the coal and the open hatched, the early morning sunlight was beaming through the hatch. I heard a few voices, and I removed a large piece of coal to one side, and started to peep. I quickly replace the coal, as they came a bit closer and stopped. A voice shout, "Come on out, we know that you are in there. Come on out! You have two minutes to come out, after that; we are going to turn on the steam hose. Come on, or you'll get the steam." I then said, "You two go on out, go on go." As I spoke in a loud whisper, Bumbie and Reds began to crawl out from their hiding places, while shouting to the ship's crew, "We're coming out, don't turn on the steam!" Bumbie and Reds finally got out and join the ship's crew. They all walked away, and exited up the fire escape and out of sight. Claude said, "It looks as if all is well." I said, "Yes it looks as if they are satisfy, that it's them alone."

Then one hour later we heard an engine and the ship's propeller start, and the ship begin to move. We knew at that point that we were on our way. Claude and I had decided to brave the journey. We knew that the ship was a slow one, but we did not know how many knots per hour the ship were doing. We did know that we had to stay in hiding until the ship crossed the "Gulf" before coming out of hiding.

The two of us hid in our holes for eight days and nights as we kept counting the ship's bell as it struck the time of the day or night. We kept twisting and turning throughout the eight days and nights. We finally came out of hiding and walked to the end of the coals bunker and to the open hatch. An elderly European man came out from the stoking area. He was very astonished to have seen Claude and I standing where we were. The man asked, "What are you guys doing here?"

I said, "We are stowaways." Then I asked him quickly, "Have we passed the Gulf?" By this time I had caught on to man's Scottish accent. The Scottish man said, "No, we haven't meet the Gulf as yet, we are just heading towards Barbados. Did you guys know that they caught two other stowaways in Trinidad? When did you all come aboard?"

I told him that we came onboard at Mc Kenzie while the ship was loading. By that time I saw Claude's eyes, and his eyes was turn backwards, all I could have seen was a white eyeball, like a zombie. I quickly said to Claude, "Look at your eyes." Claude said, "Look at yours."

You look like you're almost death". The Scottish man said, "You boys look like death, you must be strong. Now listed to me. I will get you some water, just sit in that corner." He went into the coal area and in no time he returns with a bucket of water. He said, "Here you are. I'll be back shortly to give you some more water." Off he went. The bucket of water was standing near to both of us feet. I said, "Go on, Claude, drink." He said, "You go on drink." I took a hold of the one-gallon bucket and lifted it up and drank the entire water as I lay the empty bucket to the ground. The Scottish man, our savior, returned and said, "You finished the water already?"

Claude answered, "He drank all of it."

The Scottish man said, with great amazement and stamped his foot to the ground, "you what! You know what you just did? You could have killed yourself with shock. You are very strong or our God is close to you all. "I will go and fetch you some more water." He took off for the water, and was back by the time you say, "Jack the

Ripper." He gave Claude the water and opened a paper, took out two large Christmas puddings and gave us one each. We both thanked him several times, and told him he was a," God-sent".

The Scottish man said, "Listen to me, boys. Don't let anyone know that I was giving you food and water."

We both responded, "No, we won't. That would be very stupid of us." The man said, "I will tell you all when to come out after we enter the gulf. The ship is a very slow one, only five knots most of the time."

We retuned to our hiding place. It didn't take us long to fall back to sleep, after drinking that amount of water and Christmas pudding, we were so filled.

The ship continued on its journey, and Scottish man took care of our food and water until it was time for us to give ourselves up and report to the ship's captain.

It was time for us to come out of hiding and report to the captain, for the ship had long entered the Gulf. We were taken by the mate to the ship's captain, who was sitting on the bridge while speaking to one of the AB seaman. The captain asked us, "Where did you boys board the ship?"

I said, "McKenzie sir."

He asked, "How did you get food and water?"

"We brought some salt biscuits and water on board." The captain said, "Well, you boys will have to work on the ship for your meals. The mate here will show you where to sleep and what job to do."

Claude said, "Okay Captain and thanks." The mate took us downstairs from the bridge on to the deck. He took us to the back of the ship, which is called (Off) and opens a door. It is the Anchor Chain room, the mate said, "I will fetch you some blankets. This is where you can stay." He then went away. The anchor chain was coiled up in a circle and was cold. He retuned after a while as we were sitting on the cold chain. He came back with two blankets and gave us one each. We were given food and water by the mate. He said, "We normally start work early in the mornings to beat the sun. You boys know how to chip and paint, and Sugie?"

We said, "Yes, sir." Now that was that, throughout the trip to Scotland. We kept thinking of the slowness of the ship. We spent Easter on the high seas.

After a while, we arrived finally in "Burnt Island," not far form Cooper of Fife. As the Blairesk docked and the gangway was let down, two policemen came onboard, followed by the immigration officials. We were handed over to the police, who in turn handcuffed us and put us into the police car. They drove us to Cooper police station and charge us for boarding the ship without a passenger fare. After which we were taken to Cooper Court house, in front of a Magistrate. The Magistrate read out the charges and asked us, "Are you both innocent or guilty?" we said, "Guilty Sir."

The magistrate said, "I can see from the papers here in front of me, that you two have a clean police clearance, also you all were in the army during World War 11. And was demobed." I served in Africa in the army as well. I have seen what the Colonial System has done to too many people. It's a shame. That is why guys such as you two have to stowaway in search of a better way of life. The shipping company wants me to prosecute you- well my hands are tied, I am sorry. I therefore have to pass a sentence of 28 days in prison."

After serving the sentence, which became an experience to both of us. We were given travel documents to travel from Cooper to Edinburgh, and a letter to take to the Colonial office in Edinburgh. We reported to the Colonial Officer and gave him the letter. The officer was a black Barbadian. He told us, "Lets me explain the job situation. Jobs are very difficult for blacks to get in England and here as well. I can get you a job as a seaman, working on the railway line laying tracks, or working in the coal mines." We both told the officer that we rather work in the coal mines.

The officer said, "Okay, I will make arrangements for you to go and have training and then you will be sent to a mine. I will telephone the YMCA and make arrangements for you to stay there and have your meals. I will also contact you there, and then you will come back here and report to me."

We received a telephone call from the Colonial Officer to report to him. When we got there, he said, "You boys have a seat. I have everything laid out for you. I managed to get you into the training at Muircock Hall in Fife. The training will take six weeks, after that you will be sent to a pit in Newton Grange, in middle Lothian. The wages will be five pounds and fifteen shillings per week when you start working in the coal pit. In these two envelopes, you will find enough money to last you while training. Also, here are your travel tickets. You can take the train in the morning. Mr. James Austin, here is your package, is everything understood?" We all said, "Yes Sir." The officer said, "I wish all of you the best of luck." We departed from the Colonial Office and returned back to the YMCA.

Mr. James Austin was walking along Princess Street while Claude and I were window shopping. We then bumped into each other and introduce ourselves. James told us that he was in the British Air Force. He later got demobed out of the service in British Guiana. He also mentioned that while being in British Guiana, he observed that the streets were crowed with ex-service men. Also, with the poverty which faced him in Guiana, he then decided to migrate back to England. So we all decided to visit the Colonial Office.

The following morning the three of us were bound for the train station, for training in the mines in Dunfermlin. The training was very hard and rugged, but we stood the hardship for the six weeks and were finally sent to

"Lingerwood" coal mines, and there we started work. We lived in "New battle Hostel."

Living and working in the small village of Newton Grange and staying in New Battle Miners' Hostel was not easy. Most of the workers who were living in the Hostel were from Poland and was working in the coal mines in that area. Most of them were nice to live with, while others were very difficult to live amongst. There were only five blacks staying there.

The Polish were very racial indeed. We stood our ground against them. After a year, while we were sitting at a dining table, two of them came across from where they were sitting with four others, and said, "You guys get up and go to another table that way," and pointed to a little distance away from our table which was in the center of the dining room. James Austin said, "What is the matter with you? Go back to where you were with your friends and cool down."

By this time, one of the two pushed James out of his chair onto the floor. The five of us leaped onto our table, moving from table to table and kicking and punching who ever joined into the brawl. The manager and some of the staff came and quite down the fighting in a short space of time, all of the Polish no goods came to their senses and respected us.

Working in the Linger Wood Mines was very deep indeed. It was five miles under the sea bed, drips of water would always drip from between the rocks after blasting the rocks, so as to show up the empty pockets after digging out the coal. I must say this, after working in a mine with about ten men to a crew, we all would be using a pick axe to dig the coal out of the pocket. Also a spade, to pick up the coal and throw it on to a conveyor belt. We would all try to keep the rhythm as we worked removing the coals from the coals face, I said on my second day of working, "Oh my God! Why did my mother give birth to me?"

During the weekends, we would travel down from the small village which was known as Dalkeith to Edinburgh, so as to get away from the people who thought that they were more superior to us the Blacks. Edinburgh was a big city, and one could find all sorts of entertainment, it makes life much easier after working all week as we did. But, I can assure you, going to the big city of Edinburgh, we quite often was prepare to face some degree of humiliation.

Let's begin with going to see a movie film in one of the cinema. Claude and I will be walking on the sidewalk, and saw a long line of people- all white most of the time. The people were standing as they que up in the line to go into the cinema. We would walk from the front of the line, so as to join the back of the line. While listening to racial overtones coming from East West, North and South Someone in the line shouted "Civilization" from the song which lyrics went like this, "Hey Jimmy did you see his cong tail?" Then everyone would burst out laughing down the line. No, that's not an easy thing to be faced with. Again I say, 'No, not many people can live with that kind of insularity. I have seen many a black person, who had to endure such situations, such as that, and worst.

When I first came to Scotland, I was faced with the greatest amount of humiliation a human being can be confronted with. Let's begin with jobs in 1948; a Black Man could only have gotten a job in the Coal Mines, the Railways or Washing Dishes in some Restaurant. There was no other job other than becoming a Seaman, and even that was a bit difficult. Only certain ships were available to the Black Seamen in England, in those days, I was then working in the Coal Mines in Newton Grange, and living in New Battle Miners Hostel for two and a half years. A couple more blacks and I were there at the time, we would sometimes leave the small village just to getaway from the people who thought that they were more superior to us, the Blacks. We would all hop on to a bus to travel from our little village which was known to us as Dalkeith to go to the Big City of Edinburgh, where one could find more life and places to enjoy ones self.

But from the moment a black person boarded the Double-Decker Bus at Dalkeith, to travel to Edinburgh, the passengers on the bus who were White, would all start singing Danny Kay's old Tune, Some of the words of that tune went like this 'Bonga, Bonga, I don't want to leave the Congo.'

They would sing that tune from the moment the driver select the first gear and the bus pulls away. The tune is normally started by one person, and then picked up by the other Whites joining in singing, before we arrive at our destination. They would not stop until the bus reaches St. Andrews Bus Terminal, then, before the singing would come to an end. The white passengers would repeat that particular song, over and over throughout the twenty minutes journey. It was not just the tune, but the dirty remarks, which were thrown at us, between the words of that song.

Another one of my experiences was, one day I was walking along the street when for some apparent reason, a little boy about 10 years old, walking with his mother dashed across at me, taking his finger and rubbing it against my skin, and then he rubbed his hands together to see if the black on me would rub off. The boy shouted to his mother, 'Mummy it didn't come off." I simply glanced at them both, and kept on walking. In a short time I grew accustom to their behaviour, I quickly came to the conclusion, that I was here, and it was all happening right here. But yet, I was not to let that worry me.

Many times children of all ages would come up to me and say, 'Mr. Sambo, have you got a tail wrapped around your waist? Now it depends on the mood, I am in at the time. Sometimes I will not reply, at other times I would tell the child, "Listen, when you go home, ask your mother to open her legs real wide, and you'll see a little Sambo looking at you from between her legs."

Because we got to find out that it was the parents of these little white boys, who trained their children to come and ask us such foolishness. Also, that we Blacks, were animals with long tails around our waist. They were also taught by their parents, that Black people lived in Mud Huts from where they came, while others live in trees, and swung like monkeys.

That was the system in most of the British Isles, thousands upon thousands of Black People had to endure. My first two and a half years of working in Scotland kept me away from some of the humiliation which was yet to come. Not until leaving Scotland and going to London to find work and a place to live.

# 14

## *London*

WHEN I ARRIVED IN LONDON along with my buddy Claude Roberts, who had stowaway with me from British Guiana to Scotland. We both went in search of a place to rent, which would be an uphill task, since we were black. I remembered an African Student Hostel, which I used to stay at whenever I visited London, which was just when I took a two weeks vacation, during summer.

After we both settled into the Hostel, we start inquiring about vacancies. We decided to buy the daily newspapers and go through the classified ads and write down all the places listed for rent. We took one pound and changed it up into pennies at the newspaper stand. We would both go into Campden Road and use two separate phone booths.

In all, we had about thirty ads. Our times of calling were very frustrating. My conversation with one of the land ladies went like this, 'Good morning, I am ringing in connection with your Ad of rooms to let, is the double-room still vacant?' 'Yes," is what most of them would reply. Next question, "What is your nationality?" I replied, "I am a West Indian." The reply came immediately, "I'm a very sorry, but we do not rent to blacks."

On other calls it was either, 'Are you black or light, or where do you work?' Have you got any children or pets?" Then finally, after completing the thirty ads in calls, it will be 98% of a negative attitude. The 2% who would say, "Come around and see if you like the place," they too gave us butterflies in our stomach.

When the Land lady answered our calls, after saying, "Good day," they then shouted, 'it's the man about the double room, Harry! She would say, "Hold on a minute my husband will see to you." She would hurry away, while her husband quickly says, "Oh, you're the guy for the room? "I'm sorry, but it's already gone. I let it and my wife didn't know." This is referred to as a double act. The wife didn't mind about me being black, so she said, yes. Come and see it." But when the husband comes home from work, or wherever he went, he was the one who objected to the renting of the room to blacks. So when he finally sees the person who really wants it, and they turned out to be black, the situation becomes a cul-de-sac.

At other times, the wife would bluntly refuse to come to the door to answer blacks who needed somewhere to live, not because they don't want to rent blacks, for they knew their husbands would not allow it. So the husband had to come and face the blacks themselves. In those days, the white man was very rude to us blacks, showing neither respect nor remorse.

We eventually found a place in London, after searching all over, in a bright neighborhood, Paddington. Finding somewhere to live was a big headache, but our surprises continued. We had to register at the Labour Exchange. The Ministry of Labour was strict with their un-employment rules. We were requested to register, which we did. Thrice a week we signed in our time and days, which would then qualify us to be given at the end of the week, one pound, fifteen shillings -$8.00 US money. After taking our letter from the labour Exchange to the National Assistance

Board, they would then give you a total of two pounds and ten shillings, which must pay your rent, buy food, and also we must keep some of it to be used as bus fares and sub-way fare to go in search of jobs.

Not that there were many jobs, we still had to report to the Labour Exchange, so if a vacancy pops up, we would in turn go wherever we are told to go, so as not to get cut off from our benefits, which uses to be a six week suspension. That rarely happened to blacks, for we knew how important that weekly benefit was. Getting through with a job after being sent by the Labour Exchange was always negative. Why? Because we were black, the Foreman on most occasions would sign my card showing that I did report, so we can get our benefits at the end of the week. The Foreman would always say to us, "it's not me, it's the boys who you would have to work with." So he also knew how important signing that card was, and he would only be willing to do so.

It was simple as that, no signing of the card, no money. The foreman would state on the card that, the vacancy was filled. I would then go back to the Labour Exchange and report what had transpired at the place where they sent me, only to be doubted. It was like throwing water on duck's back. It made no difference, my buddy Claude was getting the same results in trying to obtain a job, remember that both of us were sharing a double room. It was nicely furnished, situated at 26 Norfolk Square, Paddington London, W2.

Claude and I realized that, not working, was a way of life for all the blacks who was in England. Life in those days was very crucial. It was only in Scotland that one will find blacks working. Some on the railways, others in the coal mines, apart from others washing dishes, the majority of blacks were forced to be idle. The British government did not lift a finger to do anything about the situation.

After a while, hardships for some of us began to decline for that was when the white prostitutes started to pay much interest in black men. In all of the British Isles, the white woman became very sympathetic towards us the black men. I say men, because one could have walked the streets of Scotland or England and only witnessed half a dozen black women. Some might had even been students, meaning that they belong to the middle-class and they would only had acted snobbish as the white themselves. This is where the white prostitutes stepped in. They became friendly with some of my buddies and me. I started a relationship with one such woman, not because she was selling her body to give me money. I got closer to her after realizing that she had to withstand many difficulties into getting that money to help us. She will have to stand in the cold weather- snow, rain or dense fog, these "ladies of the Night." As people would normally address them, would endure much just to let us have a comfortable life. Things started blossoming for a small number of us. The whites, who were busy trying to push the blacks into ghettos, found that a number of West Indians, including myself, were enjoying life to the max.

Blacks such as myself were not knocking on doors to seek a place to stay. We were now buying homes. We, West Indian pimp treated our women well. For we saw in her something totally different from the American version of a pimp. We saw in them a person who understood that it's not because we were black, who gave them the right to treat us as filth, but after all we were all of God's creations.

So they began to reach out to us- my buddies, for they themselves felt a state of insecurity. Just for being prostitute, and that much dirt of words that were hurled at them. An American interpretation of a pimp, is one who sees the woman as being inferior and dumb-witted, and could only get a man if she "Pays him off." On most occasions, that leads to suicide, because of frustration, anger, helplessness, and the use of drugs, which most often are forced upon her by her pimp.

With us it was totally different. We never forced any of the girls to do anything they did not want to do. We would be with them, just as though they were our wives. Some of my buddies branched off to pursue an education in law or medicine. When the whites saw what was happening, they started branding all blacks as pimps, or they called them pounces. No more names like "Sambo," Nigger," or "Darkie." Some of these people, became pimps by design and not by choice. They educated themselves, and then returned to their native land of birth, more equipped, creating a situation of hate wherever they come upon people who may be white. Remembering those whites didn't like blacks in the old days when they were there in the white man's country.

Only a person such as myself can see where that came from, because I was there. We all received the same treatment from some of the English people. I have visited African students during my stay in London and would sometimes see them kneeling down on the floor, same time crossing both their index fingers as they raised their hands kissing their index fingers making, "as an oath," "When I go back to Africa, I will make sure that all the whites that are in my native land, pay for the hostilities that we endured coming from them, while being in their country, England.

One student would say to me, "Danny, my friend, you have never traveled to Africa. To see how the white man treated us. We would allow then to live well, we have treated them with kindness and with great tolerance. Yet, they never paid us the respect we deserved. Now that we've come to their country, look at the way they treat us. Is it not time for us to educate ourselves and return back to our homeland?"

I would say, "Friend, if that's what you need to do, I do give you my support."

They saw the white man as a bunch of hypocrites. To blame the black leaders who run their administrations the way they do, we must first remember it was the white man who started it all. The British government turned a blind eye to all that was going on, in and around them and should certainly apologize to all those blacks who had to live amongst, the whites. To the few white people who saw us as no different to them, I say 'Thank You, and may God richly bless you and your generations to come." As for the "ladies of the Night," my highest regards go out to you all. I know it was because of poverty, and also treatment by your own people that led you to do what you did. May God continue to shine your path as well as your generation to come.

For every good white, there were one thousand whites that were up to no good, only making us blacks feel we were inferior to them. Life was not easy, do believe me it was rough. Just imagine, being eighteen or twenty years old, and were placed like a disable person in a country. No work was given to you because of being black, places to live were not really available- because of your color, something you have no control over, along with the race stigma. Had it not been for those prostitutes in England, many of us would have died from the cold winter, lack of food, and clothing.

I would never speak a bad word about a prostitute who was in England at that time with me. These wonderful people did not need to know you in order to buy you a meal or become friendly with you, and give you money for you to pay your bills. The minute you become their man, they took it upon themselves to support you. Their lifestyles were well understood, for 98% of the prostitutes came from poor, large, English families.

Those families never really had a chance in life, neither did their children. Many of them came from homes that were bombed-out, where their homes had neither doors nor windows, no bath facilities, no electricity, and just a small gas light. The parents had to boil water on the coal stove in order for the children to take a bath-which occurred sometimes only once a week, other than taking a daily sponge bath, of just damping a cloth and cleaning your skin. Parents found it costly to boil water on a daily basis simply because it was too expensive. And, their meager wages did not permit them to do so. Their houses were fitted with cardboard at the windows, old newspapers were stuffed into creases. The whole living conditions probably forced many of their poor white girls to leave their homes in search of greener pastures. Unfortunately, the first job they found was selling their bodies for a price. In that way, they could afford all the things that were missing in their lives and put their past behind.

The elite of England were exploiting the colonies that were under their rule-Colonialism, and were enjoying it all, while their brothers and sisters were left to grab at the crumbs. Not forgetting to mention us, Colonials. It's rather funny the way a few people can ruin the lives of millions of people.

I wonder from time to time when will this all ceased. It looks as though there is no end to it all. All of the British colonies were drained of their wealth. All riches were gathered and then sent to the motherland, England. Our native land was left hanging on a string, and people started to leave their homeland, including my buddies and me. We didn't have the means, financially, necessary for us to travel the legal way, which is why we decided to stowaway on a ship.

Had the British treated black people as humans, they would have been the center of attraction that America has become. Take a look at America and see how the whole world wants to go there. Had America allowed the British to sponge off of them, they would have been a backward nation, like many of the British colonies, such as my native land, Guyana.

If one was to take a look at the size of Guyana of being 83,000 square miles, with a population of just a three quarter of a million people, ever was that amount ever higher from 1948 the year of my departure from

British Guiana to present day 2005. Now tell me, "How can England allow so many of her people to be poor, starving, and homeless and out of work? When she had Guyana in the palm of her hands, not forgetting to mention other rich colonies in Africa. In my native land of Guyana, know as the 'Eldorado' with all its minerals and resources like rice, sugar, timber-and most of all, lots and lots of gold and diamonds. Yes gold, as in G-O-L-D. The big question is, "Why didn't the British extract all those resources which were at their disposal?" That money could have made life better not only for their brothers and sisters back in England, but also us, the ones from the colonies, such as Guyana.

The British were busy amassing wealth from all over the world. They looked after only the elites of England, while they made life difficult for us foreigners. The U.S.A., on the other hand, was allowing people from all over the world. America started to build from a slow process to a rapid progress. America became the most cosmopolitan country in the world. How can the African and the people of the West Indies have any respect for the Englishman?

How could they expect to gain respect? Just like, "How can the Romans gain respect?" After plundering the world, I have seen many atrocities handed out to human beings around the world, and I always ponder as to, how. And, why? If these past rulers had any sort of compassion for their fellow beings, they would have alleviated the standards of those people they governed.

What the whites did was to introduce politics into our lives and changed the future of our people. I, the author of this book, gave twenty-five years of my life to the Englishman- and got in return, nothing.

I do not know who was responsible for this colonial system, but whoever were, they were definitely mad. What they did was turn back the clock of millions of people worldwide. Just give it a thought.

# 15

## *Jean*

THE YEAR IS 1953 IN the midst of London heat wave. After leaving Scotland and arriving in London, I was introduced to Jean who was four years older that me. She had a friend whose name was Flowers. Now a country man of mine was going out with Flowers at the time of me being introduced to Jean. I started to go out with Jean while living in Paddington, and sharing an apartment with my friend, Claude Roberts. We both were busy looking for work while collecting unemployment benefits. A job was not easy to get in those days in London, because of racialism amongst most of the whites. The girls took advantage of that situation, the prostitutes of course. So, Jean and I had a relationship.

It was here I became a victim of circumstances. By this time, I was eager to have a girlfriend. I was unaware of what was really happening in London. Being an attractive, young black man, I became a drawing card in the eyes of the prostitutes. So Jean was my first girl friend after leaving British Guiana. While in Scotland, I had no girlfriend- it was all work and getting myself all dandy, clothing wise.

Now, Jean would invite me to her apartment and quite often try to get me to move from my own Paddington apartment. But, I stood fast all the time while being with her. Some how, I did not see Jean as being the ideal woman for me. She was drinking gin and tonic water every night. She would always smell of liquor when she got home. I had my own apartment in Norfolk Square, Paddington. By that time, I started to go into the West End of London with various friends. Also, singing in various small Clubs. Then Jean became pregnant just after 18 months, and said, "Darling, I am pregnant."

I said, "Are you?"

She said, "Yes. You look a bit worried."

I said, "No, I am not worried, I was just thinking that I do not have a job, and I am living off my unemployment benefits and assistance board money. Also, you have to work and give money as well; it will be a great burden on you."

Jean said, "It will not be a burden on me or on you. Stop thinking about it, you might get lucky and find a job."

I said, "I might find a job?"

Then one day, I took a friend whose name is Joe Walker, to Jean's apartment in Bainsbridge, Campdentown, I was fixing a drink, while Joe was standing in front of the mantelpiece looking at photographs. But Joe saw two photographs with Jean and I, being together. Joe Walker shouted to me, "Come here Danny." By that time I was going to Joe with the two glasses of drinks and about to join him, now I stood next to him, Joe walker said, "I know this girl." Joe by this time was pointing at the photo with Jean and I, and said, "I didn't know you knew this Benie, I said, "That's my girlfriend." Joe said, "I know her, she hussles in Hyde Park. She's cool boy." I said, "Are you sure, Joe?" Joe said, "Sure, I am sure." I said, "But she told me that she was working as a hostess in the Stork Club. I didn't know that she was a prostitute. I believe that she was working in a club."

Joe said, "Do you remember the old folks use to say to us back home, "Eye no see, heart no burn? So, what will you do? She didn't want you to know. She likes you,

Danny. Forget about what I told you. It's all life. We are a victim of circumstances."

I said, "I guess you are correct Joe."

Joe Walker and I sat and enjoyed our drinks and vacate Jean's apartment. I went to my music lesson and Joe went home.

Time had pass by, and Jean was about to have her baby. The houses were being renovated because of the bombing by the Germans. Bains Bridge were about to get a slight face-lift, including three homes on the street, as well as Jeans' home.

The contractors and work men came and started work next door to Jean's apartment. I then inquired about a job since they were about to start work on the third floor houses.

I got lucky and was hired as a plaster's mate. Jean then given birth to our child, a girl whose name was Gloria. She was a lovely little child, and I stayed with Jean for at least eighteen more months. By which time I couldn't stay with her much longer and the construction project in the street came to an end. And we parted our friendship, as I decided to go out of sight, and go to Paris/France.

# 16

## Nancy and Kay

THE YEAR IS JUNE 1953 summer. The place is in London West-End, Piccadilly.

During the Friday evening while being at home in my apartment which was situated in Penny Wear Road in Earls Court, just off the Earls Court Road. I was feeling somewhat bored at the time. I decided to go to the London West-End and visited a Club by the name of "Club Eleven." I then got dressed looking very sharp indeed, and I caught the Piccadilly Line Subway and got off at Piccadilly, Circus Station. I then walked a couple blocks as I was directed to do so, as a couple of friends had directed me before, and had spoke very highly about the Club Eleven, Now cutting a long story. When I finally arrived at the Club, I paid my money at the door after the doorman open the door, and let me into the Club. The price to enter was ten shillings in those days.

Entering the Club I strolled across the edged of the dance floor as people were dancing. I went and sat at an empty table which I saw was not occupied. When the band stopped at the end of the tune, and all the dancers had returned to their respective tables, etc. A waiter came over to my table and enquired what I would like to drink. I placed my order, a whisky and soda. The Club was a Jazz Club and at times the band would play most of the latest tunes. The place was jumping and lively. The crowd was a mixed crowd. Between 18 years to 35 years old, with a few elders' of 45 years.

By this time the waiter brought my drink and the bill. While sipping my drink I kept looking around the club. During that time I saw two young ladies sitting at a table. They were gorgeous. One of them had caught my eyes. I waited for the band to start playing another tune; at that point I got up and went over to the two young ladies and asked one of them to have a dance, I said, "Can I have the pleasure of this dance with you?" she said, "sure." So off we went on to the dance floor, and started to dance. She was a fine looking woman, well dress, and looked as if she had a lot of class. The other young lady had looked the same as well. While dancing with her I asked her, "What's your name?" she said, "Kathleen, I've never seen you in these parts before." I said, "This is the first time I visited this club." She asked, "What is you name?" "Danny Daniels." I answered.

By this time the tune came to an end and the band stop playing. I walked her back to her table and returned to my own. The band started to play, and continued to play tunes one after the other, three sets of tunes.

But in the middle of the third tune the waiter came to me and said, "The two young ladies would like you to join them at their table." I told him, "Thank you, what is my bill?" I paid the waiter and off he went. I got up and started to stroll across to join the ladies to accept their invitation. I saw a young man got up and rushed over to Kathleen and her friend. I quickly said to myself, "oh no, I was beaten to it." But sure enough the young man had asked Kathleen friend to have a dance. But somehow she refused him, and by that time I had arrived at their table and the young man walked away.

Kathleen said, "Have a seat. This is a very close friend of mine, Nancy meet Danny." Nancy said, "I am please to meet you." I said, "Please to meet you Nancy." We then shook each other hands as I was sitting down. Nancy quickly said, "Come sit between us, and keep us warm." I got up from sitting where I was, and sat between them.

I said, "Lets call the waiter, I will order a drink." Kathleen said, "I will call the waiter, and the drinks will be on us, not you."

From now on I will refer to Kathleen as Kay. She beckoned the waiter to our table, and asked me, "What would you like to drink?" I said, "Whisky and soda, thank you." By this time the waiter came to collect the order. Nancy said to the waiter, "let's have a half bottle of gin, and tonic water." Nancy, asked, "How long have you been in London?" I replied, "I've been here about two years. But I've been coming and going. I've just return from Paris." Kay asked, "Where are you from?" I said, "British Guiana." Kay said, "I saw you the moment you walked into the Club, and I said to myself, I would like him to come and asked me for a dance." And I said, "And here I am! Thanks for the invitation to your table." By this time the waiter came with the drinks and laid it on the table, and asked, "will this be all?" Nancy said, "This is fine."

An American Serviceman came and requested Nancy to have a dance, he said, "Honey can we have a dance?" Nancy said, "Sure honey, let's get going." We all then laugh because of the way Nancy replied to the American, and the way she said it.

They both were off on to the dance floor and they were dancing to hell and go, enjoying themselves.

The evening was nicely spent. We all had a nice dance and drink. Then at 5 a.m., "God save the King" began to played by the band. Then the lights started to blink on and off, telling us that it was time to go. Truly speaking by that time I had enough, and it was indeed time for me to hit the sack (bed). The waiter came and the bill was paid.

Because, while I was in Paris, France, I was living a hectic life. I use to go from night club to night club in search of work as a singer. I would go to 1 or 6 during the course of a night, and I would do singing in Clubs, such as "Spivys." Eartha Kitt the famous singer, would be running the club while Spivys would go on vacation. I would go to the White Elephant Club, Lido, in the Champs. I would keep moving from club to club in search of work. But my first audition would be commencing after the paid singers goes on break time. I would then audition by doing two or three songs. The crowd had loved it. I would get tips after my three songs.

When we came out of the club Nancy said, "Lets get a cab and you all can drop me off home." Nancy shouted, "Taxi" a taxi cab pull up in front of the club entrance and we got into it and off we went. As we drove off Kay asked me, "where about are you staying Dan?" I said, "Earls Court." Nancy said to the taxi driver, "drop me off at Sloan Square, you two live near to each other." Kathleen and I continue to travel home. While traveling I said, "I will take you home first then I will come down to Earls Court." Kathleen asked, "are you sure you don't want me to drop you off first, and then drive on home to North End Road, where I live? The journey would be shorter and less money."

By this time Kathleen had arrived and told the driver to stop, she said, "this is where I live." She pointed to the house, "Are you free this evening?" I said, "Yes, I am free." She said "Okay, meet me in the Sugar Hill Club at 9:30pm. Do you know where the club is?" I said, "Yes, I know it." I gave her a kiss on the cheek and open the Taxi door and let her out of the Taxi. And she smile as she said, "take care." I said, "You as well." The Taxi drove off after she went into the house. I told the driver where to take me home.

The following evening, I kept the 9:30pm date; at the Sugar Hill club. We had a few drinks, and I said, "Come to my place and see where I am living." Kay said, "lets go." I paid the bill and off we went. When we arrived at my place, we sat and spoke for hours. Kay said, "I wanted to invite you in." I asked, "why didn't you?" Kay said, "Well you said, you will drop me off and go home afterwards, so I said maybe you were tired, so I didn't." I asked, "are you free and disengaged." She said, "I am married, to an African, his name is Frankie Johnson." I asked, "So, where is he now?" She said, he's in jail serving three months. But I am finish with him, he's a no-good. He doesn't want to look for a job or try to learn something to earn a living. I do know that people can't get a job easily but all he wants to do is to wait on me to go and get the money so that he can go and gamble every day and night. So I can't take it anymore." I said, "I can see that you are all stretched out." She said, "I can see that you are different to him." I then said quickly to her, "yes, I am totally different to the way you described him. I have started to work in my home at the age of 12 years old looking after six animals after school. I then started to take care of myself at the age of 15 years old. I came to Scotland and started to work in the Coalmines, 5 miles under the seabed. I work there for a few years and build myself. Because I came here as a stowaway, the only clothing I had was the clothing on my back. So I worked years and build myself. I worked and build myself six suits, etc. then I leave the coal pit. I came from a very poor family; my mother gave me away to my Godparents who brought me up, as they would say to me from time to time, "from three months of age." "So after leaving Scotland, I came to London, so as to improve myself, find a job and go to school. But its like you have said, jobs, accommodation, etc, it's not easy for a Blackman, you have said it. And you are so correct."

Kay said, "I've also had my portion. I will tell you about it at another time." I said, "I would like you to stay over, instead of going home to an empty house. Kay said, "You do have a valid point, an empty house. Okay. I'll take a bath, you'll show me around." I then showed her around the apartment.

We retired to bed, and the following morning Kay went home. We continued seeing each other. A month had passed by. So we became closer to each other. Kay then said to me, "listen to me, I will help you to get what you need. But do understand this; I may not want to be with you forever. I might want to move on, please don't feel funny if I should change that way."

By that time I became a bit stunned and confused by what she said, and the way in which she spoke to me and described her possible intention. She left me thinking for a while. Because I had never heard anyone spoke in such a way. I started to turn over her words and statement carefully. I said to myself, this girl must be mad, I didn't take her seriously. I will change her; I will make her love me. Let her wait and see, she will find out later. Kay said, "Why are you so quiet, what are you thinking about?" I said, "nothing."

"Let me tell you a bit about myself," she said, "I was born in Algate, East London. I came from a very poor English parents. My mother had died, and my father was a motor mechanic, and work by himself in a small garage, my mother died leaving my father with nine children, four girls and five boys. The births of the nine children were one and two, also three years a-part from each other." "Somehow my father couldn't cope with the expenses; we were going through great hardship in trying to cope with the support, to provide food, clothing, rent, light and gas to cook with for the home. The bills were getting on top of him. So the eldest sister had to run the home while the father works in his small garage. The eldest became the mother. The second eldest decided to hit the streets and became a prostitute in London West End." Kay continued. "Then one day as usual practice, I would take my fathers' lunch on the way back to school while he works on various cars. When I arrived at the garage the door of the garage was closed. Normally the door would be open. But on that day when I knock on the door I heard a car engine running in the garage. I kept knocking and calling my father. I decided to break open the door, and go into the garage, I saw my father lying under the car while the engine of the car was running. I pulled him out from under the car, the exhaust fume had killed him. I rushed back home to get help and told the others." I said, "Kay that was a very sad experience, it makes me feel so sad."

I started to think after Kay had told me about her father's death by carbon dioxide fumes. While thinking I came to realized that, I was nowhere around Scotland or in England, she was very young and still in school. Life can make one take a sudden turn during their life. Kay said, "Danny, things in the home begun to get worst and worst. Not enough of anything. So my second sister by that time was trying to do her best. The War with the Germans was making things hard here in London." "So, I decided to go out with my sister to be a call girl, so that we can make ends meet, Darling that is my life."

Time had passed and Kay husband came out of jail. But she was not around at home or anywhere else to receive him. She didn't even tell me that he was out of prison. It came to my attention when a few of my friends began to tell me that they saw him in the West -End. Johnson by this time would stop various black males on the streets of London West End. He would asked, "Do you know my wife Kathleen Johnson? I heard she's with a Trinidadian. I am trying to find her." He was very desperate. He also stopped me and asked me the said question, his eyes was red as if he was crying for days when he stopped me and asked me, he said, "Country man do you know my wife Kathleen Johnson? I heard she's with a Trinidadian." I said, "I don't know her. I am sorry." Kay was keeping out of sight from her husband. A couple of months had passed by, and Kay was living with me in Penny-Wearn Road. It so happened I was with a girl by the name of Jean, and I had finished with her because we couldn't get along. So I went to Paris so that I would be out of sight, out of mind. So when I return to London from Paris. Jean heard that I was in London. The news was given to her by some of my own associates because they like to see her harassing me about the place. So finally she ran into me and Kay. So Jean came over to Kay to start trouble. But I had mentioned her to Kay. So Kay was waiting to see her since she was a trouble maker and getting on vulgar at the said time. Jean came to Kay and said, "What the hell you doing with my husband?" Jean was in the company of two other girls who was her friends. Kay said, "Come bitch, come and take you husband with your drunken self, come near to him, you think people scared of you. Come I want you to take a step closer." I said, Kay come lets go." We walked away from Jean and her two friends. So finally that was the end of Jean molesting me. By this time we had save enough money to buy my first car. So I went and bought a Vauxhall car. The police was on my tracks while we were living in Earls Court. So we moved quickly from Earls Courts. I had started to work on a film by the name of "Gordon of Khartoum" (Four Feathers) a friend of mine by the name Elario Pedro of Nigeria came two months before Kay's husband was released from prison, and said "Daniels tomorrow there will be next audition for a big film coming up. So try and be at Leister Square rehearsal room at 2pm." I said, "Okay, I will be there." So I went to the audition the following afternoon and I was chosen as an extra. We were given a week to get ourselves ready to start work on the film which was an Epic. The film studio was called Sheperton Studio or British Lion, I was told to report there, so I did. That was the first film I was about to work in, also the first film studio as well.

On my arrival in the studio I was told to go to the wardrobe and collect my costume. I was also fitted as a Devonshire guard defending a Barracks, controlled by the Arabians against the British. I was only an extra at the start of shooting the film. I was a Rifleman. It was three days working on the film, during our lunch break;

I was sitting among Claude Roberts, Elario Pedro, and four other boys in the group. We were at the back lot of the studio grounds. The crowd must have been over five hundred Extra's sitting in groups, covering a far distance. Our group had finished eating lunch and was breezing out and chatting about the amount of work which will be needed. We all suddenly heard a set of voices shouting, "Hi you there!" So we all turn around and look into the direction of two males and a female. They kept walking towards us, passing several groups, while continuing to shout, "Hi you there." And each member in every group kept pointing to themselves, and that continued until they arrived to the group I was sitting amongst. Then one of the males said, "My name is Zulton Kodah, and this is Mr. Terrance Young, and Miss etc, etc," I do not remember the woman's name. Mr. Kodah continued, "Since the past three days we've being watching you defending your post, and you do stand out. Where did you learn to use a rifle?" I said, "During my service in the South Caribbean Force. "A British outfit" Kodah said, "Were you in the army during World War Two?" what's your name? I said,"Sylbert Vincent Daniels." Kodah said, "What a name …what do the boys call you?" He quickly point to the boys. I said, "Danny Daniels." Kodah said, "That's it.! Do you know to speak Arabic? I said, "No, Kodah, but you're willing to learn?" he said, "Yes", I replied. Kodah said, "have you done any acting before?" I said, "No," Kodah said, "But you're willing to learn?" I said, "Yes." Kodah said, "Have you ever ridden a camel?" I said, "No." Kodah said, "This young lady will teach you Arabic. Come with us." I got up and follow them into the production building and office. Mr. Zulton Kodah then said, "I want you to play a part in this film. You'll be leading some men up and down the mountain in search of General Gordon, (Anthony Steel, and Laurence Harvey.) We will give you a film contract; you will have a change of clothing, and a dressing room. You don't have to go and sit with the Extra's". I said, "Okay, Thank you."

Terrance said, "We know you will do a good job. I am the director of the film, and as you know my name is Terrance Young." Kodah said, "If you need anything come and see me, I am the producer. Bye and good luck."

By this time a week had passed and I was still working, playing the part. Mr. Zulton Kodah came to me on the film set and said, "I am going to give you a letter to take to Mrs. Cole, at the London School of Dramatic Arts. You are to tell her I send you. Also you are to go there and take the evening lesson, while during that time you can do your film work during the day." I then said, "Thank you very much." Kodah said, "Have you heard of Sidney Poitier?" I said, "Yes." Kodah said, "I built Sidney with the film "Something of Value," I can build you as well." But Mr. Zulton Kodah had left England and gone to Hollywood to start work there. So he was not around to help me. But I kept on doing as he advised me to do, which was to go to Drama School, and at the said time keep on working in the film industry while attending London School of Dramatic Arts. I would then work as a film extra. Also I was trained as a stuntman and I kept on going. I was later cast in a film by the name of "On the Fiddle," to play a guy by the name of "Trinidad" that was Sean Connery first film so to speak. Then shortly after that Sean was chosen to play James Bond in the film "Doctor No", Now, I have seen from those days that I was living in a white man's world. I finished drama school and I went into the acting field getting a few parts as a cameo actor. I would get cameo parts one after the other. I became a great cameo artist so to speak. I often can remember the saying, "who god bless, no man curse." Well it's a true saying.

Now getting back to Kay, we were getting on fairly well, and then suddenly some changes took place. Because the Police was keeping watch on me at Pennywearn Road in Earls Court. I came to realized that I was under their surveillance, so I told Kay, and she said, "Let's move from here, and go to Notting Hill Gate. I went in search of a place and I found one." So we move to Arundel Gardens. But while things appeared to us that all was going well.

Early one morning around 7:30a.m. we both heard a loud knock coming from the front door, followed by a voice, "Open up Police!" we both got out of bed as I shouted "Okay, just a minute." We quickly started to get dress and the police shouted, "Come on open up the door, come on!" I went and open the door and let the three police into the apartment. As they enter into the apartment one of the Police had a paper in his hands, he then open the paper and said, "Is your name Sylbert Vincent Daniels?" I answered, "Yes." The Police said, "Well I have a warrant here for your arrest for living off of Kathleen Johnson. Come let's go." They took me to Nottinghill Gate Police Station and charge me for living partly off of Kathleen. But while writing the police report. A police officer came to me and said, "Didn't you know that Kathleen has a husband?" I replied, "yes" the police officer said, "That's how we know about you. We also know that you are not like a lot of the others depending on a woman to support them. You're always working, and helping out. That is why we are charging you on partly, because of your associating with her. She's a call girl and if she give you a cigarette or buy you a cup of coffee with her money, that is called "partly." I was taken to court and was given three months imprisonment.

By this time three months had pass by, and I came out of prison. But Kay was still living at the said apartment. And she took good care of the car paying the hire purchase, and put the car into a garage for safe keeping. I had nowhere to stay when I came out of prison, so I ended up staying at Kay. Also she had saved up quite a bit of money during the three months. So the following morning I went to Nottinghill Police Station and asked to see the Police officer whom I had seen when I got arrested, also it was he who was in charge at that time of the station. So a police sergeant was the one I spoke to as I said, "Good morning sergeant my name is Daniels. I would like to speak to the officer whom I saw when I came here three months ago." The sergeant said, "I remember you Daniels, hold on I'll get him." The sergeant went into the back and came back out followed by the officer. He came out from the desk area to the front, and close to me, and asked, "you want to see me Daniels?" I said, "Yes sir, I came out of prison yesterday, I would like to get a "Hawkers Licence because I would like to buy and sell." The officer said, "Okay, go and get a form, from the motor vehicle officer and you will fill the form, then you will bring it to me. Then you will take it to the church on Landrook Grove Road and asked the Minister to give a recommendation and go and register it." I said, "Sir, I have nowhere to stay, so I am asking you, if I stay by Kathleen while looking for a place, will there be any trouble?" the officer said, "Okay, you can stay at Kathleen for two months, no longer, no one will touch you during the two months." I said, "Thank you very much.

Kay and I continued living in Aurendell Gardens for a month while Nancy and her went in search of an apartment. They would easily find a place easier, than I would. Black folks didn't get places to rent easily. Nancy and Kay got lucky and found an apartment in Hendon.

A week later after Nancy and Kay got the place. They took me to see it and to introduce me to the landlord and landlady as Kay's husband. The house was a maisonette, and the couples were Jewish and they had occupied the bottom floor and Kay and I occupied the top floor. The two of them were a wonderful couple in their early sixties. The husband asked after I was introduced to them both by Nancy, "Mr. Daniels where do you and your wife work?" I said, "I am an artist, I work in the film and on TV. Also as a dancer and singer, my wife works as a waitress as well." He said, "That's nice, well I hope you all make yourselves at home. You can come and signed the contract when you are ready."

So by that time we finally moved in and all was well. During the period of six months I was given an announcement by Kay, she said, "We've been living here just about six months now.. I am expecting a child darling." I said, "are you sure?" Kay said, "very sure." I said, "well my love, we have to do some serious planning, now that you are expecting a child." I had received my Hawkers Licence and I was buying and selling. Also working in the film as well, so we were doing very well." We both were looking forward towards the coming child. Kay was just about three and a half months pregnant.

Then one afternoon around 5:30p.m. When I arrived home and opened the door. I went into the house, and as I was about to go up the stairs to my apartment, when suddenly the landlady open her door to her apartment, and came over to me looking a bit worried as she said, "Mr. Daniels, two white gentlemen came and asked who's the woman living upstairs with, I told them a Mr. Daniels." I said, "I don't know of any two men who can come here asking for me. Thank you very much." She went back into her apartment, and I went upstairs. I began to think about the two men. They must have tailed Kay after work and saw where she was living. Also saw the lights went on and off, and realized she lived upstairs. I am not easy to trail. I have too many activities. Not only that, because I was always on the alert, paying attention to my car mirrors, also to vehicles traveling at the back and along side of my car. I would know that I was being followed. So I would become highly cautious. I knew what I was doing. But funny enough the law makers could not see that two people who loved each other had decided to share a relationship which was based on companionship, along with understanding. Especially, as I saw it, I was working and earning more than Kay, during that time. I just couldn't accept the fact that I was living fully or partly off of her earnings. I saw myself as being a victim of circumstances, so was Kay. We weren't hurting anyone else, other than ourselves, and that we weren't doing anything other than work.

Anyway I decided I was not going to leave her. So I went to an Estate Agency in search of another apartment the following day, and this time I intended to move from Hendon and go to the other extreme, across the river Thames. I was lucky in getting a place to move quickly. I got the place in Brixton Summerlayton Road. I was unaware of the area until we moved in. The streets were heavily crowded with black people, most of them were unemployed, they just couldn't get a job, also there were a few white people living in the streets, which I saw after moving into the street two days later. But to my surprise, I got out of bed and I went to my living room window and looked onto the street. I said to myself, someone had stolen my car. Now, I have to go to the police station at a time when I am trying to keep out of the police way and sight. I went into the bedroom, and broke the sad news to Kay about the car. She said, "They stole the car? This is a bad street. What are you going to do?" I said, "I will have to go and report it to the police."

I later went to the Brixton Police Station and reported the missing vehicle, I said, "Good day my name is Daniels." The policeman at the desk said, "What can I do for you?" By that time I had glanced through the window and saw my car parked at the back of the police compound. I said, "I came to report a stolen car from Summerlayton Road. But I can see my car at the back of the station." The police said, "You have the papers for the car? The car was not stolen. We had a telephone call saying that a strange car was parked in the street since a couple of days. Let me see the papers." I handed the document for the car to the police. He took the papers along with my driver's license and look at them. He then gives me back my documents and said, "Go to the back and get the car." I drove back to Summerlayton Road to see Kay, to let her know that

I received the car. Kay was very pleased to hear the good news.

Kay asked, "So what you decided to do today?" We can't live in this street, you will have to go back to the property agent and see if we can get another place." I said, "That is what I've decided to do after I drop you off." I finally drop off Kay to get her hair done. I immediately went to the estate agency, and told them about the situation in Brixton. The boss of the agency said, "Just a minute Mr. Daniels." With a paper which he took out from his draw, and said, "I have a place which came in this morning, here it is. We have a property in West Dulwich, which has a semi basement and three floors above. The building has eight years remaining of its lease and the owner would like to sell the lease and the building for seven hundred pounds. The three floors are rented, one at two pound and ten shillings, and the other two floors at three pounds each." I said, "I will get that lease." He said, "I will call the woman and make arrangements. Come in tomorrow and I will have some news for you." I went back to the agency and we finalize the purchasing of the building. The basement had to be furnished. Kay and I decided the place was ideal after I took her to see the place. She said, "Will you have all that amount of money to buy it and to furnish it?" I said, I will try to meet the target. Months went past quickly and she stopped working because of the child she was expecting. I was so glad she wasn't working and was at home. I didn't have no fear of the police, and during that period I landed a T.V. series by the name of, "White Hunter." That of course made my day. I was one of the regular part players, I began to shine in the series, and at one time I played two different characters in the same episode. That was great fun to me; I really enjoyed it because it took a lot of talent in order to do that. I saw it as nothing while doing the various characters in the same episode. I was working by this time six months on the series, we then had a break of four weeks off, and then return back to work. Kay by that time had given birth to a bouncing baby boy, after she took in with labour pain at 38 Croxted Road West Dulwich London, SE 21. I had to quickly put Kay into the car as she was crying. Because her water bag was burst at the time in the car as we were traveling from Dulwich to Paddington Maternity Hospital on Harrow Road London. It's like I've said, Kay had given birth to a bouncing baby boy, during the evening after I came away from the hospital. This was two hours after we arrived at the hospital. After the baby was born I received a telephone call saying it was a boy and my wife would like me to name the boy. So I then named the boy "Malcolm Daniels", I went to the hospital the following day and signed the papers. Kay and her son finally came home after two days and all was fine. She stayed away from working for four more months to look after the child. I had started back working on the "White Hunter" series. We were enjoying life all through that time I was still buying and selling. I was also saving as though I was crazy, by that time I had saved about eighteen pounds.

So, I decided it was time I try and invested some money. So as to stop Kay from being a call girl. Because I knew that type of life was no good, time was coming for her to stop being a call girl. But Kay by this time was becoming fed-up being at home and not working. So one day after the boy had completed being five months old, she said, "Darling its time to get back to work. I've manage to find a foster parent in Wimbledon who seems to be very nice". "Her husband is from your home, Guiana. And they are very interested in looking after Malcolm. I took him for them to see, Nancy went with me to see the people as well. So, I made an appointment for you to go and see them this coming weekend." I said, "Okay if that is what you want to do, then its okay with me." I often would go the distance with Kay just to please her. I said, "By the way, today I telephone my lawyer, asking him to keep a look out among his clients, if a property would come up for sale, and to let me know. I told him I would like to invest some money." I continued, "Darling you can't keep on working as a call girl all your life and I keep on running and hiding from the police. We have to stop living the way we do." Kay asked, "What did the lawyer say?"

I said, "Well it looks as if my luck is in." The lawyer said, "One of his clients' at Westminster Building Society has two properties for sale, one situated in Colville Terrance W2 London. That property has six floors vacant, and the asking price is three thousand, five hundred pounds for a twenty five years lease. The owner is thinking of selling the free hold. Seven hundred and fifty pounds is the down payment, over the twenty years lease.

The other property is situated in Talbot Road W2, London. That one has five floors and with three floors vacant, the other two floors is rented, one floor is rented at two pounds, ten shillings, and the other rented at three pounds monthly. The asking price is three thousand, five hundred pounds as well. Also it's a free hold. The down payment is seven hundred and fifty pounds". Kay quickly said, "But we do not have that kind of money. It's a very good bargain Danny. What did you tell the lawyer?" I said, "I do have the money. I have sixteen hundred pounds plus, I will have three months to closing to save as well. I am doing a series and getting thirty pounds a week, plus I am buying and selling, which I do in the evening and during the weekends". "Listen young lady, when I buy items in the East End from the wholesalers, I can make two hundred percent on each item, I buy and sell. That's before I add on a ten percent hire purchase on the credit charge." Kay said, "Tell me this, when you sell those things you give the people hire purchase?" I said, "Yes, not only that, I usually go around to all of the big stores in the West End bond in Oxford Street, and check out all of their unusual and latest styles, prices and all. I would then go to the various clothing factories, and wholesale dealers and shops, at a cost of adding my prices, also my ten percent. And when

DANNY DANIELS AUTOBIOGRAPHY

I sell I would asked the buyer to give me three quarter of what I pay. And the remainder is paid to me within two to three weeks, and I am selling the items well below store prices." Kay asked, "Who do you sell to?" I usually sell the girls and their boyfriends. Also the girls' family will see them wearing the items and ask for me to go and see them so that I can sell them various items". Kay, burst out into laughter and said, "You are very smart." I said, "You call it smart, it's not smart, it's being clever."

Let me say this, like I said to you earlier that my luck was running beautifully, I told the lawyer that I will take both properties. Because I have the sixteen hundred pounds. Not to mention the fact that the Jews in the east end likes me and I love them as well. I would only have the money to purchase the Aylon Coats, but I would have customers who like 6 or 7 coats, order for a weekend. Now, I will tell one of the factory or wholesalers who is a Jew, and they would say can you pay me next week when you come back? I see that I can trust you." I said, "Yes, I will pay you next week when I come back." I would then be given the item or items. Now that's because I was trusted in the eyes of the Jewish person. I would stand to my word of trust. I became a trusted person amongst them. They would say to me you are one in a million. Do keep it up.

Kay would work for her money. But I would never depend on it. I would only make promises on my own money which I've earned. I did not look upon myself as a pimp, punk or a jigelow. As the law would deem me to be. But of course Kay would work and earned ten or fifteen ponds sterling each night and give it to me. Not from her hands into my hands, no, no! Quite often when she came home I would be asleep. She would take out the money out of her hand bag, and then put the money on top of the mantelpiece. Then Kay would say to me after I am awake in the morning, "your money is on the mantelpiece". The money will always exchange from her to me by way of the mantelpiece. I would use that money as a backup to things for her, our son, and so as to get her to stop doing what she was doing, such as a call girl. Anyway Malcolm was handed over to the foster parents and Kay and I would visit him every weekend, and during holidays we would have him home with us.

Time pass by while being with Kay. But Kay sat me down one evening and said, "Danny, I think I will stay in the apartment where I work, and do not come home here so often. Otherwise you will get yourself in trouble with the police, and that you do not need." "So from next week I will do as I said." I replied, "you do have a point, and I totally agreed with you." Kay said, "Do you accept what I've decided?" I said, "Certainly, I do, so you will come home on weekends, and we will go and see Malcolm, Okay." She said, "Yes, we will do that."

Quite often, I would be in agreement with Kay. So as to have a happy relationship with her. Very rare we would argue with each other. Basically, we would get on as an ideal couple, who were made for each other.

By this time my TV film series came to an end. So Kay and I took off to Spain, so as to have a vacation. We had a wonderful vacation during the two weeks we spent together. After which she flew from Spain to London, leaving me in Spain to spend an extra two weeks. I returned back to London at the end of the two weeks after enjoying the "Bull Fights" with my Spanish friends. Also going to the various nigh clubs, and listening to the various "Flamingo" music and dancing.

When I returned to London, I found everything was in order as the three of us had wanted it to be. Kay had started back to work. Earning her ten to fifteen pounds per day. And J.S. also was at work earning her twenty five pounds per day to give me, and the remainder of money which she earned each day, she kept it to take care of her other wishes, or expenses. By this time a few months had pass by and Kay began to complain about how things was getting bad, money wise, and she couldn't make enough to pay her rent for her apartment. So I said, "Nothing stays the same forever, not to worry. Things will change," She said, "I hope so, because it's driving me out of my mind." By this time, I was trying to cheer her up. Not knowing what's to come later. She had her plans all worked out. I of course was still buying and selling, and I was working on various television plays and films. Kay and Nancy would keep on telling me how bad things were from time to time. When ever I saw Kay during the weekends she would give me twenty pounds. I did not care much for Kay to give me any money, because I was collecting the rent from the houses, plus I was working, etc. and not to mention I was getting money also from J.S. I therefore would pay the baby money each week and also take care of all other finances. Then several months later Kay and Nancy came together at Croxted Road where I was living as a bachelor, and we three sat down speaking from one thing to another. Then suddenly the conversation took a change as Kay switched by saying, "Darling, by the way one of my clients wants me to go to Switzerland on a vacation for two weeks. He said he will buy me a new set of clothing and pay my expenses. We will be going soon. What do you say about that?" I said, "Its Okay with me." By this time Kay was about to go on her vacation. So, I told her when she returned. She's to start sewing a set of new curtains for all of the windows in the various apartments. So that we can have new change of curtains for the summer time. She had agreed to do so, and off she went after I had told her of my trip with J.S.

Kay came back from her vacation before J.S. and I did. So after my return from Spain with J.S. to London I went to the two properties to see how things were going. Because, I had left my friend and an accountant, Mr. Hector Karham, to look after the two houses and to collect the rent from tenants. I then went home to Hectors' and all was well done by him. I did not see Kay. Not until four days later after our return.

I was at Colville Terrance speaking to one of my tenants, when Kay came from around the corner, and stood to one side, as I was conversing with the tenant. At the end of my conversation, Kay came to me, and I said, "Hello darling, what's going on?" Kay said, "I just came from Andre and Barbara." I asked, "How are they?" Kay said, "They are fine." My tenant finally took off as she said, "I must say bye to you too." I said to Kay, "I am going to lunch, would you like to join me?" Kay said, "Come let's go." We got into the Corvette, and drove to Paddington to La Hoare Indian Restaurant. My 'Corvette' car was a 1960 model. Also during this period the year was 1960 during mid summer, and my corvette was the only corvette in England.

Kay and I finally arrived at the restaurant; I parked the car, and we went into the restaurant. After we got seated, an Indian waiter came to our table and took our order, and off he went. There was also another couple in the restaurant. It was very quiet and peaceful, "so to speak." I said, "How long have you return from your trip." Kay said, "A week and a half." I said," We got back four days ago and I've notice the curtains have not been done." "How was your vacation?" Kay said, "It was fine, I forgot to do the curtains, I want to tell you something. But I don't know how to tell you." I said to Kay very quietly and surprise, "Since when you would like to tell me something, but don't know how to tell me?" By this time the waiter came with our order and laid it on the table, and asked, "Will this be all Sir?" I said, "Yes, thank you." I started to share the food, Kay said, "I am in Love." I said, "You are in Love?" Who are you in love with?" How long did you know this person?" Kay said, "He's a wrestler, I don't know him long." "We started to eat." I asked, "Are you sure you love him, and what about him, does he love you?" Kay said, "Yes he loves me." I asked, "Where is he from?" She said, "He is Italian." I asked, "Did you tell him, that you have a child and it's a black child, so that you will see if he really loves you, and you love him." "What does he have?" "Here you are, all ready to walk out from what you and I have accomplished, to start all over again." Kay simply sat eating and having a broad smile on her face, as I continue to eat my food as well. Kay then said, "No, I did not tell him about Malcolm, you don't have to worry, I will help you. I know you have the free hold to pay for; I will help you pay for it. I don't need what you have." I said, "you don't need what you have?" "You don't want anything? You will regret it, you will be wanting; you do not know what you are saying to me." "I love you, I hate to loose you, and I do not have you on chains. But I'll tell you what; I will give you a month to reconsider, and to find out if you do love this wrestler." "At the end of the month, if that is what you want to do, then I will have to accept it." By this time we had finish eating and I paid the bill. Kay asked, "Where you heading to now?" I said, "I am going home, I have a few thing to do." Kay said, "I will come by you later, is that alright with you?" I said, "That's Okay." I took her to catch a taxi on Edgeware Road, and we went our ways.

But later the said evening Kay came and let herself into the house and joined me as I was sitting watching television. We later got ready and retire to bed, and lay speaking to each other. Kay said, "Let us be still friends I will still help you." I said, "I wouldn't want you to still help me, I wand you to help yourself darling, take care of your money and your life." Kay quickly said, "I'll be okay, don't worry about me." I quickly said, "You will regret what you are doing, and telling me you don't want what we have, after starting from nothing. You will be wanting. You can't live by going from man to man." She started to make love to me while saying, "Let's not keep on talking and worrying about me." I came to realize she wanted to change the subject. So I did, and we continued to make love.

While Kay and I continued to see each other and having our sexual affairs, I caught gonorrhea. So I went to University College Hospital so as to get treatment. But to my surprise when I arrived at the clinic and the nurse said "Okay, Daniels drop your trousers let me see." I did as I was told to do by the nurse. He started to examine me, he said, as he was taking smear on a small piece of glass. "Yes it looks as if you do have a "Leak," gonorrhea." He asked with great surprised, "and what is this cut on the head of your penis?" I said, "It look like a hair cut." He went into the back and he brought back another piece of glass. He then took a curve bit of wire and started to scratches the small cut until it started to bleed blood. He took another smear on to the glass once again, and return to his lab at the back which was enclosed. A few minutes later he returned to me and said, I told you when you came back from Paris a few years ago after going with a beautiful French model, to leave the girls alone and stop the stroke catching. But you and Lord Kitchner will not listen to me. Now you have Syphilis and Gonorrhea." I said, "What! Are you serious?" He said, of course I am serious, you are lucky, if you did not get the gonorrhea so that we could see that small cut and the cut had dried up and start moving into your blood stream. You could end up as a cripple." I quickly asked, "So it can be cured?" He said, "Yes it can, but you have to listen to me, and do exactly what I tell you to do. I will start your treatment today. The treatment will consist of arsenic or penicillin, iodine, streptomycin, for those three have to be mixed together and box up well." I asked, "Arsenic isn't a poison?" He said, "Yes it is poison." He said, I will have to give an injection every day for one year. You must not miss a day, if you do miss a day, I will have to start all over again. Also no sex, until I tell you that you can." I was treated, and he asked, "do you know the girl or girls who you had sex with during the last month?" I said, "Yes, I usually go with two girlfriends." He said, "Okay, tell them to come here or go to Paddington Hospital, and to give your name so that they can get tested and treatment." I said, "Okay, I will tell them."

The following day I went to J.S. and Kay and told them to go and have a check up, because I was founded to have the two diseases. But two days after I had told them, I decided to check up on them to see if they went to get a check up. They both told me that they did, and they were founded negative, I was very surprised and worried. Because I had never had sex with any other woman over a year or longer than a year.

But by this time Kay month had arrived. Kay had started to telephone me at 1 and 2am. The first I received at the end of the month were as follows, Kay said, "I am planning to bring Malcolm to live with me. I would like you to give me Colville Terrance, So that me and Malcolm can live there." I became shock by her request. I said, "How can you ask me to give you Colville Terrance, a six floor rented apartment building?" "You are not thinking, or you have someone else telling you what to come and tell me. Now this is what I will do. I will buy you and Malcolm a house. A two floor house, you can live on one floor, and you can rent the other floor. But I will buy the house in Malcolm's name, that way you will not be able to sell it or give it to a man, and the property, will always belong to both you and Malcolm." "Then later on when Malcolm reaches twenty one years of age, he can give it to you, so that you can give it away. Now you can go in search of a house, and you can come and tell me and I will go with you and see it, and I will buy it, so just do that and let me know." She said, "Okay, I'll do that, and let you know." I said, "Then it's settled."

But after consideration I come to realized that Kay was been tutored by her lover. Two nights later Kay telephoned me again at 2 a.m. I was fast a sleep with J.S. in bed next to me. When I picked up the phone, Kay said, "Listen I can't wait for you to buy a home. I want Colville Terrance, if you don't give it to me, I will go to a lawyer, and tell the lawyer and the court that I bought those houses with the money I hustle and give you to buy them." I then was convinced that the Italian was pushing to get what we had. I said, "Okay go to the lawyer and court and do what ever."

J.S. was wide awake while I was speaking to Kay, J.S. then questioned me. I told her, and JS said, "You will be having trouble with that woman, she wants to claim all the money I give you as well." I said, "you will have to keep away from me for a while." J.S. said, "I think that's a good idea." I said to myself it would be a good idea to stop dealing with Kay and J.S. That was the end of me and both of them, in so deciding, I got up very early in the morning, because I could not go back to sleep after Kay had told me about lawyer and court. I twisted and turn in the bed before getting up early that morning. I had to put on my thinking cap, as the saying goes. So when I decide to go on the road early that morning, I went to an estate agent and put the houses up for sale. So by afternoon the sign board had appeared at each property. Two weeks later we had a buyer wanting Colville Terrace property and Talbot Road property. To buy them all at the said time. So Kay could not blackmail me no further. Well three months later the places were sold. But then Kay came to me and said, "I want to speak to you." She came to Croxted Road at 2:30am Kay said, "I am sorry about everything, I want us to make up and forget it all which I've said and done." I said, "I am not a machine, that is turned on and off, I can't trust you again." Kay said, alright, can't I sleep here tonight?" I said, "Sure, the time now is three thirty, it's difficult for you to get a taxi this late so you can sleep."

We both woke up the next morning, and Kay sat up in bed and pulled out a long bread knife from under the pillow. She kept on pointing the knife and saying, "I was going to used this on you last night." I said, "You want to be wrong and strong, and kill me on top?" We got out of bed, ate something, then we hit the road all in silence. I got rid of Kay for a while. Until I got married, she attack me and my wife with a large brick, she ended up in court. That's in another chapter.

# 17

## J.S.

I WAS IN THE MIDDLE OF BUYING one of my two properties, when I met this beautiful girl who I will refer to only as J.S. I discussed with her my intention of purchasing this property. She was pleased to know that I am ambitious and serious-minded. I had sat down and told her of my plans as a young man. She became very interested, and offered to help me achieve my goal. She stood by my side, and helped me financially. Being the first woman to help me more financially than any other woman. Despite of knowing I had another woman who had a child for me, but myself and the woman were not living together. J.S. had appreciated me quite a lot. Kay, who was the other woman, also knew of J.S., who was just like J.S. not bothering with whoever I was friendly with. J.S. and I began a relationship in no time; she was just twenty three years of age, with a height of 5ft 4ins, fair in complexion, statistics 36-24-35 with green eyes, she was like a movie star. I guess that's what attracted me to her.

I was working on a TV series called "White Hunter" starring American Rhodes Reason. He also starred in the TV Series "Bus Stop". We should have seen him more often on screen, but I don't know what happened to his career. I had a beautiful contract in that series, while working alongside Rhodes, who played the "White Hunter." When

I left the studio, I would go home to take a bath, change into some fresh clothes, and off I would go to one of the Clubs in the West End of London. I couldn't go to bed early, so quite often I would hang out at one of the Clubs, take my supper, also have a few drinks, take a few dances then go back home to bed, so as to wake up early in the morning, to be at the Film Studio at 7 a.m., to start filming.

Myself and a friend named Harry Baird were sitting in my ivory XK 120 Jaguar Racing Replica Sports Car, in front of "The Sugar Hill Club" chatting. Suddenly a white car pulled up along side us and stopped. There we saw sitting in the white car (Ford, Zodiac) two beautiful girls; we continued our conversation after glancing at them. One of the girls was known to us, being a girlfriend of a Trinidadian. The other girl sat quietly, then after five minutes of chatting. I heard a voice shouting, 'Danny", I quickly acknowledged it was the girl whom I knew was the Trinidadian fellow's girlfriend. Harry and I were just talking about work, which we had ahead of us in the Studio. Again, the girl shouted, "Danny one minute." Leaving my friend in the car, I strolled over to the white car, while she was rolling down the car window. As I stood by the window, I leaned my head slightly into the car, she said to me, "Danny, this is a very good friend of mine, J.S." The new girl quickly replied, "I am very pleased to meet you." She continued, I am a great fan of you, and your friend Harry Baird, but especially you." By this time I got the message. It was a beautiful summer night. So what I did, I decided to use that as my cue, as I said, "What are you two doing, driving around on a beautiful night like this?" J.S. quickly butted in, "We were looking for one of the clubs that we hope to see you at." "Do you fancy going to a party later on?" I then asked, "How late do you mean?" "I have to face the camera early in the morning." J.S. said, "About midnight." "Is that Okay with you?" I looked at her for a few seconds, and then asked,

"Where shall we meet?" J.S. answered, "I'll meet you alongside the B.B.C on Regent Street, after I finish work at 12 o'clock." "I will be there?" I quickly said, "See you at twelve..... Now don't be late, I don't like to be hanging around waiting". J.S. then smiled like a Cheshire cat, as she said, "I'll be on time darling."

The Scottish girl then smiled as though a great battle had been won. She then said, "I won't be coming to the party with you two... I have to go home to my old man, (boy friend)". The Scottish girl then turned to J.S. and said, "J.S. do you know that I was living near to Danny in Dalkeith?" "He was very popular in all of the night spots as a dancer." J.S. asked, "did you know each other?" The Scottish girl said, "No, if I had known him then, he would have been mine." I laughed, and then the two of them joined the laughter. I then said, "I'll see you girls later." I returned back to my car, my friend Harry and I went into the Sugar Hill Club where we ordered something to eat and drink. After leaving the Club with Harry, I drove him home. Harry was happily married to a beautiful girl, where he himself was a nice and clean person. He did not mess around with other women. He would go out with the boys to various clubs, but would then leave and go back home to his beautiful wife.

It was almost time for my date, so I drove straight to the B.B.C on Regent Street. She was on time, I like that. I pulled up alongside her and asked her, "how far do we have to drive, to get to the party?" her reply was, "it's a party for two, I told you that, so as to get with you ..." "Are you mad at me?" I watched her for a few seconds, as I thought to myself a woman would go any length to get a man she wants. Then I said to her, "of course not." "Where are we heading to?" "Do you want to come to my place?' she then asked, "How far do you live?" I said, "Dulwich." "Its too far, come to my place, follow me." She put her car into gear and pulled away swiftly from the side of the curb. I followed closely trying not to loose sight of her car. In Europe, people are known to be fast drivers, of course those who drive.

We finally arrived there, which was located in Roy College Street, N.W. London. She then pointed to a suitable parking spot, with her car parking a few yards from mine. We then got out of our cars, and headed upstairs to her fourth floor beautiful apartment. I felt a bit uneasy as I was going up to her place. I never did liked going to a woman's home, who I had only met for the first time. One can never tell if the woman is living with a man, or if she was single and not married. So being aware of the complications which can arise, if another man is involved. That makes me very uneasy. She sensed my uneasiness as we were climbing the long flight of concrete stairs, which leads to the hallway. J.S. turned to me and said, "Danny, its' Okay you don't have to feel scared, I live alone." I then tried to cover up my fears by saying, "It's alright I'm not scared." The building was very quiet, and everyone had seemed to be in bed at that time. Upon reaching her apartment door, she took out the keys from her black leather hand bag, after opening the door; she walked ahead of me, kicking off her shoes, placing her handbag on a small table. While my eyes surveyed the interior settings of her apartment, I noticed a small lamp sitting on a beautiful stand, also a stereo set which was on, and the music was very low. Honestly I can say I was still feeling a bit nervous. At least being there for the first time which caused me to be with that fear. She then turned on the bright room light. She then said, "make yourself at home... have a seat." I was standing in the middle of the room, with my hands in my trousers pocket, as I glance around the room, to see if there were any signs of a man living there with her.

I decided to move over to her mantelpiece instead of sitting where she suggested I should sit. I then noticed two portraits of a little boy, sitting on top of the mantelpiece. As I walked over for a closer look at the little boy, I immediately saw the resemblance of the boy as being her brother, or child. By this time J.S. was moving around the stereo, selecting special music she probably was intending to play for us that evening. I turned away from the portraits as I asked the question, 'who's the little boy?' she looks at me and smiled". As she said, 'it's my son; he's away at boarding school." She had just switch over from radio to record, placing the selected record on the turntable. I strolled over to one of the sofas' and sat myself down. I did not see any signs of a man living there. But yet I could have seen a few closed doors which lead off to the sitting room, and separated other closed rooms. She came over to me and stood in front my sofa, and asked me "what would you like to eat or drink?" I got hold of her and eased her towards me on top of my legs, and she sat and hugged me up. We both began to kiss each other, by this time I became more relaxed, and felt as if I had known her all my life. She was like a little doll up against me, as we kept fussing about with each other. Then suddenly as she kisses me at the side of my ear, she whispered to me. "You haven't answered my question as yet." I then said to her in a very low tone of voice. "What are you going to have?" She whispered once again, but this time straight into my ear. "Anything you have." I said, " Gin and Tonic with ice." She immediately got up, and at the same time she said jokingly, "yes my master, your Gin and Tonic is coming up" and she walked into the kitchen and switched on the lights. She then shouted from the kitchen, "are you sure you don't want something to eat?" "Quite sure." I shouted so that she can hear me clearly. She replied, "Okay, darling, when you do, you only have to say, and I'll fixed you up something."

After a little while she came out of the kitchen, and collected a gold finish trolley from out of the sitting room, and she wheeled it back into the kitchen, and collected the drinks, then brought it back into the sitting room. We sat there. For two hours drinking and talking from one thing to the other. She had taken me on a conducted tour throughout her apartment, in-between drinking and changing the records to a new set of records. She was living in a two bedroom apartment, and the entire place was nicely furnished, and was decorated to match the curtains and furniture. She was a very clean and tidy person. As it was getting late, and I had to be up early in the morning to pick up Harry Baird, and then head out to Twickenham Studio. I then told her it was time to hit the bed, and we then went to bed. After clearing up the place and getting ourselves tidy for the bed. While we were in bed making love, she told me of her marriage, and of her husband, who was away serving a prison sentence of five years, for stealing several cars. The husband was due to be out of prison in ten more months. She also told me that she visits him, and that she was due to see him that very same weekend. And in so doing she had decided to tell him there and then, that she was not going to be with him any longer. She said that there was no future of them being together. She said he was only twenty seven-years old, and he had been in prison before, after only spending two or three months out of prison. She pointed out to me that her husband was the head of a West End gang of car thieves, and sometimes the gang can be very rough. She further said to me as she began to sob. "Danny you don't know how bad my husband and his friends can be. Have you ever heard of a black man who was found in the canal in College Road, Campden Town?" I immediately went cold, because at the time I was very friendly with a girl who was living facing the said canal. That girl became my first child mother in England. She later got married to a US Flight Officer, and went to America with my daughter. We couldn't get on, so we decided to part, and just be friends. I said to J.S. "Yes, I remembered the incident, I was on Baynes Street quite frequent when they discovered the body of the black Man in the canal." She quickly said, "were you? That boy could have been you, since you were in the area that often." I said, "yes, it could have been me, I also thought that at the time." She then said to me, "it was my husband and his gang who committed that murder." I quickly sat up in bed, bracing myself on my two elbows as I turned my head, to look at her, and took the bed sheet and dried the tears from her eyes, as I spoke to her. "Stop crying, the damage as already been done." "Now tell me this, since you felt so strongly about it. Why didn't you go and tell the police about it at the time?" Her reply, "I wasn't with them, when they did it. I had over heard the conversation when they got back to the house. I had just gotten married about eleven months, and I was expecting my son at the time. So, I was at home, and he was out with his friends, then later on, himself and three others came back to the house to drink and talk. So while they were drinking and talking; I heard my husband say." 'That is one nigger less; the canal is the right place for him." "So I turned to one of the boys, and asked him, "what you all up to?" Then they all burst out laughing and my husband said to me. "We were at the Tea Cart at Campden Road, and a nigger was there buying himself a cup of tea, so we waited until he got his tea, then one of us went near to him and knocked it out of his hand. So he decided to do something about it. So we give him a good hiding. So as to teach him a lesson. We then lifted him, and throw his body into the canal." I then ask her what was her reaction to what her husband had told her. She said, "I screamed at him, and his friends. I told his friends to leave my home… and I called them a bunch of murderers. Then my husband turned to me and asked." "Which side are you on?" and he called me a nigger lover, and all his friends began to laugh, and I just walked out of the room leaving them."

By this time she had stopped crying, and I had laid my head back down on the pillow. I began to relax a little bit more. All this time while wide awake, with all sorts of thoughts flashing through my mind, as she continued her conversation. She said, "I went into the bedroom and packed a small case with a few clothing, then I got dressed. A little before I was dressed, my husband walked into the bedroom, and saw the suitcase lying on the bed as I was getting ready. He immediately got a hold of me and ripped off all of my clothing, and started to slap me in the face... as he started to shout and scream." As he asked, "where the hell do you think you are going?" I told him that I was going to my parents, until I got a place of my own. He said, "you are not going out of this house, otherwise it's me and you, then next thing I know, you and your family sending the police on me." "Well I'll tell you this, if anything happens to me or one of my friends, you will be in for it." I said to her, "so you got scared?" her reply was "Hell yes, are you not scared of those bunch of gorillas?" I said, "maybe." She questioned me, why did I say {maybe} I said, "well I am not in you place, so it's hard for me to say what I would have done, had I been in your position. I further pointed out to her that I am not one of those people who go around saying what they would have done, had they been in the other person place? Because another person can never have been in the place of the next person.

Each person is different. And a person can only be that person and no one else. She said, 'Why couldn't I have met you before? You have a wonderful mind. I heard a lot of girls talking about you." I quickly butted in. "What do the girls say about me?" Her reply was, "Well it's a lot of nice things they usually say about you, I am not going to... Because you might get swell headed, and I might end up loosing you. So that's my secret." I said, "Okay, I'll let you keep your secrets." And we both laughed it off. The time was near 4:00 a.m. and the traffic was beginning to build up, with the post office, newspapers, milk van, the market, trucks and other vehicles outside.

So we both decided it was time to get some shut eye and go to sleep. So that we did. Then the clock started to alarm early in the morning. So I ended up having one and a half hours of sleep. Then we both got up. She fixed me my breakfast while I took a bath and got dressed for work.

We made a date to meet each other after I had finished work, we continued seeing each other, because we were both very fond of one another, and we both got on fine. Then eventually we became more and more attached to each other. I told myself I would not leave her for any other woman, once she did not change towards me. Once again J.S. appreciated me for being that way. J.S. had decided to share me with Kay, who was the other woman. Kay also knew of J.S. and she felt the same as J.S., in the sense of sharing me, and not caring who I was with. Kay was also helping me financially, but not in the same sense as J.S. Kay was like my wife but we weren't married, because she was only separated from her husband. She was a bit wild, and made no secret of her wildness to me, from the first day we started dating each other. I can remember Kay saying to me after three weeks, while we were going out with each other, "Danny, You know I love you, but I'm a funny person, I could love you, and be with you today or a year, but I will not stay with you all the time, forever." "Ever so often, something just comes over me, and then I want to change my man." "So do not ever feel funny if it should happen. I will help you to get the things you want in life. But not because I do that, I may want the same things." I could not have had understood what she was saying to me at the time. I guess I was too young to understand any of it. I was twenty-five years old; my experiences with women had only just begun, especially with European women, so to speak. Yes, European women are different to an American or West Indian, or a Chinese, etc. I will go into that much later. I said to Kay, "Ah, come on, you don't know what you're saying, you have changed since the few weeks being with me." "So, you might even change, from changing man after man." She simply smiled at me, but did not comment on the issue any further. That for example is a European woman. She will make her point to her man, and she will avoid very much having an argument against her point, if her man or husband should disagree with her. She is very quick to make peace with her man, and not try to show too much fuss, she is on the opposite side of her man. She tries to get the best out of a relationship while she's in it. That was something I was yet to learn about the English women at least. The English women will be that way with her man for years once she gets the best out of that relationship. But the moment that relationship begins to lack her expectations, then that's it. The man could be a millionaire, it does not matter, whatever, she will leave that man with only the clothes on her back. Then go and start life all over again, with a road sweeper, once she feels happy with that road sweeper. Instead of staying with the millionaire, most English women do not put comfort and money in front of their happiness. Like in the case of an American woman, or West Indian woman, however, is the opposite. So, getting back to Kay, I had taken her statement very lightly indeed. I shouldn't have done so.

Had I not, I would have been one of the richest black men in the world today and more clever. Instead I thought of Kay, as being my wife. I had built for her, the child and myself during the six years I had been with her. But while doing that I thought I could have steadied her, and give her a life of which she was not accustomed, such as respectability, a beautiful home, and lots of money and children. But she was not that inclined. Instead she ruined three lives to a certain extent mines, hers as well as our child's. At the age of twenty-five, I did not need to work for anyone. Kay had tried to turn me into a pimp of hers. When I met her she was on the streets. I did not mind that as I pointed out before. That was her life and I had my life to live. I sat her down and told her it was not a good life, therefore she should think towards giving it up and living a respectable life. When I used the word respectable, I do not mean it in the sense that most people do. I have better sense than that. I do not mean because she was a prostitute, she was not respectable, because I have seen many women who were not known as prostitute, and were married with a family, yet at the same time they were jumping in and out of bed with different men, without using any form of prophylactic. Some of them do that, and call it love, and they looked upon themselves as being clean and decent. While some are doing the same thing, they become pregnant for one of these men, and in turn they will give the child to the husband as being theirs. While there are others taking small gifts from these men who they sleep around with. Then there are others who will take the husband's money and keep other men on the side. Now, in my eyes those women I do not have respect for.

My respect is greater for an English prostitute, I say English prostitute, because 90% of the English prostitutes I have seen or heard about, will not go to bed with a man, unless they themselves put on the prophylactics on the man, no matter how much the man was willing to have sex without them. Then its only a few who would go to bed with a man, without using any form of protection, and those women usually get a hard time from the other women, and in no time everyone gets to know who those women are, who rides 'Bare-back,' as they call it. So in short, we know the reason behind the prostitutes doing such a thing.... its money. But the other women are doing it for love, and that's what the English prostitute calls it. 'Free Love', Kay uses to give me ten pounds, six days a week in those days it was a lot of money one can say. Apart from that money, she had to get money for food, hair, clothing, and rent for her apartment where she was staying. Whatever was remaining out of her money, I was free to do whatever I so wish.

So what I did was to save it towards buying a home for us. I was working at that time as an extra, and a Stuntman, so my money in the film world was great. Some days I will make no lower than eight pounds to fifteen, twenty-five pounds depending on the various works I do. So I can say, I did not need a woman to keep me, for as I used to tell all of them. Do not, ever feel you are keeping me because, no woman can keep me. No matter what help a woman was giving me, I will always go out and work for my living. That way I was independent of any woman's help. Secondly, I would be in a position to help the same woman, if she was sick or anything had gone wrong with her." That had suited Kay. She realized that I wasn't a pimp in the true sense of the word. I had never supplied her or anyone else with a man, so that the man can pay her. To go a bit further, I have never seen her or any other woman who I was friendly with, on the streets with another man; I never went nearby to where they were doing their business. My knowledge of what they did was enough. To see was another side which I never cared to attempt, because I had placed their profession as a job they choose, and I could not have had supplied anyone of them with the life style which they had been accustomed to, financially. So my intelligence taught me not to try and lecture to them too strong.

Because after the lecturing, money talks, and at that time I had no money. Their white brothers were not giving me any work in the first place. So that was how I became involved in that life. While doing my film work as an extra, and a stuntman. I decided to get a Hawkers Licence to sell. So what I did was to save up some money to place a deposit on a car. I went up to London East End, to the Jews, and other wholesale stores, and buy men and women's clothing, and sold it on a weekly payment credit system.

So after working in the studio, I would go around in the evenings, and sell or deliver my orders. The days I am not working in the studio, I will do the same. So I did that for a couple of years, and save up all the money I can put my hands on along with working as a film extra, a stuntman and a salesman. I enrolled into drama school where I was trained as an actor. After which I then changed over from working as an extra and stuntman, and started to work as an actor. It was a year later after becoming an actor; I purchased one of my two properties. So when I met J.S. the negotiations of purchasing the two properties were six weeks old.

I already had my down payment for both properties in the sum of five hundred and fifty pounds for Talbot road, and seven hundred and fifty pounds for Colville Terrace. Talbot road property was being sold at 5,500 pounds and Colville Terrance Property was being sold at 7,500 pounds. I also had my solicitor's fee and stamp duties, all in hand a surplus of 700 pounds towards furnishing the two places. So I was banking on making some more money from my series. By the time, full completion of both properties came through at the end of the three months.

So while I had all those plans in hand I ran into J.S. as I've mentioned above. So on our second date, which occurred on the evening following my staying the night at her apartment. I went home to 28 Croxted Road after I had finished in the studio my series for the day. So after I had gotten home at ten from work, I tidied my two bedrooms, and living room apartment. Then took a bath, and made supper for J.S. and myself, also a bit extra food, should anyone phone and say that they were coming over, or just passing, and saw the lights on in the apartment, and decided to stop by.

I was expecting J.S. to arrive at about midnight after she had finished work. So at five minute to twelve, there was a knock on the front door, and the door bell rang. I answered the door, and let her into the apartment. I showed her into the living room, and gave her a seat. I then asked her if she would like to have a drink, she said, "yes, but I would like to have a hot bath before." So I took her into my bedroom, and showed her where I kept all the towels and linen. I then gave her one of my bathrobes to wear. And said, "Make yourself at home. I'll run the bath for you." She thanked me, and I then left her and went and run her bath. I prepared a cologne bath called "Fuego De Amor." Fuego Deamor means, 'fire of love,' in Spanish. I always kept several types of colognes, and perfumes in my bathroom. Because I loved pouring various colognes or perfumes scents into my hot bath water, while the water is steaming into the bath tub. That way my body and my apartment are nicely smelled, so I usually let my girlfriends do the same, whenever one of them takes a bath in my home. She came out of the bedroom and headed towards the bathroom, as I left the water running and mixing up with the cologne and bath salts. She asked, "Danny, what's the name of that smell, it's beautiful?" I told her the name and she said. "I meant to ask you the moment I step into the apartment; the smell was all over the place, and what a gorgeous apartment you do have."

"It makes my apartment looks like a hog pen." I said, "Ah, come on, you too have a nice apartment." She replied, "most of the things you have are from abroad, it's really nice and so comfortable." I replied, "and so is yours." The point is I have the opportunity to travel all over the place being a movie actor, so I usually buy various things when I go abroad." She said, " I must let you do the same for me, whenever you go abroad." I said, to her as I throw my arms around her shoulder and walked her along the rest of the hallway to the bathroom. "Come on, your bath must be ready, and I must go and check the dinner." She said to me as she arrived at the bathroom door. "I will see you later, darling." She then went into the bathroom and took her bath. I was busy then in the kitchen preparing the supper as I was hungry, because it was getting late, much later than my usual supper time. While I was in the kitchen I heard the telephone ringing in my bedroom. So I went and answered the phone, it was Kay on the other end of the line. She said, "I wanted to know what we were doing this weekend, are we going to visit our son?" I told her yes, we can and then we can go down to Brighton visiting. "How are you, is everything alright? She replied, "yes, fine, and you?" I reply. "Oh, I am fine darling." She then questioned, "How come you are home so early, are you feeling sick? Or do you have a visitor?" I told her, "No, I'm not sick, I have a visitor." She then said, "I hope I didn't interrupt you." I said, "No, you didn't. She then said, "Okay, I'll see on Sunday morning, I must go now." And we told each other bye, and we both hung up. I had an African friend who was living in Brighton, and sometimes we would go up there, and spend the day with him and his girlfriend, so that's what we had planned to do, to visit our son, who was staying in Kingston-Upon Thame, at his foster parents. It was now Friday night going into Saturday morning, as Kay telephoned me trying to tell me in so many words. Do not get too tired up for Sunday. Because on Sunday she would like to be with me, and to go and see our boy. In any case that was fine with me. How many women will allow their man to do as he likes, to me she came first, she had always leveled with me, and I the same with her. That, J.S. had learned from her girlfriends, before she had decided to be friends with me. By this time she was out of the bathroom, and she was in my bedroom making herself look prettier. She was really pretty, so she didn't wear much make-up. In any case, I never did like a woman who wore a lot of make-up as though she was on the stage, or in a film. All of my women had to be very pretty, and lady- like no matter if they were a prostitute, let them be a prostitute by profession, but not by sight. It gave me a kick to have a beautiful prostitute, and at the same time one who knew her table manners, the right way to dress and matched her clothing,  also to carry on a sensible conversation. I was much moved and intrigue by such a woman, most of my women have been that way. I can remember many times, some of my friends who were from rich and noble

149

families, some movie stars and ambassadors; they all would watch my girlfriends with water running out of their mouths. As they turn to me and said, "where did you find this Madonna? This time, how do you find them, Danny?" my reply was, "I usually search, when I find beauty such as these, I placed my claim. No matter in what corner they maybe, I cannot resist." My friends then say to me. "Neither would I". Now, I knew they weren't telling me a lie, because all the time I would be with them and with my girlfriend. They were busy trying to served them and me, while we were at their parties or where-ever, and on top of that they will be trying to pull my girlfriend from up under my nose. Sometimes they would tell me to my face. That they find themselves very much attracted to my women, and then they will try and pull them away from me. I would then laugh and pass it off, as I would say to them. "Well you know me; go ahead there are lots of fishes in the sea." And deep down in my heart I meant it. I never felt funny against another man if one of my girlfriends or a wife had left me for another man. Because, I look upon such a thing as being part of life, so to speak. Women had trained me into such an acceptance. I am very thankful to them. Very few men had started life with the same woman and ended up in being old and gray with the same woman, and the same goes for a man. So that was something I had learned at a very early age. So I made no pretence about it. A person can have a very good friend and that friendship can last for a life time, but you as well as I know that seldom happens, and that's a fact. So I like to think practical, it makes life much easier, and one looks much younger and lives longer. At present while writing this book, I am fifty-one years and six months of age and not one person in this world who did not know me would believe my age. Everyone thinks I am thirty-three years old. So my way of thinking must be right. I look very good for it considering what I've been through. By this I had laid the table and the supper was served. J.S. and myself were sitting at the table having supper when suddenly she said, "I heard the phone rang, who was it, Kay?" I replied. "Yes, that's right," she said, "is Kay mad because you are seeing me?" I replied, "No, not at all, she do not get mad with me because I am going out with another girlfriend." She said, "I knew she didn't, I don't mind you being with her either, but just keep it to the two of us. We will be a family of three. I will help you to get all things which you want. I'll give you twenty-five pounds every day, six days a week and the rest of my money I will keep." She was doing all of the talking, and I was listening while watching her, as we were eating. I had selected a set of Latin long playing records which was playing on the "Gains Bourough" Grundic Sterio Set, that set was an important part of my job. It was fitted with a tape recorder, radio, and record player. The tape recorder was the most important section with my work as an actor. I would rehearse and practice on the tape at least three times a week. That allows me to have full control of my recording voice. I knew the various tones, level etc. of my voice. By using that set three times a week, I was a very dedicated actor. My work came before any thing else, other than health. Because once I can work, I can have anything that money can buy. So while she was laying her cards on the table to me, I was also listening to the wonderful Latin music in the background as she spoke to me. She continued her conversation, "I am saying that if you should see some beautiful girl who fancies you and you fancies her, not to mess with her, but let it be a one-night-stand. Don't be with her like Kay and I, you see what I mean darling?" I then asked her "Why do you allow me to have another woman as a one-night-stand?" She replied "you know why as well as I do, every man at sometime sees another woman who becomes attracted to him so then, if its easy pickings he ends up having an affair with the woman. Isn't that true." I said, "Quite True".

Unless the man is not normal, or he's sick, then he will not fancy another woman." She quickly said "you know people are very funny, they simple try to harness too much of nature laws and rules. That is why the world has so many problems. Won't you agree?" I replied, "I do agree with you all the way, by the way, not changing the subject. But since we are talking about problems it came to my mind." She quickly inquired. "What?" I continued, "You told me last night that you'll be going to visit your husband this weekend. I take it, its tomorrow? She replied, "yes, tomorrow, Saturday, why?" I said, I remembered, you saying last night, that when you visit your husband this weekend, you are going to tell him that you are finished with him. Well I want you to give me your promise, that you will not tell him that while he's behind bars. Too many people go around doing things like that, and it only upsets the individuals while they are locked up in jail." "It's very cruel to do such a thing to anyone." She said, okay, I'll wait until he gets out, and then do it. Okay darling?" I said, "Well! Would you like some more wine?" she replied, "Yes, thank you," and I then poured another two glasses of wine for both of us. While pounding the wine I heard the front doorbell ringing. So I hurried up and finished the pouring of the wine. Then I went to the front door to see who it was. As I opened the door to see who it was. I saw a policeman in uniform standing at the door, I said, Good evening or good morning whatever, and he quickly said, "Daniels, this is the third time I have to tell you about your cars parking on the road with no lights, I gave you a ticket before." I quickly butted in and said, "But the car is parked under the street lamp in front of my entrance. Secondly, I came home early while it was still daylight and I forgot to put my lights on at 9:30pm" he said, "No excuse, Mr. Daniels I am going to give you a ticket." I said, 'very good, write me the ticket." He took out his book, and wrote me up a parking ticket which reads, [Failing to comply with the parking lights regulations on the public road when parked.] He handed me the ticket and left. I took it and closed the door, as I went back into the house. I then pulled on a weather jacket and a pair of shoes and went outside and removed the car. J.S. had parked her car around the corner off of the main road. Because, I had told her to do so, the morning when I was giving her the direction to my place, while I was at her home before leaving for work. So her car was fine. I knew that policeman; he didn't like me at all. At this stage I didn't too. I will tell you later on. I had a garage across the road which belongs to the Lambent Bourough Council, so I was sub-letting the garage from them because; most of their tenants did not own a car. Most of them couldn't afford to buy such a Luxury. I finally parked my car into the garage and returned back to the house. During all this time of living in Croxted Road, I was being confronted by a lot of jealousy, from people in the area. But no one had dare say a funny word to me, instead they all took their jealousies and turned it around as they tried to become friendly with me. Some of them will stop and talk to me as I would be standing outside cleaning my car. Some of them will say to me, "oh, that's a beautiful car you got there." I wouldn't mind owing one like it..", "I saw you a couple of days on television. Tell me something, do they pay a lot of money when you work like that on television or films?" I usually cut them short, by saying, "yes they do, and it depends on the length or size of the part." I could well understand the way some of them felt. Let's face it, many of them had tried to suppress the blacks by not giving them work in the country, and then suddenly many of the blacks were driving in beautiful cars, living in homes of their own, also dressing nicely and always sharp and clean all day long. While they were working everyday, and hardly could pay their rent or buy a suit at the end of the year. The money which I was being paid for a days work in a film as an actor, it took the ordinary Englishman five weeks to work for it and to take it home as take home pay. So I knew the way they felt. After trying to kill the 'goose' (the blacks), and then the 'goose' escaping from their pressure. I sympathize with them. After I got back into the house I found that J.S. was in the middle of washing up the dishes after she had cleared the table. That's another good point which I like about the English and German women. They do not go to sleep and leave dirty dishes lying around in the house all night. Instead they always wash the dishes and tidy the place before retiring to bed for the night. That is also a habit of mine. So I began to give her a hand with the dishes as most Englishmen would do. Please do not misunderstand me, not every English or German woman normally tidy up before going to bed. But most of them, 90% do. In America it's the reverse. I'm yet to meet one who does it. I still might meet one of them. So getting back to the topic. We did the clearing up and then retired to the living room where we had a few drinks, before going to bed for the night, after drinking and talking from one thing to the other. Our relationship had been set, and we both understood what was what. So we continued seeing each other.

# 18

## *Jackie and Me*

WHILE BEING IN POTTER'S APARTMENT one afternoon in the year 1960...around May month. I was introduced to one of the most beautiful woman I had ever seen in a long time. She had just arrived from South Africa, where she had been living in Johannesburg since the age of five years old, with her mother and sister.

She was white and had been born in Northampton, England. When I met her in 1960, she had just finished her 21st birthday before leaving South Africa. She had long golden hair, which touched her waist line. Her hair had natural curls, and therefore she had no need to go to any hair dresser. Her beauty was excellent; she was beautifully built from head to toe. The mere looks at her made my dream come through.. of the sort of woman I can see myself walking up the alter with to say "I do." She was the apple of my eyes, the fire in my life, and the light of my life. Somehow, I felt that I could spend the rest of my life with such a woman. She was very, very, lady like, and didn't speak much. I knew she came from a very good back ground and family.... Just by looking at her.

I decided in my mind, she I must have! I kept sizing her up to see if she had any faults which was visible to me. I just couldn't find any, as I sat there looking at her, unnoticeable to her of course.

Her name was Jacquline Duthon Peters. I did not make much of her on our first meeting. I quickly said to everyone who was in the apartment, "Goodbye." I then leave as if I was in a hurry, and at the same time as though she meant nothing to me. She gave me the impression as though one had to be very careful not to make too much of a fuss with her, otherwise, you are liable to loose or scare her. She wasn't the type that was easily taken to people. She had a sort of snobbish look about her, which was due to her upbringing partly, as I saw it then.

I went to the 'Club GiGi" on the following evening to see Potter or Joan so as to find out more about her. As I pulled up outside the GiGi and parked my car. Potter was walking up the stairs which led into the basement to the GiGi Club. He saw me and quickly said. "Hi Danny! Come follow me home, I have to collect some drinks for the Club." I said, "Okay lets' use my car."

Potter and I got back into my car and we drove off to Colville Terrace to pick up the drinks. Potter always leaves most of the drinks for the Club in his apartment. Because the area in which the Club was situated was in St. Stephen Gardens and around that area places were been broken into by the various thieves. So he took no chances with his club, and stock. While Potter and I were together, this is what I had wanted. He told me all that I had wanted to know about Jacqueline. He said, they had grown almost together, but her mother was a very fussy type of woman and she never did liked him. Because his family was poor and her mother had money, and live a life with maids and servants. He said, "You know the type?"…. "Black maids and servants, the mother doesn't have to work. Her husband died and left a bundle of money for her, and all she does is laze around all day long, and the maids and servants wait on her- on hands and knees." "But Jackie, she is different, she's a nice chick. Like you fancy her?" He asked me surprisely. I told him, "Yes, she seems like a nice girl." He quickly said, "And very special, she and Joan were mostly friends, it was through her I got to become close to her." I asked, "How long is she planning to stay in England?" His reply was, "Three or four months, she just arrived from the States from a vacation. I think she's planning to go to Spain when her mother gets here from South Africa."

We returned back to the GIGI Club with his drinks, I gave him a hand to take it into the Club. When we got there, I saw Jackie and Joan standing behind the counter serving the customers who were in the Club, and spending their money like, 'mad'. Joan was a beauty herself. She looked a bit like Jacqueline Duthon Peters, who I will refer to as Jackie. When I first saw Jackie, I thought it was Joan's sister. Until, I was introduced to her as being a friend of Joan and Potter. Quite a few of the boys had tried to make a play for Joan in the past, while she was working in their Club. Potter and I knew of it. Although they were aware that Joan was Potters' woman, and at the same time Potter was very friendly with them all. They would still try to make a play behind his back for his woman, which I thought was very dirty. I could never go to bed with someone who was close to me, as a friend (woman). There is no feeling in me as such for a woman. All my life, I've been that way. That is why most of my male associates like me, and think very highly of me. Once there was a slight friendship between me and a male friend, also if he had introduced me to his wife or his woman… and I knew that those two people were together-then that's it, I could never go to bed with her for the rest of my life. So you can imagine how the drinks were flowing from across the bar to all the customers who had fancied themselves as dating the girls behind the bar.

Also the money and the cash register were busy changing hands, and being Jackie was a new face in the Club, it was like 'hell let loose in the joint.'

157

Potter and I went into a corner where everything was quite. We sat there drinking and talking from one thing to another. While lots of money were being made to go into his pocket. After a while, we were joined by Tom and Becky and a couple more friends of Potter, the moment they came into the Club. That table where we were sitting was reserved for Potter, his Club Staff and close friends. No other person was allowed to sit there. The club had several tables and the tables were served by a waiter and waitress. Most of the stroke catchers were crowded around the Bar, because that's where most of the single women who came into the club, normally sat, and was sitting that present time.

It was very funny, ever since I was growing up I never like having to compete for the attention of a woman against other men- somehow that puts me off of the woman, I am still the same way. By this time, Potter had decided to go and assist the girls, one at a time from behind the Bar. So he told me that he'll be sending over Jackie to take a break at the table where I was. Becky and Tom and the others were moving around the Club speaking to various people they knew. Potter left and Jackie came and joined me. As she sat down, she said, "Good evening, how come you're sitting here in the corner and not dancing like the others, or doing what they are doing?" I asked, "What are they doing, may I ask?" she replies, "well you know flirting, the amount of guys that were trying to date me and trying to buy me drinks." I said, "That's what happens when you are a woman. Especially beautiful woman, as in your case." She then smiled as she said, "Thanks, for the compliment. Joan tells me that you are a Movie Star." I then reply, "Well not a Star, but an Actor." She then questioned, "But isn't it the same thing?" I said, 'far from it.. When we have much more time I will tell you the difference, would you care for a drink? Or is that like taking tea to China?" She asked, "what do you mean, by taking tea to China?" I told her, "It's a saying. In your case you are working amongst all those drinks in the Bar. You might become sick of it by now, seeing it all the time." She said, "oh, I got it. You mean china produces tea, so no one will take tea to china." I said, "That's it." She said, "Okay, this Chinese will take it." I asked, "Then what will you have?" She replies, "A Brandy and Coke, please." I said to her as I got up to go to the Bar to get the two of us a Drink. "A Brandy and Coke coming up."

She then smile once again as I turned to leave the table. She had one of the most beautiful smiles, as she smiled both of her dimples appear on both cheeks and soon disappear as she becomes serious. I went to the Bar and edged my way through the Friday night crowd, which was blocking the front of the Bar in order to get served. Joan saw me as I was edging through the crowd. She came over to me and asked, "What would you like Dan?" She always called me Dan, instead of Danny. I guess she liked Dan much better that Danny. I told her what I wanted and she quickly served me. As she placed the drinks in front of me, she asked, "What do you think of Jackie?" I said, "I think she's gorgeous, I am crazy about her." She said, I guess she's the same about you. The first day she met you." Don't let her know I told you. She's a bit shy." I said to her as I give her the money for the drinks. "Thanks for telling me." And she went to the cash register, and I to my unfinished business, Jackie! On my way back to the table, I saw one of the guys standing at her table trying to speak to her. But the moment he saw me, he quickly moved away and gave me a smile. I then joined her at the table and we continued speaking to each other. She said, "Some of the guys in here scares me. They can never take No for an answer. Instead, they just keep on pestering me for a date."

I laughed at the way she said it. She was a bit scared; I guess she had never mixed with the type of crowd which was in that club. All classes were in that club, especially just before closing. The drinking hours in England were very strict. All Bars, Pubs, Clubs, were limited to 10:30pm drinking licenses. So what most small Clubs uses to do, is to close their doors at closing time and continued serving drinks over the limited time. They made more money that way, because all the people who were locked in, will simply order doubles and triples and drink it up much faster. As they try to consume the amount they wish to consume before the place was officially closed. Of course only the smaller clubs which were situated in the off beat areas, could have taken those type of chances to violate the club and liquor Laws. Because if they were caught and their Club licenses were taken away.. They usually register the Club into a new name and then apply for a new license. Then they are back in business. So because of the late hour drinking in the smaller clubs, the customers will flock into them. Jackie was not familiar with those types of situations in the Clubs of London. The late rush into those clubs was tremendous. By this time her break was about finish, so I told her that I'll be seeing her the following day. She then returns back to work. Then I told Potter the same, and then leave the club.

After a week had pass and Jackie had gotten to know me more or less. I started dating her. We went out with each other almost every night. She would work all day as a private Secretary in an office, and then on some evenings she will go and work in the Club. So as to give Joan and Potter some help. Then after the club was closed at eleven in the evening. Then we will go all over the place to various Clubs.

She had liked going out a lot, to different places, and so was I. We became very attached to each other after a few months. But while the places were going through the legal process of being sold to new owners. I sat down one day and told her of my intention in getting rid of my properties. She had agreed, with me in selling the places. I pointed out to her that selling the places was one thing, but after that was completed, one had to be very careful with the money obtained from the property sale. Such money would have to reinvest. Otherwise the money will soon disappear.

I then told her of an idea which I had in mind to invest the money which I will received from the sale. My idea was to lease a building in Old Oxford Street, just past to Tenham Court Road; it was very good locally for the type of business which I had in mind. The business was a small boutique, specializing in leather goods from Spain and other places. She thought it was an excellent idea. Therefore, I ask her if she would be willing to work along with me so that I may get it started. I suggested that she should run the store while I was out buying the various stocks which we both agreed upon to sell in the store. She accepted the entire idea. So that was settled.

She had told me previously that she might only be staying in England for a period of one year. She had liked South Africa because of the beautiful climate, and wages which were being paid over there, as against the wages which were being paid in England. I told her that I understood, had I been in her place I would think exactly like her. Because one always try to get the best out of a country one chooses to live in. But, since I was Black that was out of the question, for me to think about going to a place like South Africa. She pointed out to me that, that was one of the things she did not like about South Africa.

There were too much racial barriers. She said at times she would go out shopping in her car, with the maid which they had. The name of the maid was Sophie. Jackie said Sophie was never allowed to sit in the front seat of the car next to her while they were out shopping or otherwise. Another thing which she pointed out to me, that a black person could not go into any of the stores, and try on a pair of shoes, hat or any other clothing if they were to try-it-on for size and then found out it was too large, they would have to pay for it, and keep it. I asked her, what happens if the black person were wearing a clean pair of socks while they were trying on the pair of shoes?" She said, "I had nothing to do with the way in which he or she was dressed, it goes for all the blacks but not the whites?" I said, that was a shame for the blacks who were living in such a place. I said, "How can you live in such a place?" Her reply was "What can I do?" "It did not affect me, a white person can live like a King or Queen. The Whites who did not approve of the system could not voice their opinion otherwise, they would be put into jail." She further stated, "I had lots of arguments with my mother about it. Sometime I would sit down to the table in our home and eat at the same time as our maid, Sophie. But my mother would get mad about it and told Sophie to leave the table. So as you can see, even in my home I had trouble in trying to change the general system of the whites or should I say, most of the whites". "I wrote my mother and told her about you. I told her that I was going out with you. But so far she hasn't reply. I know, she'll be very mad about it." I ask her, "What about your father?" she said, "My father is not alive. It's a very said story!" She continued, "My father went out to Johannesburg before us. He went out there to start his own business which he did. Then after he sends for my mother, sister who is younger that I am, and me. When we arrived in South Africa my father came to the Airport and met us. He then droves us to a beautiful home which he had built for us. He spent a couple of hours with us in the home.

After which he then leave to go and attend to some business a few miles away. So while he was traveling on the road, there was a storm during the same time. So he was caught in the storm while traveling." "The storm got hold of his car and blew his car into a tree and killed him instantly on the spot. That was the last we saw of him." I asked, "How long was he in Africa, before you all went out to join him?"

She replies, "Quite a few years. He had built up a large Haulage Transport Business; also he had owned some apartments to let." I said, I am sorry to hear of such a tragedy, it was a tragic event for yourself and sister, to have faced on the first night of your arrival in a strange country". "I can imagine, being seven years old at the time, especially."

After going out with Jackie a couple of weeks. Joan and Potter had sold the Club and went back to South Africa. But before Potter had leave Colville Terrance he asked me to give him a smaller apartment at the top of my building. The apartment was like a small penthouse. I gave it to him and he moved out from the other apartment down-stairs into the above, but after a few days living there, he departed and went to Africa, leaving Jackie alone to live in it. I guess why Potter did that because he knew I did not like messing around with my tenants. But he must have felt since I was going out with Jackie while he was my tenant, he will secure her into one of the apartment, but he will be fronting as my tenant for her. It was a clever move of his. Also he knew that the building was changing hands very shortly. I didn't mind about the entire affair. Since the place was changing hands.

Had it not, I would have searched for a place elsewhere for Jackie, so as not to mixed business and pleasure at the same time, as I pointed out before.

I finally sold the two places, and paid off all my bills owing against them. I had just barely recovered all of my capital, which I had put into the two properties. I went across to Spain to check the cost of my various items which I intended to buy, so as to stock the boutique I intended to open.

The prices were all reasonable after my research into it all. I then returned back to England to go ahead with securing the premises in Oxford Street. But before I went into it. I discussed the idea with Jackie once again. She then became a bit apprehensive as to whether she'll be able to run the place as a Manager, while I will be working still as an actor, and being the buyer when I am not working as an actor. In short she became scared of the responsibility. So I then decided not to go into the business. Instead, I continued working as an actor and put the little money into the bank.

I kept on dating her. Then her mother and sister finally came to England on a vacation. By this time I was going out with her about three months before the mother arrived in London from South Africa. Jackie had found a larger apartment and had removed from Colville Terrance. The larger place was selected to accommodate her mother and sister who were being expected to stay in Europe for at least two months. It was decided upon before Jackie had left Africa, that she will return back to Africa with her mother and sister after they had spend a European vacation. But since meeting me, all that had changed. She extended the time of staying in Europe, as I state before, nine months to be exact. She did not inform her mother of those changes before she arrived in London.

Instead she waited until she had arrived in London, and then discussed it with the mother. By this time Jackie had become very much in love with me. But yet she had the thought of still returning back home after she had spent the time which she told me she'll be spending. I kept that in thought in case she had decided to go through with it. At least she was very honest about it all. So I did not build up my expectation too high, in the sense that we may be together all the time.

But some where at the back of my mind I was hoping that she had a change of heart in going back home. I was the first man to have ever seduced her. The beginning was very difficult for me; it took me three months sleeping with her almost three to four nights a week before she finally gave into me. I can remember while trying to seduce her the second occasion. Somehow, It got into my head that on this occasion this was it. We both had wanted each other. She was all relaxed. Then the moment I tried to go much further into the act, suddenly, out of the blues.. Wam! She punched me in the right eye. I saw so many colours after receiving the blow in my eye. I became very furious with her. I then return a similar punch into her eye. I didn't say a word to her for the rest of the evening. All I did was to turn my back against her and lay still until I dozed off to sleep. When we both woke up the following morning, and looked at each other. She first burst out laughing as she watched me. I said to her, "What the hell are you laughing at? You're like a tiger in bed." I am not going to try again to make love to you.. You are too dangerous." She said, "I told you it wasn't easy." We both ended up laughing at each other black-eyes. Up to that point I didn't realize that she had never gone with a man before.

At times when I kissed her and she got all worked up, she would start to tremble like a leaf. I thought it was the fact that I being black and she growing up in a place like South Africa, which had caused her to be nervous, and being scared. But that had nothing to do with it. She was simply scared because of not having the experience of having a sexual relationship before. I must say that was my first relationship of trying to have sex with such a person-as they call them, 'a maiden!' I hope that will be my first and last as I told myself then. But after a few weeks later everything was Okay.

Finally her mother had arrived in London. The sister came two weeks before the mother. So I had met the sister we got on very fine. Then when her mother came to Jackie's apartment on that first day. I was sitting in her apartment; Jackie had asked me to be there when her mother arrived. She was a bit nervous while the time was drawing near for her mother to show up from the airport to the apartment. So was her sister. I saw the state in which both of them were in. I felt it was my place since I had known better.

To excuse my presence, before her mother had arrived. I knew what a racist was like. It was like taking a totally blind person to a ball game, and expecting them to see the game and enjoy it. One cannot sit down with a racist and try to compromise with them. It just doesn't work, that I knew. A racist never, never changes their out look. That is a fact!

I sat down with Jackie the day before her mother was due to arrived in London. I told her not to expect her mother liking me… or seeing me as a man and not a black man which she dislikes. Her mother was old and set in her false ways. Her prejudices had been in-bedded in her mind from childhood. Such a person does not change, and one cannot expect them to change. I am black, and being the receiver of such prejudice from people like her mother. I suggested that I should go and not wait around to see to her. But Jackie was very stubborn, she insisted that I should stay and see her mother. I did not want a confrontation with the mother, because I can't stand to be insulted by anyone. Especially, when it comes to my colour. I see my colour being just as great as any other colour. I see myself being just as great as anyone who is in my class or category.

I will defend that with my life, against any one who tries to abuse me because of the colour of my skin. I am not responsible for nature's rule or gift to man. So that is why I will defend that gift. But Jackie meant well! She didn't know better in regards to the situation. Finally, her mother and her ex-step father who went to the airport to meet her had arrived outside.

Her sister who was so nervous, and at the same time been checking at the front window from time to time. To see if and when her mother arrived, she was the first one to have seen the mother and ex-stepfather pulling up in his car. The sister shouted, "Jackie they are here." the sister was about seventeen years old if I remembered correctly. Jackie and I went across to the window and looked out. We stood there for a few seconds and looked at the mother and ex-stepfather as they walked from the car towards the front door. I quickly said to Jackie, "I'll phone you back later, I'll see you." I then kissed her good-bye, I then walked out of the apartment. Jackie said, "Okay promise?" As I moved so sudden and unexpected. She hadn't time to think or to argue with me. I replied, "Promise?" Then through the apartment door I went. The apartment was situated on the second floor of the building.

On my way out I passed her mother in the hallway as they both had just closed the street door behind them and started to walk along the hallway. As I walk pass them I said "Good afternoon!" The ex-stepfather replied. That was that. I got into my car and then drove away. I rang her back later the same evening to find out how she was getting on. She told me that everything was fine.

Also that her mother was on her way to North Hampton, where she was originally from. She's going there to visit relatives. So Jackie wanted to see me the same evening. So I drove back over and spent some time with her. Then I went home. The mother had planned to take the two girls to Spain on a vacation. So after spending a couple of weeks in North Hampton they then returned back to London. They all took off for Spain. They spent a couple of weeks in Spain and then returned back to London. They had a splendid time while being in Spain. We both had missed each other while she was away.

Then while the mother was still in England, Jackie told me that she had a discussion with her mother about me. Jackie said, "My mother made it quite clear that she didn't want to meet you." She also did not like the idea of me going out with you.

She was very frantic about it. She also said, "That she would not sit on the same bus as you, or any black person, much more sit in the same room and breathe the same air as you." As she finished relating all that her mother said to her about me. I then said, "I told you, you cannot teach an old dog new tricks, your mother is too old and set in her ways, for you and I to try and reach her. I have seen many people like her in the past. I will not waste a single minute in trying to prove to people like her how wrong their outlook can be. So you can go ahead and try to prove and fend with your mother. But do not ever ask me to do the same. Also as long as we are together, your mother must never set foot in my home as long as I live, please remember that. I do not need to be friendly with a mother-in-law or father-in-law. But I do know this, if my mother were to say the things yours' said. And she was speaking about you, or any woman I was with, my mother could never had set foot into my home as long as you or whoever I was with that she did not like. Because mother-in-laws or father-in-laws can be very dangerous. Just remember what I've just said. Jackie did not reply to my statement.

Now those words were very strong words, which came from Jackie's mother. Words such as those I would always remember and the person who used them to me. Such a memory I will carry to my grave. Lets be realistic, it's only a sensible person who would always bear those words in mind, so as to protect themselves and those who are around them, who needs protection. That is why I told Jackie there and then, about not letting her mother set foot in our home, if we should reach that far. I know me and I know my limits. So I always use to try to teach any woman whom I'm with. My limits, and my likes and dislikes. I find doing that makes my life becomes an easy one. Because the moment she slips once, I will tell her. If she slips twice, I will remind her. Three times then I know its time I should put a final stop to it all. That way I have no more such problems. So that I may deal with the problems which I have no full control over them in trying to stop them. That's the way I am. I will also continue to be that way until I die.

Three days later Jackie and I went in the afternoon, where she had to meet her mother on Regent Street, Piccadilly, as I pulled up into the car in front of Sawn and Edgar Department Store on Regent Street, her mother was standing in front of the store waiting. I stopped the car in front of her mother, and she got out and joined her. I looked at the mother and then drove off. That was the last time I saw her then, while she was in England in 1960.

Summer time Jackie mother and sister finally left England. They went back to Johannesburg, South Africa, we were left in peace. Jackie had changed into a smaller apartment, which was situated in Chepstow Road, London. I was still living alone in Croxted Road. Time had began to pass, it was now 1961. Somehow Jackie had gotten notice to move from her apartment in Chesptow Road, because of me. The owner told her, that the other tenants were complaining to the landlady. Because Jackie had a black boyfriend who were seen visiting the house. So because of me she was given notice to vacate the premise. Well, Jackie had searched around to find a place. Then after trying to find a suitable place for three long weeks, time was running out on her, she had to leave the place in a matter of a couple of days. Because her months' notice was up in a couple of days. So I told her, not to start panicking, because if 'push came to shove' as the saying goes, 'you can always move into my apartment until you find somewhere else. I, at the same time was expecting to go to Rome to work in a film for three months. The British actor strike had just started. So work in England for actors was very difficult to get at that time. So the Film 'Cleopatra' was looking for dancers to go and work in Rome, on a three months contract. The money was good. So being an ex-dancer, I decided to audition as a dancer. I did, and got the job. By this time money was beginning to get very low on my end. The Actors Union Strike was heading in its sixth month, at that time. My car payment was beginning to pile up on me. Because I had only bought my Chevrolet Corvette car about eight months before. This was three months before the strike had started. So because I wasn't able to work properly owing to the strike. I was heading towards bankruptcy. Jackie decided to move into my apartment and at the same time look after it while I was in Rome.

But while the two of us were staying in the apartment during 1961 summer, just before I took off for Rome, one early evening while we were in bed, in the back bedroom which was my bedroom. The other bedroom which was used as a guest room, was situated at the front of the larger bedroom. The curtain was fully drawn, but the top of the window was slightly opened so as to allow some air to enter into the room. As we lay there we weren't asleep, then suddenly I heard a voice said, "you in bed with another woman?" I quickly looked towards the bedroom window, and I saw Kay's head sticking out in between the curtain and hanging over the top of the opened window. She quickly pelted a brick towards us while lying in bed. By the time I got out of bed, another brick followed the first one very quickly, not to mention the fowl language, which I will not repeat. But you can use you imagination. I rushed over to the dressing table which was standing in front of the same window. On top of the dressing table, were several large bottles of various colognes. I got a hold of one of the bottles and threw it at Kay. But she saw me as I got out of the bed and rushed towards her at the window. So she quickly pulled her head away from the window.

When I threw the bottle after her, it missed her by inches. By this time, I became very furious. Then I saw her rushing around to the front of the house, by walking along the side entrance which leads from the back of the house to the front. I then quickly slipped into my dressing gown. But while doing so, she came to the front door, and began to hammer against it with her hands, while she was shouting all sort of abusive language. By that time, I was at the front door. As I opened the door she quickly swung around and was heading down the flight of treaders, when she suddenly slipped, falling on her arm. She then began to scream as though her arm was broken. I closed the door as I saw her struggling up quickly onto her feet, and down the remaining treaders, and towards the gate which leads to the road. At that moment I did not realize that she had broken her arm, but when I saw her fall, I had wished that she had broken her neck. Because there and then I had seen a different side of Kay, which I had never seen before. I also knew that she had intended to make my life a misery. Since, she had made the greatest mistake in her life. Kay immediately walked around the corner to West Dulwick Police Station with her broken arm, and made a statement to the police. Telling them that I had strike her with a stick and broke her arm. It appeared that the police had told her that they could not do anything.

Since they were not present when the incident occurred. So therefore, it was a civil matter of assault, and that she would have to take out a summons, to take me to court. But while Jackie and myself were in the in apartment speaking about her attitude, neither of us knew that she went to the police then. Until a policeman came and knock on my front door. After hearing the knock, I went and answered the door, and saw a policeman in uniform standing at the front door. The police man said, "Mr. Daniels, I am here to investigate a complaint which was made by Kay." Of course the police called her full name, instead of saying Kay. He continued by saying "Kay stated that she was here, and that you started an argument, and after which you strike her with a piece of wood." The police had arrived at my home about twenty minutes after she had left. I told the police that it was a pack of lies which she had told them. I then told the policeman exactly what had taken placed. He listened to me very carefully, and then reported back to the station. I heard nothing more from the police. But around two weeks later I had received a summons from Kay for assault. I went to court on the summons. When I appeared in court and give my version of the incident, to the magistrate, she was found guilty of harassment. She was placed on one year probation to keep the peace, and she was told by the magistrate not to leave Earls Court, where she was then living, and go to West  Dulwich again, or say, or do anything to me. Then that was the end of the case.

A week later I went to Rome. But before I went, I returned my car to the finance firm, so that I could cut down my expenses before leaving. Jackie was then left alone in the apartment, all the time I was away in Rome. I invited Jackie for a two weeks vacation in Rome, she could do so at my expense. She accepted my offer. She was expected in Rome six weeks after I had started work on the film.

# 19

# Rome/Italy

THIS WAS MY FIRST VISIT to Rome. It was during the summer of 1961, when all the various contingent of dancers arrived to work in the film 'Cleopatra'. I was very excited to have been able to make the trip to such a great Ancient City. Ever since, I was a child and attending Sunday school and ordinary school, I read and heard about the great city, and its protective wall, which was built around the city of Rome. Now, I was working and living in that city.

The British Black Contingent of dancers was consisted of one hundred seventy-five males in total only one was female. We were then integrated with fifty black American dancers, thirty of them were females. We were known as the Wa-Tusi Dancers in the Film.

The Film was being made in Cine Film Studio which was located just outside the walls of Rome. It was a very large studio, one of the largest in Rome. Most of the British Contingent was placed in the same hotel which was called 'Hotel Bar-ba-ri-na' in Plaza De Barbarina at the end of the Via Vinitta.

Each morning we were transported from Barbarina at 7:00a.m. to be in the studio for 8:00a.m., then at 3:00p. m. we were transported back; rehearsal was from 8:00a.m. to 3p.m. In the studio, it was very tough indeed. Because during that time, the sun in Rome was very hot, and all of our dance routines were fast moving African dances. But we all loved and enjoyed it. At the end of each day we were free to go visit all the interesting sights in and around Rome.

The White dancers came from all over the world Brazil, U.S.A., South Africa, Austria, France, and Germany. Just like everywhere all the female dancers were carefully chosen for beauty, shape, built and also dancing ability. The men were about the same; the white dancers were about three hundred and thirty in number and were staying hotels nearby. When we first arrived in Rome, all of us would board the first or nearest bus at our convenient. This means, if I felt like riding on the bus which was parked in front of the remainder of buses, and at the same time that bus had enough space for me, or a friend of mine, we both will then choose the same bus to travel on.

We all did that without any stipulation of the company, for the first three to four weeks. Then one day we heard from Charlie Hingis, the person responsible for transporting us, that the film company had stipulated to our agent, to inform us all that the whites must travel on one bus, while the blacks travel on another. Now, that news came to us the British Contingent with great shock. Ninety percent of us were West Indians; the other ten percent were Africans. We West Indians were not accustomed to that sort of racial segregation. I was the British Equity Union Representative, on that production being an actor, and being senior to all of the others who had traveled from England under a British contract. I was called to the Union and was given the position as Union Shop Steward which meant that all of the dancers, no matter where they were from, came to me with their troubles and grumbles. It was my duty to listen and advise them. I was known as the middle man. I was in the middle between 20th Century Fox who was in charge of the production, and the artistes, who were dancers and musicians. Because the British contingents were the largest from any one place, those who came from other countries of the world, nominated me to represent them with the power given to me by the British Equity Union.

I had no choice in the matter of representing the other artistes from the other countries. All of their contracts were similar to us who came from England. Only those who were living in Rome were different.

The news of the segregation was brought to me around 11:00a.m. One morning, by two of the West Indians from our group. They both said to me, "Have you heard the news about the buses? Mr. Charlie said that all the black boys must travel on separate bus from the white girls, and the girls on a different bus." I then questioned the two boys carefully, "and what about the white boys?" The two boys replied, "Well the white boys had traveled this morning on the second and third buses from town, and they all rode on the buses with the black and white girls." I said, "That cannot work! if the production wants to make a rule like that, to protect the girls from the boys, then the black girls must be also protected from the white boys." "I will find out more about it." I quickly went over to Mr. Charlie's Office to discuss the situation. Mr. Charlie told me that he had received orders from the film company that such segregation must be implemented, to protect the girls from the boys. I said, "How come our girls are traveling among us and among the white girls and men? Why aren't they protected?" He said, if the black girls want to travel with the black boys they are free to do so" I asked, "what about the Whites?' Are they free to travel on any bus like they did this morning." He said, "I suppose they are." I then said, "Since you are supposing, you better go to the production office and get it all straightened out. I want you to call a meeting with whoever wants you to implement those rules. Let the meeting be called at 2:00p.m., which is after lunch". "Also tell them I say that no man or woman from England will be working until it's all settled." He then said, "Okay, I will take your message, but they will be very annoyed." I replied, "So are we, Mr. Charlie." I then left him, and went to the stage where everybody was sitting around waiting to have a run through with their dance routines. I then went to a few of the dancers, and asked them to go and spread the word around. The dancers were more than five hundred in numbers that was summoned to the meeting immediately. In no time the entire cast was gathered. I then inquired from the entire group, who were in favour of the segregation, and who were against it. Everyone was against it. I called a vote for a sit-in, if the production did not remedy the situation in the right way. Such as, all the males will travel together, like-wise the females. Regardless of what colour. They all voted in favour of my suggestion.

Then while we were having the meeting, at that moment one of the Italian workers' in the studio came on the stage with one of the Italian newspaper. The heading on the front page was, "Little Rock Came to Rome", and the Italian gave us the newspaper to read. It was the midday news, but how the newsmen got such news, I do not know. But I do know this, the Italian media do not joke. Richard Burton's and Elizabeth Taylor's names had appeared in the Italian newspaper the moment they winked at each other. I was working with both of them on special shots; I did not sense that they both had eyes for each other. I was one of Liz Taylor's marble bearers, also one of her two fan men. So I was quite close on set and in shots with both people. But there you are, that's the Italian newspapers, they have a way in getting the news. The publication was plastered into the daily for about three days. It was a very good thing that I called the meeting, and made a first stand against what had started; otherwise the Italian newsmen would have made a series out of the incident. That would have been very bad publicity for the film, away from the other publicity which the film had.

While we were in session with the meeting, some of the producers and directors were also standing around listening to us. So before Mr. Charlie had taken the news to the Production Office, some of the top guns already knew of what was going on amongst us, in regards to a sit down strike. I can tell you this, I wasn't popular after that. Mr. Charlie called a second meeting with members of the production and us, and then in no-time the entire rule of the segregation was removed. Then everything was back to normal as though nothing had happened.

But then I was a marked man from then on. I did not realized that, why should they bear such a feelings against me. Every production has a shop-steward; such a position can be a powerful one, especially when employers trample upon workers rights at the same time disregarding the union rules. Then the shop-steward is given the power to act for the workers. Such a power I did not asked for. It was the film company who gives rise to my power. So they should not be mad at me. But I said before, they were. I uses to blame the film company, but in actual fact it may not have had been the fault of 20th Century Fox Film. It could have been the idea of one or two mischievous persons, who works for the said company.

Then at the same time the one or two individuals, decided to exercise their position and their racial tendency, in many cases that usually happens, and when it does the firm or company is the one who gets the blame for such a person(s). But 20th Century Fox was no fool; the company soon solved the situation, by allowing us to travel on whatever bus we choose. This is the way it should be, we the blacks had in our midst a very young female dancer. She was fifteen years old. But the white dancers were all over twenty-one years of age. So as you can see, which one of the female groups that had needed protection from the male. Plus, the white males were traveling on the same bus with the fifteen years old girl along with the other girls. I really cannot understand some people, they goes around making rules which suits themselves, and they never think about those who their rules affects.

We were rehearsing from Monday to Friday. Saturday and Sunday were our rest days. But by God, we needed those two days rest. Because by the time our choreographer finishes with us, for those five days, we needed all the rest we could get. We had one of the best choreographers in the world, his name was Hermis Pan. People like Gene Kelly, Fred Astaire, they had worked under Hermis Pan in various Hollywood musicals. Pan was a great dancer himself.

He will set the routines one after the other, at a slow pace, then he will walk you the dance through the steps one, twice, and then at the full pace. Anything he gives you to do, he's capable of doing it himself. He was a great man to work with. We all ended up working with him, for four and half months on the production. I too had enjoyed working under him and the rest of directors in the film.

We did have a few misunderstanding on the production while the film was being shot. I can remember one of the greatest misunderstandings of all the others, was, there were so many of us as I pointed out before, that each day of the month which had arrived, it was one of us birthday. So members of the dancing group at the end of our working day celebrated his or her birthday, after rehearsals, which continued sometimes after heading back to the hotel. Because of my position as 'Shop Steward', I was singled out as the one who encouraged others to drink during our lunch breaks. An allegation that was not true. Now those bent on causing further strive, accused me of being drunk, two so-called officials from the production office fired me, ordering me off the set.

I then leave the set and the two big guns, I went over to a group of dancers from England, I told them what the big ones had said to me. While I spoke to them, I stood up on one leg as I did in the presence of the so-called officials. The group immediately said, "They picking on you because of the bus incident. So if you are fired then we all are fired". "Call the entire British Contingent together, and let's have a vote on it." I said to them, " go ahead and call everyone, I will go and see Mr. Charlie as I leave to go to Mr. Charlie, the boys went around to muster the group, and they also told the other dancers from various countries.

Mr. Charlie was away, but he had left his wife in-charge, while he was away on business. Mr. Charlie was a very busy man; he usually supplied dancers to the various night spots in Las Vegas and to the Blue Bells Dancers of Paris. Also other known places in the world. So the supplying of dancers to 'Cleopatra Film' was only a side line to him, which comes and go. Not many films like that were made every week or year. So, Mr. Charlie was often away from Rome. Mrs. Charlie listened to me as I told her everything. She was very annoyed when I told her, she and Mr. Charlie were French, and their homes were in Paris. They both knew what attitude was building up amongst some of the Americans in the production office, those in high position. Most of the racial feelings, which some of the white Americans in the production office were executing, arise from the fact, that a world-wide search for the most beautiful girls were conducted. As I said before, all black and white women dancers who were chosen for that film were all beauties. So after a week or so almost all the girls and boys, were going out with each other. I myself became very close and friendly with one of the white dancers from England. She was a ballet dancer; we were going out with each other. Also my relationship with Jackie was no secret to her. Some people did not like the blacks and whites mixing especially since the girls were beauties, and some of them were trying to date some of the girls, but the girls had preferred going out with us black boys. We were much more fun. Secondly we were black, which made us being different in their eyes. The girls felt like having a fling since they were close to us, and found out that we had no tails like they were often told. We dance well, we all dressed well. It was like that, simple attraction, Mrs. Charlie Knew all those things. She went to see the "Guns' and to find out what was going on. She told them that they could not fire me otherwise if they do; they are liable to have a general strike of the dancers on their hands. At first the they would listen to her. They were too busy trying to line up the shot which they were mostly concerned with at that time. Instead they told her to wait aside, and they will discuss it at a later time. So while they were pretending to be busy, we held a meeting with the British Contingent, and excluded the other dancers from other countries. They sat around in the meeting and listened, but did not vote. I told the British group that I was accused, and fired for being drunk on the set. I also did my same performance of standing on one foot, after the other, while addressing the group. Everyone agreed that we should call a vote to strike, in sympathy of my dismissal. They decided that if the company will not reinstate me into my job, then all of them will cease working on the film. Then after the vote was taken the decision became a unanimous one, in favour of all to strike.

We were a great team, we stood no nonsense from anyone. As we made the decision final, one of the American male dancers who were black, said to us, "You guys are crazy to make such a firm stand against such a big company like 20th Century Fox. They will fire the whole lot of you." One of our boys said, "What will you Americans do in a case such as ours?" Most of the Americans said, "I will not sacrifice my job for one person when I have my hotel, and other bills to pay. Because the person who

I might be doing it for may not pay my bills." That was the worst thing they could have said. Because the British Group soon put them all to their places, by saying, "We do not think the way you black Americans think. There is such a thing as a common interest and our common interest is at stake here. We know he's not drunk and all of you know he not drunk. So lets suppose it was one of you what would you all do?" None of the Americans replied to the question. One of our girls who was white quickly said, "That's exactly what we are talking about, not one of you had a common interest at heart I can see where you all are from, its dog eat dog." "We try not to be the same as you all, if he goes; we'll go, that's the way it is. If he was drunk it was a different matter". "Even then we might have thrown a collection to raise some funds to give it to the individual against their lost of pay. Because not one of us here are a drunkard."

One of our boys joined in and said, "It's a good thing that it wasn't one of you Americans who were involved, because we would have taken the same stand. But by the looks of it we would have been wasting our own time on you lot." By this time Mrs. Charlie came over to us. I then asked her, what did the production officer tell her?" She said, "I have to go back and talk to them." One of our girls quickly said to Mrs. Charlie, tell them if Daniels is drunk, so are all of us. We will all strike if he gets fired for being drunk as they say." Mrs. Charlie questioned, "Is this true? Is it a general stand amongst you?" I replied, "Yes it is, so you better tell them right away. Because they'll be calling a rehearsal of this shot any moment now. So let them know." She went back to them to discuss the situation. Ten minutes later, I was called to a group of authorities on the side of the set. As I got there, some of them were having an argument about the film having too many bosses, and that the film was behind schedule, and too much of money were being lost. Then one of the directors turned to me and asked, "What this about, you being drunk and being fired?" I then told him who said so. He then turned to the individual and asked, "Can you see he's drunk, where did you get the idea from?" the individual turned to the director in question and told him, "one of the assistants came and told me that he and a few more of the boys were drinking and they were drunk." The director said, bring that assistant to me. Daniels, you go back to work. I will get to the bottom of this." I told the director, "Okay sir," I then went back to my group and told them the outcome, and that the strike was off. The assistant was spoken to by the director in question. Then that was that. We had no more such trouble on the production. The point was this, they were too many people who were trying to snatch power on that production. I have never seen so much money being stolen and wasted on a film before.

Hundreds of Italians became rich over night while Cleopatra was being made. The film extras were so many that they were split up into alphabetical groups. Each alphabetical group, were given a cardboard placard with a letter A, B,C, etc, written on the placard of each group, in each group were a hundred and fifty people or more. Then each group had a male, who was in charge, he was know as a 'Campo Groupo' many of the Campo Groupos' were given the pay-chits which had to be given out to each of his extras for that  day's work. The film extra will then retain that pay-chit until he or she finishes work at the end of the day, then the film extra must get his or her pay-chit signed by those who are being given the authority to do so. But what I saw happening, was that a lot of the 'Campo Groupos' were having extra pay-chit, and was giving it to special people for them to cash in, and they could spilt the money between themselves, and the person who cash it in. Many of us were approached by various 'Campo Groupo' to do the cashing in for them. But I spread the word around our group, not to become tempted, in such a fraud. Some 'Campo-Groupo' was having as much as fifty and sixty pay-chits, to be cashed in at the end of each day. It was like money falling from a tree. People who were very poor became very rich. They were buying motor cars, houses, and all manner of various things. Sometimes it's not a good thing to be poor, and to be in the bread line. But it allows you the poor man to see how the rich makes a fool of themselves at times with their money, and the way the man in the bread line can cheat him out of his money.

It teaches you the poor man, if you should become rich, not be a fool, and to be more protective with money. So that's one of the ways in which the Cleopatra Film had lost a lot of its money.

While all that was going on, we the various artists from abroad, had become a drawing card in all Rome. The various Italian nobilities such as Counts, Countesses, etc. not to mention some of the Bold and Idle Rich. They would all sneak into the studio ground, those who did not make it into the studio would be seen parked in front of the studio gates at the side of the road daily. Between the hours of 3:30 to 5:30pm. They were waiting to catch the beautiful women and men. We the men were carefully selected because of our beautiful built, height, muscles and dancing abilities. We the artists attracted the homosexuals, lesbians, and the various sexual fanatics. To walk on the streets of Rome was sometimes difficult. Men and women in all sorts of cars will stop their cars in front of you, as you were about to cross from one section of the street to another. The first question they ask, "Are you in the film Cleopatra?" then everything else in the book follows, in order to catch you. We would sometimes keep our head straight or turn the nearest corner, so as to get away from the individual. But that was useless; they would continue to drive alongside the sidewalk, as you walked along, still trying to pick you up. If you decided to turn into a one-way-street, the molester will then drive around the block. Come down the right way into the street, which you had dodged into. Then they would continue where they had left off. Many of those who had sneaked into the studio while we were rehearsing, they would hang around, until we all would get a break to rest, or to have coffee or whatever. Then finally the lurkers would then descend upon us like vultures seeking their prey, in which case they would come up to a group of us as we were sitting, and then they would pull out their card and hand it around. They would invite large groups of us to a party which they will throw, especially for us, so as to catch their choice. We were ever more going to those lavish and grand parties, which was quite often held in great big villas and mansions which stood in its large imposing grounds with statues all over the villa or mansion, not forgetting to mention the double swimming pools, one indoor and the other outside in the grounds. The parties were thrown every weekend. We would find it difficult to plan our own parties, because of the clashing with the lavish ones. That was the period when 'Mohair' cloth and suits were in style, or just coming into style. So most of us had to go to the well known tailor establishment, and ordered ourselves four or six tailor made mohair suits. So that we can look nice while keeping up with the various parties or 'Dulca Vita' life. We all could have afforded the cost of four or six suits; it was a matter of spending two weeks of our pay. And yet we had more money left in our hands.

After spending three weeks in Rome, I decided to get myself an apartment, because I don't like the idea living in hotel rooms, and eating in restaurants very much. Sometimes eating out is okay. But I also love cooking and eating the best. Because of that, I decided to move out of my hotel. After finding an apartment to share with one of the girls, who was a dancer. My intention was to share with one of the boys. But when the time came for him to part with his money he found that it was too much for him to part with. Also that it was too much for him to do. So, one of the black girls took the 'cheapskate' place instead. They were many of them who were like that, they wanted to live nicely, but they were too mean to themselves to spend their money towards the beautiful things which they would like to have out of life. I am the opposite of such a person. If I need or want something, and I have the money, I buy it. I live in this world once, and during that time I will try to have all the things I can afford, while I am alive. I cannot bring myself to think like a lot of people. Such as to deny myself, in order to save for the day, when I get old and gray. The way I see it. I do not need to live, or cannot live in such a way, when I am young and healthy. When I get old, I must enjoy all the things which youth could have allowed me to enjoy. I do not want to become old, miserable, dissatisfied, and empty of great memories.

My friend whom I was sharing the apartment with, her name was Beryil Cunningham. She was from Jamaica. I had known her in London, we use to run into each other at various casting interviews, from time to time, and I would say hello to her, and short conversations. I never did know her very well while seeing her in London. But just before I had arrived in Rome. Beryil was there, she had arrived with the early bunch of dancers, before we did, to be exact. Beryil's group had been in Rome four weeks before us. She was a model in London, instead of an actress, or a dancer. She was just starting to break into the acting field when I first saw her in London. Then about a year later she was casted into a television play, which I was in, playing the part of a boxer by the name of 'Sandy Johnson' for Granada TV, in Manchester England.

So when we got here in Rome to do Cleopatra, I saw Beryil. She was staying in the hotel where they took us, as I got talking to her in the hotel on the first day I arrived. She told me that she was selected in London, after doing an audition. Then she came to Rome, and started rehearsing for three or four weeks, somehow she found it very hard to keep up with the dance routines, and some of the other girls. So the company terminated herself and two other girls' contract. She decided to hang on in Rome, since she had fell madly in love with the City. She was also hoping to pick up work elsewhere, and in Cleopatra, when the camera had started to roll. Beryil was a beautiful black girl. She had a lot going for her. So in no time she did start to pick up lots of work in films, and modeling in Rome. Also she later got work again in Cleopatra. She was like a sister to me while we lived, and share the same two bedroom apartment. Because I had a steady job, I did not let her buy things such as food, soap and other things for the apartment. I bought them all myself so as to help her out. Her work was coming more or less in and out, it wasn't very consistent. So I saw it as being the least I can do to help her out. We had paid three months rent in advance, for the apartment. So that had more or less cleaned her out. There was no affair which existed between us, all the months we were living together. Many people could not have understood it.

It was so hard for them to have believed it. But still they are people like that. Sharing a place with Beryil was marvelous. She was very tidy and clean. She was never any trouble. We had never one day had any sort of argument, or ill feelings against each other. Many times she would be in the apartment, and I wouldn't know that she was at home. She would stay in her bedroom while I was in mine, or while I was in the kitchen cooking. She didn't like to cook much, so that was never any trouble to me. I would do most of the cooking for both of us, or if we had any guest. If she had her guest she will then come out into the living room and that's when I'll see Beryil, or if she was going to the bathroom or kitchen. That how we both lived together. Not to mention sometimes we would sit down to the dinner table and eat together or have a drink. Other than that I very seldom see her in the apartment. As I've mention before, I was going out with one of the dancers from our production staff, her name was Wendy. We both took a liking to each other while working together. She was a darling of a girl. She was very beautiful and attractive. Wendy was a ballerina; she was one of the Blue Bells Top Dancers in Paris. She was an English girl, and came from a very decent and understanding English family.

Wendy was a great dancer. I often sat down during rehearsals while she and the others were dancing, and I would admire her as she floated along into the air using no effort whatsoever. She was beautifully built and very gracious. It was very hard not to be tempted by so many beauties around you. That's a fact. I would like to have met the man who would not have being tempted by all those beautiful women. I guess such a man would have to be with one foot in the grave and the other out. Or otherwise wasn't normal. The temptation was very great among us. I must say it had been a great experience on my part to have had a girlfriend in England, and not leave her for one of the other girls whom I was working with for all those months. I guess the reason why I wasn't that tempted was the fact that I have had many beautiful women in my life. I had also learned that beauty was only skin deep. There was much more to a woman than beauty. But then it's quite alright with me to say that. But who wants an ugly woman? I never did have eyes for an ugly or plain or simple looking woman. Let's face it, it's a wonderful thing to wake up in the morning alongside a beautiful looking woman in bed, it helps make your day which is ahead of you. Also it's something to look forward to, as you place your key into the lock of you front door, before walking into the house to face her. As I said I am in this world once. So let me have the beautiful things.

Don't tell me about heaven and what's up there. No-one has never ever been there and back to tell me or to convince me of what I will have when I get there, or hell. To me heaven and hell is right here on earth. So while I am here I'll make sure that I choose the best of the two.

By this time I was going out with Wendy for two weeks. Jackie was about to arrive in Rome for her two weeks vacation, as I promised her. As I said before that Wendy had known of me and Jackie. Wendy knew that I couldn't be quite sure of Jackie not returning back home to South Africa. So our affair was like touch and go to both of us. We allow our relationship to ride, and not make any firm plans. Wendy had an English boyfriend who was one of the dancers on the film. He was a homosexual or should I say a by-sexual. Somehow, he became more involved with the other men who were like himself, and were working on the same film. I guess he being what he was, it became no secret to her. As far as I know she's been with him ever since they were working together in Paris. That much she had told me. So I never questioned her no further about him. As I pointed out before, I hate having to question a woman about anything of her past love affairs. Especially, when it comes to another man who was in her life.

To question her you will never get all the truth, she will tell you the things she think you want to hear. So I do not question them about their past relationships. If it's to do with me, and it's very important then it a different matter all together. As the time was drawing near for Jackie's arrival to Rome, Beryil and Wendy suggested to me that I should throw a big, welcome party for Jackie on the same Saturday, as she was flying into Rome. I went along with both of them and planned the party. Some of the dancers, when they had heard of me giving a party for Jackie, they decide to pitch in and make it a big party.

On the same evening of the party, I went to the air terminal, and met Jackie while the surprise party was in full swing. So when we got home to Via Val Savio, she was very surprised to have walked into the apartment and find the party. She was very pleased with the 'home-coming' which was given for her. But later on that evening the atmosphere has changed a slight bit. An associate of mine whose name was Vernon, and one of the dancers, had fancied Wendy, but she did not care much for him. So, what Vernon decided to do unknowing to all, was to wait until Jackie and myself had returned from the air terminal, then while he was at the party along with Wendy, he decided to make a play for Wendy, as she was busy in the kitchen fixing a drink. Jackie was sitting in the large bedroom speaking to some people. I was standing outside on the verandah or what is called the balcony. Then suddenly, I heard a bit of noise coming from the direction of the kitchen. As I listened carefully for a few seconds, I could hear Vernon voice as he shouted out "can't you see Danny hands are tied?" his woman from London is here. So he can't do anything" I quickly went into the kitchen to investigate what was all the shouting and my name was being called about. As I entered into the kitchen, I saw Vernon standing in front of Wendy, Beryil standing on one side, and a few more people. Beryil said to me, "Danny, Vernon is taking liberty with the girl, he telling her that your woman is here and you have no time for her." "Because she told him to buzz off, he wants to hit her. And at the same time telling her that you cannot do a thing about it" I then told Vernon to leave Wendy alone, and do not push his luck too far. I said, "Do not feel because Jackie is here I will allow you to take liberty with me or Wendy. So go out of the kitchen and leave her alone." Vernon said to me. "Like you want to fight me over the woman?" I quickly said, look I don not want to fight you or anyone else, but if you do, it's okay, with me. Don't think that my hands are tied as you may think." "So let's forget it. Do not break up the party." He went out of the kitchen peacefully and I took Wendy aside as she was in tears at the time, and I spoke to her. She was okay after a while. Jackie heard the whole argument. Because I went into the bedroom afterwards. As I walked into the room I had notice the strange look which she gave me as I entered. I then asked her if she wanted a fresh drink which she accepted. But she did not ask me anything about Wendy there and then. A week later she said, "I heard that you have a girlfriend on the film set. The girl which Vernon was arguing with you over. Is it serious between you two?" I said, "How can it be serious when you are here? Had it been, you would not have been here. So don't you start getting all sorts of ideas." She was a bit cold for the rest of the day. But hadn't said anymore about it. She stayed with me for two weeks, and afterwards left for London. I ended up spending two and a half months after she had gone back to London. Wendy was still working on the film for two months out of the time I stated. She was finished two weeks before I was.

In short I had covered everything which I had wanted in my contract. The manager Mr. Bonpani, had agreed to all of my requests, including allowing me to return back to London, to spend two weeks before they were ready to shoot the film. So I spoke to Tony in English. He translated what I had said in Italian. The manager had agreed, and told Tony to tell me to report to wardrobe section for my clothing to be made.

That appointment was made for the following day, which I did keep, and I got measured for my various clothing.

So I was told to return in three days time for the signing of my contract. Now this was the second time for Tony and myself returning to the office. The production manager and Tony had gone over my contract with me after which I signed it. As they read my contract to me they told me everything I had asked for was in the contract.

# 20

# Jackie MY FIRST WIFE

I HAD NOW TURNED A new page in my life style. The opening of the page had stated "until death do us part".

I was now married to Jacqueline Duthon Peters. She was my first wife, and I had hoped she would be the last. Marriage to me was a very serious thing. I was now prepared to please the woman who I had married, and our children. I had become a one-woman man; my heart had been filled by all the other women with whom I had tried to make life with. To me, this was the last woman in my life, 'until death, we should part.'

The secret oath which I had taken within myself, should my wife die. I will then bring up our children alone as I live with them. Until such time that they reach an age, to fend for themselves. This woman who I had placed a ring on her finger, and took the marriage vows, I was in love with her.

That which I had known, I had settled for, no more or no less. That was the marriage contract I had examined and signed on the day I married her.

It had taken me from the first day that I met Jacqueline Duthon Peters, to the day and hour of our marriage, for me to read and properly examine that marriage contract. After so doing, it was obvious that I had approved of her along with what she had presented to me… and last but not least, the marriage contract. So as you can now see I was one of the world's happiest men.

It was now July 1962, and my two weeks in London was finished. So it was time to leave my newly wed wife and, returned to Rome so as to commence work on my film. As I said good-bye to her and leave to board my plane for Rome, I was full of contentment like I've never felt before. I was no longer free to do the things which were best suited to me alone. From now on I will do all the things which will be suited to my wife, child or children, then myself. As you have noticed in the last sentence, I did place my wife in front of her children. I will later go into that. But before I do let me say this, "I still think that way, I have always placed the mother of my child in front of the child". "My vow is to my wife, after all it was not to the child, (vow).

I did not place my weeding ring on the finger of the child, and said, at the same time, "Until death do us part". The child or children comes second to my wife. It is her and myself who produces them. So if we are capable of producing one, it may be possible to produce two or more. This means, if my wife and my four year old child were traveling on a ship, and I was with them, while the ship was sinking… and at the same time I had a choice to only save one of them. It means that I will have to save my wife. That also means if the wife is young and healthy, we maybe able to fill that gap of the lost child by producing another, or others. That's the way in which my mind works. To some people I would look in their eyes as being stupid, or crazy. But in fact I am not. I am what they refer to as having a logical mind. So when one thinks logically….. The example which I have just given you, it means that the logical mind will save the producer instead of the product.

So since I have gone that far with this example, I will go a bit further for the minds which are against my first logical example. So we will take a further look into this second example.

Let us assumed that you the reader has a factory which produces several products in that factory, you have got a set of machinery which values half a million dollars each, and standing in another section of the factory is a set of products which value a few thousand dollars. Now your factory is on fire…. But you've got enough time to save the machinery or the product, but not both, which one will you save? Try and work out that answer.

But in so doing it will prove to you if my way of thinking is right or wrong… The answer to that example – is machinery! By saving that, you will be saving many millions. But if you choose a cheaper product you will be only saving a few thousand. So don't follow your stupid brain to play tricks on you, by allowing you to think because you have saved the product which had only worth little money, that you'll be able to buy new machinery.. Yes, you will be able to resume production much easier, simply because, it will cost you less to get started. The other way around have seen you losing millions instead of a mere hundred thousand or so, to buy materials. In short the example is: with the machinery already saved. Production goes into motion once again. ( the machinery is the Producer, whilst the Product comes from the machinery). So as you can see and well understand is that the example will be like the first.. As in the case of the wife and the child. Secondly, I can't find the comfort in a child to that in which I can find in my wife. My wife can grow old with me and comfort me, while my child may leave me at an early age, and never to look back. So can a wife, but I am not speaking about that type of wife. I am speaking about a perfect and true wife. Now, will you please remember those two examples which I have given you. Remember it because it's very important that you should. In any case by this stage you the reader should know me, and the type of person I am. I am no different to the way in which I have described myself to you in this book. So I will continue to give you some more account of myself and the life ahead of me.

By this time I had arrived in Rome and was all set to start work on my film. I was home in my apartment in Via Val Savio. Beryl and her boyfriend the Count was there with us, so while we were talking, he said to me, "Danny did you collect your contract as yet?" I replied, "Yes, a couple of days before I went to London, by the way, it's a good thing you asked." The Count quickly asked, "Is anything the matter?" I said, "No, but I would like you to read it for me and translate to me." He said, "Okay, go and get it." I went into my brief case, and got hold of it, and gave it to the Count. He took it and started to read it. Then suddenly he shouted "What the hell is this?" hold on a minute." Then he continued to read the contract to himself quietly without saying a word, like he did when he first started to read it. I waited and watched him patiently. I then glanced at Beryl who was sitting in the sofa close by him. Then Beryl shouted to him, "Come on Sergio you haven't all day, read it to us. Tell us what's wrong with it." I used the name Sergio, but that wasn't the name of the Count, is name was different... So I will use Sergio.

Count Sergio said, "Danny now listen to me, you will have to get them to change this contract. I will not let my cast work under a contract such as this". "How much did you tell them you want per day?" I said, "I told them I wanted fifty five British Pounds Sterling per day for interior work". "With a guarantee of three days work per week then when I go to exterior, I must be paid sixty-five pounds per day, with also a guarantee of three days work a week". "While we were on exterior, they will pay my Hotel bills and all transportation must be provided, period. Now, how much does the contract say?" The Count said, "Your figures is stated, but it's in Lire. For example they have fifty-five Lire for interior and sixty-five Lire for exterior". "The Lire is less that the British Pounds. Did Tony read this contract and approved it for you?" I said, "Yes, he did." The Count said, "Tony has sold you down the drain.... You ought to do something about it." I said, "I will first thing in the morning, it's too late now, and the office is closed." "That Tony is in on it." The Count said, "He has to be, maybe the money has been split with himself, and the Production Manager." Beryl quickly said, "Danny we all believe Tony was genuine, but its unbelievable what some people will do for a few dollars, I will never trust him again as long as I live."

I did not sleep much that night. Instead, I laid awake most of the night thinking about the slave contract which I had signed and possible had to work by it. I began to wonder what I have done. I got up early next morning, and prepared myself; I then caught a taxi cab to the production office. I was in firing rage as I knocked on the door of the production office to see Mr. Bonpant. I heard his voice shout, "Come on in!" As he spoke in Italian. I then opened the door and walked into his office. He was sitting behind his desk in a swivel chair in his plush office. As I strolled into his office and stood in front of him. He looked at me and smiles as he greeted me in Italian, and welcome me back to Rome. He said, "Have a seat. What can I do for you? You start shooting in three days' time, are you looking forward to it?"

He knew I spoke a bit of Spanish. In so doing I could understand and speak a bit of Italian. So that was why he was holding such a long and friendly conversation with me. I sat down in the chair facing him and place my copy of my contract in front of him. Then I said, "What sort of bogus contract did you give me?" he said, "Momento!" He picked up his telephone, and dialed a couple of numbers to an extension. He then placed the telephone to his ear and spoke to someone, whom he told to come into his office. He placed the phone down, and picked up my contract. He then started to browse through it. As a young man opened the door, and walked into his office, Bonpani said to the young man, "Find out what's the matter with Mr. Daniels?"

By this time I realized that the young man spoke English, and he was acting as our interpreter. I told the young man what I was there for, and then he told Bonpani. To cut a long story short. Mr. Bonpani pretended as though he did not know what I was speaking about. He made it quite clear that my contract was in order, and I got what I had asked for. He also pointed out that Tony told him that's what I had wanted. So there's nothing more he can do. I had signed the contract, so I had to do the film. Otherwise he will black list me into not working in Italy again. He further added there is no excuse for ignorance of not knowing the Italian Language. I said, "You can take a horse to water, but you cannot make him drink." That is an English saying. I then got up and walked out of the office… As both of them stood watching me as I leave. There was nothing I could have done. Other than not play the part correctly. But then as an artiste one does not go that far. There were too much at stake, to do such a thing of not playing a part properly.

Three days later, I started to work on the film. Then each day as I continued to work and see Mr. Bonpani on the film set it gave me a feeling of being more unsatisfied and despondent….. to do the film. Most of my early scenes were with Gina Lolobrigida. After the second week she had realized that something was troubling me. We were shooting some exterior shots outside Rome, in a section which had the feature or should I say the same distinctive characteristic as in Haiti in the Caribbean. While we were waiting for the camera to be loaded with new films, Gina said to me while both of us were standing at the back of an old castle, "What is worrying you?" Now it was only the two of us in that section of the area, but instead of me answering her question straight to the point. I began by asking, "Who me?…. nothing." She quickly said, "Yes

I know there is something bothering you, and you keep thinking about it." I asked her, "What makes you feel that?" I was still covering up and trying to pretend that nothing was wrong. She continued by saying, "Come on tell me, I could tell by looking at your face each time we do a shot. You get into character just before the take, and the moment the shot is taken, you become very serious wearing the same look on you face. So what's bothering you?" I said, "They have messed up my contract."

She questioned, "How, and who?" I said, "Bonpani and another guy I knew. Look, I cannot read Italian or speak the language very well, so when I got this part I told Mr. Bonpani how much I wanted to play the part. A guy by the name of Tony whom I knew, and who was also supplying the extras here... he acted as my translator to Bonpani." "But when my contract was all ready, and to be signed they both read the contract to me telling me all the things I had asked for were there. So I then signed the contract believing that it was Okay." "So later on, I got someone else to read it for me. The money which I had asked for is in no way being the same. So, I am doing this film for thanks." She said, "What... I am not going to let you do that, when I started in the business, I went through the same. There are too many crooks about the place." "Okay, you wait until we go into the studio tomorrow... You are not going to work under those conditions." I said, "I went back home to London a couple weeks ago, and got married. My wife is expecting a child in a couple of months. I have to send money to her, my rent for the apartment is now over due." "Plus we have a strike on in England"... She quickly butted in and said, "Do not worry, if I have to give you money to send to England to your wife, and pay your bills here, I will.... but I am not going to let you work after what they have done." I quickly said, "He told me that I will have to do the film because I have already signed the contract. Otherwise, if I don't he will black-list me from working in Italy period."

She was very annoyed as she said, "If they do not change your contract I will not do the film.. I will stop working on the film. So we will see in the morning."

By this time I had a bit of hope, Gina had given me a bit of strength, and courage. She had decided to stand behind me no matter. I felt it was very nice of her to have taken on my troubles in the way she did. As I was working with her before we had discussed my problems. I had liked her a great deal. She was always quiet and did her work well as an actress.

She never fooled around with anyone, or her work. She always be seen sitting with her secretary when she is not wanted on the film set. The interest which she had shown me that afternoon, had given me a greater respect towards her. She was a fine woman, one in a million. She had won my heart and soul. Not many people who were in her position would have become involved in someone else interest, like the way in which she did. Her mere gesture and consolation was enough at that point. She was a very unusual lady indeed.

The following day we went into Cinecita Studio where all the interior work on the film was being made. The film camera was being set up as everyone was sitting around waiting for the first shot to be taken in the morning. I walked on to the set telling everyone as I passed by them, "Good morning". Gina saw me and came over to me and said, "Do not forget you are not working. So let's get the production manager." I said, "Okay I will send and call him." I went over to one of the assistants, and told him get Mr. Bonpani... tell him I want him, and it's very urgent." The assistant said, "Okay I'll get him. But don't leave the set; they'll be needing you very soon." I shook my head so as to say, "Okay". Then he leaves to go and find Mr. Bonpani.

I then said to Gina, "Let me make an apology to the director before he calls us to shoot." Gina said, "Yes, that's good." I then went over to the director and gave him a short explanation, and at the same time asked for an excuse for delaying the film. The director was very understanding and said, 'Its alright, I am with you, take what time you need." I said, "Thank you very much."

Mr. Bonpani was not in a rush to come to the film set as he received the message. The assistant was back, and told me that he had delivered my message. The director had called the rehearsal for the shot. Then when Gina and I did not walk over to the main set. He shouted, "Put out the lights, Daniels and Ms Gina are waiting to see the production manager, where is Mr. Bonpani?" The assistant director shouted, "I'll get him." Then off he went. In no time Mr. Bonpani and the assistant director was back on the set. Mr. Bonpani came over to me and asked, "What is the matter Mr. Daniels?" "I am not doing the film, unless you issue me a new contract." Mr. Bonpani started to scream at me as he said, "You already got a contract, you are holding up the film."

All this time Gina was speaking to Mr. Stephen Boyd in another corner. It appears Gina was telling Stephen Boyd the whole affair. Because while Mr. Bonpani and myself was standing arguing with each other, Gina and Boyd came over to us. Gina said, "If you do not change his contract, I will not be doing the film.".. Mr. Boyd quickly said, "The same goes for me...I am English as well." When Mr. Bonpani saw that he was cornered. He quickly said, "Come on Daniels, lets' go into my office."

We both quickly rushed into his office. Then in no time a new contract was prepared and signed. This time everything was done correctly and very fast, because everyone was waiting to shoot the scene. After that everything was back to normal.

# 21

## Doris and I

IT WAS A LOVELY ENGLISH Summer Day, the month of June 1971. I was living at Lot 2 Kennnolds Croxted Road, West Dulwich, London, South East. I was in the living room enjoying a T.V. Program. The entire apartment was almost empty. All I had at that time was a Grundic Tape Recorder, by the name of "Gainbourgh", it was also a Radio and a record player, and an armchair sitting on top of a gold color wall to wall carpet. In the kitchen were a Gas Cooker and a Refrigerator. As I was in the armchair, I heard a loud knock on the front door. I got up and went to the door to see who was there.

When I open the door to my surprised, I was confronted by a very good friend of mine who lives in Barcelona, Spain. His name was Jose Valez, along with a friend of his. I then welcomed them into the house. As they entered, Jose quickly asked, "Danny, what is going on? Where are the furniture and the family? I then said, "Jose, the wife and children move away with all the furniture, and leave me with just a couple of things, lets sit down on the carpet Jose, "sure Daniel."   He always calls me Daniel, and not Daniels. Jose quickly remembered, and said. "Ah! Excused me, this is a very good friend and partner of mine." As we sat down, "Daniel, this is Ramon." Jose said, "tell me what happened."  I said, "I am please to meet you Ramon."

Ramon said, "A pleasure Daniel." I then said, "Jose, all I know, was that I was tricked out of my home by my wife and her mother. Her mother came from South Africa on a vacation. Before she went to America she planned a going away dinner at an Indian Restaurant. And after the restaurant, we all will go to see a play at one of the London West-End Theatre. The mother, Clifford, Jackie, and I were to dine and see a show on that day, the mother had planned the entire affair. So on the day in question, when I got home from work after rehearsing a T.V. Play. I saw the three children in the house, also Mauve, my mother-in-law."

As I walked into the house Mauve came to me and said, "Jackie came home sick, she said she was sick all over the train, so she went to bed to see if she will feel better, so as to join us at the theatre. And will not be able to have dinner with us. So when you go up stairs do not to wake her, I am about ready, so you will have to hurry." I said, "Okay." I then rushed upstairs so as to get myself ready.

When I walked into the master bedroom, I saw Jackie lying face down on the bed in her working clothing. I stood looking and feeling sorry for her, for a minute or so. Now cutting a long story short. We finally left home and we went to the restaurant and dine. Then off to the Theatre. Everything was fine, the play got started, and then during the Intermission Mauve said to me, "I would like to go to the toilet." I then asked her, if she needs me to accompany her up the long stairs. Mauve replied. 'No! I'll be okay you sit and enjoy the play." Mauve then took off for the toilet.

She was long gone. The play had started; it was running for at least ten minutes, into the second half of the play. I then began to wonder what had become of Mauve. So I got up, and went up the stairs to one of the usherette. I then said, to the beautiful young lady. "My mother-in-law went to the washroom area since intermission, and hasn't returned back to her seat. So, could you please check the area for me?" The usherette said, "Sure will."

The young lady went and search, as I stood waiting and hoping that Mauve did not fell or fainted, would be the girls' statement to me. Instead the usherette said, "There is no-one in the toilet." I said, "Thanks very much."

I then went back to my seat and viewed the play. I hurried home and saw all the lights on, upstairs and down. And all the window curtains were missing from the various windows. This, I saw while walking towards the house, when I opened the front door and enter. I saw the home like this, everything was all gone, Jose! It was a well orchestrated plan by my mother-in-law, before she went to America." Jose said, "your mother-in-law is a Devil of a woman, she is a bitch." Jose then said, "Come with me, I have a caravan which is park outside. I have a surprise for you." We then got up and walked out of the house. By this time we came to the caravan, which is parked, on the road in front of the entrance leading to my home, and Jose opened the Door of the Caravan. We stepped in to the new brand Caravan.

The interior of the vehicle was fantastic. A young lady was lying on a lower bunk of a bunk-bed reading a book. There were two double bunk-beds, a TV, a microwave, a kitchen area, and a bathroom area etc. Jose said to me. "I have a beautiful friend" While walking to the young lady who was reading a book, by this time Jose had stopped by the bunk-bed, and the young lady quickly put down the book and sat up. Jose said, "Danny, this is very good friend of mine, Danny this is Doris, she's from Germany. Doris came to Spain to learn Spanish." Doris said, "Danny its nice meeting you. Jose speaks about you all the time while we were in Barcelona." "We're like brothers Doris," Jose answered. "My friends let me get you all something to drink, place your order. Danny replied, "I will have rum and coke." Ramon said, "Rum and coke Senor?" He turn to Jose and Doris and said, "you two the same?" Yes! Jose replied.

Jose sat down in the sofa next to me, "Danny, Doris came to Barcelona to learn Spanish and she had a rough time, so she came to London to learn English. Doris needs a place to stay, she don't have much money." Ramon brought the drinks and served us. Ramon Said, "Drinks are served." "Daniel, you live in a big house and alone.

Being in a house alone is not good. You need someone to speak to, you need a friend."

"Doris is the ideal person, it's like the saying, pennies fall from heaven." Jose said, "Danny can't Doris stay at your place with you?" "I then replied, "Yes she can." Jose said. " We will be going to Hyde Park to camp for the night. Tomorrow morning we will bring her back to your place." I then said, "In that case I will have to give you a key to get into the house. I will be leaving home early to go to rehearsal. I am doing a TV. Play." Doris then said with joy, "Oh Danny! Thank you, I will be no problem." Jose said, as he pats me on my shoulder, "she be no trouble Dan, you will have someone to cook, wash and clean the house. Pennies from a bone." I then said, "Well it's all set. How long you will be in London?" Jose replied, "My partners and me would be leaving tomorrow, going to Russia to buy some machinery. Then we go back home". I then told Jose, "Come and get the keys to the house. Doris, I will see you when I come from rehearsal. Also you can help yourself, there is lots of food, take whatever you need." Doris said, "Thanks, we will get a few things to cook as well." Ramon said, "Everything set Doris, and take good care of Danny."

Jose then butted in and said, "That's right Doris, look after Danny. Don't forget he's like my brother. I will send a post card." Jose and I then exit the caravan as I told Ramon and Doris to take good care, I am going. That was the end of that.

Doris was home when I arrived home from rehearsal. She was very pleased to see me when I entered into the house. She questioned me. "How is it, are you hungry? I replied by saying. "Well I am very fine. I am a bit hungry" Doris said, "Well I try to cook some food. I hope you like it." Doris strolled away into the kitchen. A short while later she came out with a plate of food and gave it to me. I took it, and she took the spoon in her hands, and scoops a spoon full of food out of my plate and put the spoon of food into my mouth. She then handed the spoon to me, and said, while walking away from me. "I am going to have my bath." I then replied, "Sure darling." I continue to eat my food while doing my home-work on another script which was 'Black McBeth' and not the TV play in which I was rehearsing.

At the time, I was to start work in Black McBeth, two days later. By this time Doris came back down the stairs after having her bath. As she step down the stairs slowly and gracefully, she came and sat on the carpet facing me, as I sat in the arm chair facing her as well. She was very tempting. Doris came down stairs wearing a Mini-mini white night dress, trimmed in lace, and black lace panties which fitted nicely between the front and rear. She was actually giving me the come-on. I then got up and said to her. "I am going to have my bath," and off I went. By the time I got out of the bath and enter the master bed-room. Doris was in bed waiting for me to join her. Then the love making started.

Doris and I became very close in a week's time. But I kept my sights on her trying to learn her likes and dislikes. Sex was one thing. But by this time, I had already learned that a relationship needed more that sex. It needed compatibility, the more the better. Basically I am a very easy person to get along with, but I can also be difficult if one do not stand up to certain high human morals. By the end of the second week I started to see certain traits within Doris which needed to be changed. She had a Bohemian attitude. Taking off her clothing and tossing them into a corner. House cleaning, she did not care too much for it.

Washing dishes every other day after there's a pile up. She likes to sleep and lay on her back. Like in the bunk-bed in the caravan reading a book or magazine. I decided to teach her about my likes and dislikes. I started with her untidiness, her clothing been tossed around the room, and washing it two weeks later, after changing her clothing daily. Doris did not take too kindly to me dictating to her as she called it, when I spoke to her she said, "Don't you tell me what to do." I then said, young lady as long as you're living here, I have to tell you what to do, if you do not know what to do. By the way how old are you? "Doris replied." I am twenty-three, I will be twenty-four year old in two months time. Why did you ask" I said. "Because, I could see you at times like a little child." Doris asked, 'How am I acting like a child?" I said, "a sensible person do not say the things you do, such as, "don't tell me what to do, because if I see you don't know something and its wrong. Then it's my place to teach you. You came here to learn, correct?" Doris then said 'Correct, I am sorry its getting late, are you working tomorrow?" I replied "Yes, is only on Saturday and Sunday we are off." Doris said, "Okay come on let's go upstairs and get ready for bed. Come I'll scrub your Back." She ran up the stairs. I followed her and get myself all ready for bed.

Three weeks had pass and time was drawing near for me to go on tour with Mc Beth, the Shakespearian play. Doris was now living with me as man and wife. We were becoming closer to each other. She was no longer untidy or hot lips. She was more or less humble. Doris did not like the idea of me leaving her to go on tour. I had to assured her that I would only be away for two weeks. She also became accustomed to us going out quite often to enjoy ourselves at friends, the movies or to a concert.

I knew the way she must have felt, being in a strange country, and being in a big empty house all alone and have no friends. Secondly, she hasn't started school to do her English studies. Had she done so, it would have taken up some of her time out of the house.

Time had arrived for me to go on tour with "Black Mc Beth". I told Doris of my coming departure and what to do in the house while I am away. I also told her that I will try and come home on week ends. We arrived in Swindon and went to work after we hit the city, after been shown to our living quarters and then to the theatre. We got down to work for a couple of days, and the play finally opened on Tuesday February 8 and ended on February 19. The play did well at the Wyvern Theatre in Swindon, our cast was huge. The Theatre was very nice, but at times it would be a little difficult at the end of each performance. The bathroom area would be crowded, and a stampede to hit the shower and sink area to remove ones make-up would be a long wait. The Theatre was not built to accommodate such a large cast. But the most difficult evening of all evenings, was on Saturdays, after the last curtain call. The rush would commence from back stage to the dressing rooms. One had to be careful not to get knock down along the hall way leading to the dressing rooms. We the principal players were lucky than most. We were, two or three to a room. But on Saturday evenings the crowd of extras would come banging on our door so as to use our showers, etc. The real trouble was the running of the trains. There were two trains at nights so in actual fact we the main principles had to keep our dressing room doors closed, so as to keep out the crowd and the disturbance. So because of the weekend, and not having to return back to the theater until Monday evening, the rush was on to go home to London. Almost everyone was heading to catch the second/last train to London. If one of us ended up missing that train. It would mean missing the buses, when we get to London. That means taxi, and we hardly could afford that fare home by taxi, our pay in the theatre was small. So like I've said, transportation in London after midnight can be very depressing in those

days. Our last curtain and the last of the two trains. It's 45
minutes between the two, so one has to hurry so as catch
that last train. Then that train will put you off in London
at 12:30pm, and then one has to rush in order to get the
last sub-way or a taxi to get home. It was not easy, it was all
go, go. On my home I stopped short in Brixton and bought
some food to take home as I was feeling a bit hungry, also
to take food as well as a surprise for Doris. Stopping off
at Brixton became a regular routine each Saturday on my
way home from the theater, while working away from
home in Swindon. Doris had appreciated the surprise of
me taking the food when I arrived home. Doris was very
shocked when I open the front door and entered. She had
a broad smile on her face, she had forgotten I said to her
I'll be back in two or three week's time. I greeted her with
a kiss on the cheek as she hugged me around the waist,
and fit one of her leg between my legs and returned my
kiss, by kissing me on the lips, and not wanting to let go.
That was a prelude to sex as Doris would perform, by
rubbing her legs up against my groin, etc. She let go of
me and look at the bag I was holding. She asked, "What's
in the bag?" I said, "Food." She took the bag from me. I
asked' "When last have you eaten?" She said. "I don't eat
much… I had some food three days ago. But I've been
eating a bit of yogurt." I said "Yogurt, soon you'll be look
like a Yogurt." I then strolled across the floor and sat into
my regular one and only armchair, and said. "You have
food in the house?" She simply, eats everything off the
plate. I feel so sorry for her. She was only covering up
by saying. She did not eat much food. She had eaten
everything out of the food cupboard. So by this time she
was living on yogurt because her money had all finished
more or less. I began to guess what must have happened
to her while touring around in all the various countries,
she had mentioned. After we had finished eating, she
collected the plates, and took them into the kitchen.
While she was doing that, I then went upstairs to see if

everything was okay. As I walked into my bedroom I saw the room was very untidy.... A bundle of clothing was all stacked up into one corner, all the clothing was dirty. The bed was un-made and the sheets and pillow cases on the bed were filthy. I just couldn't believe my eyes. I said to myself how could a beautiful girl such as her, could allow herself to live in such filth. I immediately called her upstairs, when she arrived, I said, "Doris, I do not keep dirty clothes in the same room with my other clothing, plus where I sleep must be clean and tidy as well. We've got enough cupboards, come I'll show you." I saw an immediate change on her face. She became very offended by what I was saying to her but I didn't give a damn! I was not accustomed of mixing with a dirty woman. All the women I've been with were very tidy and clean. If they weren't, in the space of a week they would have to change otherwise they would have to get stepping, or I will. It was as simple as that. To me a woman should take a lot of pride in herself and her personal hygiene. Much more so than a man. We are two different sexes, and therefore we are made much different. I am not saying that a man does not need to keep himself clean, of course he does. But as I said, a woman needs to be much more clean than a man.

I took her and showed her the clothing cupboard where dirty clothes are kept. The same time I asked her, "have you seen the soap powder, Clorox, in the kitchen cupboards?" she replied, "Yes! I then continued, "do you know where the clean sheets, towels and so fort are kept?' she replies, "Yes! In here" she then pointed to the linen cupboards above the hot water tank cupboard. I then said, "So why have you been sleeping on the same bed clothing for two weeks, without changing it?" She did not reply to my last question. So I continued to remove the bed clothing, and put clean sheets on the bed. I also opened up the windows in the three bedrooms, so as to air-out the rooms. The thought of my wife not being around hit me; I began to think my wife Jackie was not like Doris. Jackie would never keep a home in this fashion. She was very tidy and particular. So Doris was a new experience. Doris by this time moved me to one side, as she said, "Give me the sheets I will do it." I moved to the window out of the way and stood as I said, "Doris I said to you before, about not having dirty clothes unwashed in the house, from one week into the other. My mother used to tell us also that most people in the West Indies believes it brings bad luck. At least, it allows us to be on the clean side. This is why I accepted it. You may call it superstitious or what you like. But I pay tribute to what she said, that bad luck is unhygienic.' so since you are with me, and will be living here, please let us keep the place as we should, clean!" Doris then shouted, "I don't have to stay here and listen to you talking to me like that." "Who the hell you think you are?" I quickly butted in and said. "Hold it a minute, you don't have to stay here, so get the hell out of here!" "Now don't you be screaming at me, plus telling me a lot of bullshit, such as what you don't have to do?" "As long as you are fucking well staying here you will have to do as I say." "So, stop your bullshit and pick up these fucking clothes in the corner, and get the hell out of here, or put them in the bath tub to soak down." "Then wash them in the morning, so don't you stand here arguing with me, so move."

I quickly went over to the wardrobe and took a look into it. To see what other clothing she had. I found the ladies wardrobe, which had housed my wife clothing. But instead what did I see. I saw a long piece of foam rubber sponge fitted into a ladies stockings, it was shaped like a man's penis. In actual fact, Doris had built a Dilldoll and was using it up on herself. I quickly shouted, "Doris! Come here!" by this time Doris had picked up the bundle of dirty clothes and was soaking it in the bathtub. When she came, I was standing with the wardrobe door open waiting on her. So as she walked into the bedroom, I quickly said, "Pick up this man made prick and hide it out of sight if you need to use it." "I can see you were living the life of a bohemian. Is that all the clothing which you were traveling with?" As Doris picked up her Dilldoll, she said, "Yes, I lost most of my clothes in Holland and in Spain. So these are all I've got." I said. "Okay Doris, come downstairs when you finished doing what you have to do, I would like to have a word with you." She said, "I'll come in a minute." I completed putting the sheets on the bed, after which I went down stairs. Then got myself a drink of whisky and ginger. I decided to have a good talk with Doris if she intended to stay under the same roof with me. It was quite plain that we should understand each other. If not she will have to go. During this time of my life. I had decided not to groom or should I say trained another woman who I had found needed it. I was becoming too old for that. Not to mention the fact, that I very seldom used to reap the benefit of such training from the women afterwards, instead I found them to become very hostile in the end of it. Then they ended up leaving me. But after a few months of being away from me, they regretted it, and then wants' us to start all over once again. But my style does not allow me ever to do so. I can never finish once with a woman, and then return to her starting all over again. Maybe that is why I have twelve children between nine women. Plus as I said before, I had many women in my life, and somehow we all never could make it. I know some people may say that I'm at fault, though I see it different. I can either allow nonsense or take a firm stand. I would always choose the latter. It's a beautiful thing to know one's self, so as to be able to analyze. Now let me go a bit further in explaining myself, as against my statement of being independent of a woman.

I know millions of women would be only ready to say I am speaking nonsense. So will a lot of men. There will be those of you who may think that what I am saying, was the type of women whom I was trying to make life with as a life long companion and didn't make it, there will be those of you who saw me as being what I am, and therefore I become a challenge to you. Simply because I was void of depending upon all the qualities that you may have seen fit and just for me or any man. So the men who would agree with you as against what I am saying. They do need a woman such as you, because they do not know better or is capable of doing better. So they have to settle for second best to themselves.

The Monday morning had arrived for me to travel back to work at the Wyvern Theatre. This was the weekend coming up, which Doris had referred to, as I was about to leave home on that morning. As I reached the front door, I give Doris a hug and a kiss. I said, "Okay! Take care now, take this money to buy what you need until I return." I went into my pocket and give her the money. She got hold of me and hugged me tightly, and kisses me once again. She said as she let go of me, "Just remember, I will be looking forward to next weekend." I replied, "Okay, I will remember that, you don't have to throw hints." She burst out laughing, and then she said, "You are a bastard, I might end up raping you." I said, "You won't have to do that, I then went across the road to the bus stop to catch the No. 3 bus. While waiting at the bus stop, Doris went up stairs into one of the bedroom and started to wave her hands to me, while I wave back to her. The bus finally came and I embarked, while traveling I began to think about Doris. As I sat down in my seat on the upper double-decker bus. I said to myself, Doris seems to be very frustrated and annoyed with me, because I had slept in bed with her for the two nights and did not touched her sexually. That why she was throwing remarks and calling me names. This would have been the second time of lying for two nights and not touching her.

I do know principles are one thing, but needs and feelings are another. So what man of integrity would have added to Doris' state of mind. I saw some of her problems, sex would have been damaging to her and to me. Had I rushed into a sexual relationship with her like she was expecting, only her sexual needs would have been fulfilled. But her fulfillment would have haunted her for the rest of her life. Doris would think after the sex that I took advantage by demanding sex from her after such a heated argument hours before. That comes like scolding a child who does something wrong, and a few minutes later you turn around and hug-up the child and then you say to the child you are sorry. That would be confusing the child, the child would then question as to why daddy or mummy hit me and sorry afterwards. Why did they hit me, so as to sorry afterwards? The respect, which suppose to exist between the child and mummy, or daddy would cease.

Integrity was acquired by me at an early age. What man with integrity would do something such as argument and sex at the said time? Doris would feel obligated because she's in my home, and in my bed fulfilling my needs, not hers'. It's only a man with no morals or integrity. Such a man who receive hurting words from another, and not be hurt by what's been said, or the way it's been said. Such a man is heartless, and highly sex oriented. Sometimes I wonder as to the way I am. But something tells me it's the best way to be. It must be the best, because I feel and look good from it all.

Our journey to the Wyvern Theatre came to an end. When the cast assembled we found out that one of the artiste did not arrive for us to start the play on time. At 7:15pm was the curtain call, (when the play should be started) we waited until 7:25pm. The absent member did not arrive. We were all back stage sitting and standing, waiting on him to show up.

The show must go on, but we were made to sit and wait for him. We waited ten more minutes beyond curtain call. The curtain was lifted, and the play got started and on we went. The theatre management was very annoyed with that artiste, so was the entire cast as well. In any case we shared and jump the lines of the missing artist.

The audience barely noticed our dilemma. All went well to a packed house. No seats were empty, as I stood and look into the audience. Running for half an hour then came the missing actor, who arrived on the stage when his entrance part came for him to be on stage. He then settle down and picked up the pace of the play. I would have hated to be in his shoes. Because for two days the entire cast would not say a word to him, he was like a man with a curse. He was given the cold shoulder. I was not him, but yet I felt it. But after those couple of days, the entire atmosphere had changed, everything was back to normal. It can really hurt at times.

Shakespearean plays are all great plays. As an actor or actress, they need to be good in order to do those sorts of plays. I've enjoyed doing it as an actor. Finally the weekend came and it was time to go back to London, to my Doris. Time had drifted by and we had completed the amount of weeks, and we had to do an extra week extension, which would have brought us to a third week playing at the Wyvern Theatre. Also the entire cast was delighted about only having to do a few more weeks, we were becoming home sick.

I was also delighted that the play was not going to run for a longer period than the week ahead. I did not like working in a theatre for a long period. The play was small in comparison to working on a film "movie" or a TV film, or TV play. Not to mention the fact, I was an actor who gives' all in a performance, lots of energy in my work. I would explore the character in all various ways. Then I will get fed up and need a change of a new character. Basically I am a character actor. I am not a straight actor, by this time you may realize that I was very independent at an early age. Thanks to my up bringing. I am not a person who becomes lonely, and need friends or people to be around me. I can be in a house week after week without going out; I do not get fed up easily. I do not get fed up with the furniture being in the same position for a very long time. I am very good at cooking, doing my laundry, sew or mend my clothing, and keeping my home tidy and clean. I am very stable minded and contented, I am not jealous, envious or selfish. I will give you an example. I have never gone into my girlfriend or wife personal belongings in search of anything. Even if I should request something from my girlfriend or wife and they should say to me "Go into my hand bag and you will see it." I will not do as I was told, instead I will pick up the hand bag and give it to her, and let her take it out and give it to me. The same applies to her drawers where she may keep her personal items. What I came to realize, is that many women do not like a man with that status they love a man who is dependent upon them, to do all most everything for them.(man)

That way it allows the woman to be critical against the man. That is one of the problem I experience in some of my relationship. I cannot change my ways, I will not change for all the money in the world. I do know I cannot be too harsh with Doris. She's a bit spoiled, so, I have to be careful. Now, as you can see, being able to do all those things very well. It makes me very independent of any woman. I am not a man who usually gets sick and needs the help of a woman. I haven't been sick in thirty-five years to be precise. While writing this book I have been working seven days a week from October 8th 1978 to September 15th 1979. I have had Christmas and New Years day off, no other days. So you can see work does not scare me, the description which I have just given you, that is why I used the term of being independent of a woman. Yet, I would hate to give you the impression that I do not need one, or can live without them, because I can't. A man do need a woman for many other purposes. By this time I had arrived home on the Saturday evening, once again from the Wyvern Theater. Doris had given me a warning on the Monday as I was leaving home.

As I entered into the house, Doris was relaxing on the carpet in front of the burning fireplace. The lights were off, the living room was lit by the glare and flickering from the smith coal fire, in the fireplace. The Grundic stereo was playing very low as one can hear the chamber music coming from the stereo. She was all dolled up. She was dressed in a mini see through night-dress, silk and lace, white color, very brief legless black lace panties, no brassiere, she was all groomed. She was like a tiger-cat waiting to lure her prey. Doris sat up as I walk towards her. I bend over and kiss her slightly on the lips. We both then rise up together, while Doris hugged me around my neck. She then gave me a long kiss on my lips, and said, "You didn't bring your dirty clothes home, so that I can wash them?" I reply, "We got our washing done up there." Doris said, "I missed you all the time you were away, I am so glad you came home." I said, "Well, we had another week more to do, before we get back to London." Doris said, "That's great let me get you something to eat." She went to the kitchen, and I went upstairs and change into my dressing gown. She brought me a nice German dish and a glass of wine in the bedroom. "Here you are darling." She said, laying the wine and food on the bedside table. And off she returned downstairs, after I thanked her and gives her a slight slap on her bottom. Apparently she went downstairs to switch off the music, kitchen light and returned with her glass of wine.

She then jumped into bed and started to sip her glass of wine as I continue to eat my meal. I said to her while feeding her a spoonful of the food, as we continued eating that way. I asked, "How was your week?" She replied, "Not bad, I went and register to start school next week Monday." I said, "That's great, you should do great, after all you do speak a lot English." She said, "Thank you, let me take the dirty dishes away." "Would you like some more wine? I will bring the bottle upstairs."

She got out of bed and went downstairs and returned with the wine. We laid in bed and continued to drink our wine. Doris then came closer towards my body and began to fumble me and started to get sexually worked up. We both got into action sexually, by this time she started to breathe very heavily while I continued caressing her. We continued our love making for a couple of hours. Doris glanced at the clock in the room while we were having sex and said. "You are out of this world sexually; we have been having sex for the past two hours." "What did your mother do while she was getting you?" I replied, "You know, I didn't ask her, it's not my mother, its self control." "I knew we were hours at it, and you love it?" she replied, "Love is not the word, I am crazy about it." We finally dozed off to sleep snuggled into each other arms.

We woke up and took our bath and our breakfast, after which we both returned back to bed. We spend the entire Sunday in bed talking to each other. She said, "You are very unusual." I quickly asked her, "What do you mean by that." She continued by saying, "Well I have never heard or known of a man who would have acted the way you did when you speak to me, then coming into bed and not try to have sex with me or try to touch me." I give a slight grunt, when she said that to me, and I smiled. I started to think how correct she was. I stopped and thought for a few seconds, I said, "I like being different than most men. That is why I like my women to be different than most women. A vast amount of women thinks that all men are the same. But we are not the same applies to all women are not the same. People vary, most men and women are controlled by their sexual organs, and then that triggers the brain cell." Then the hormones are raised and are ready to stimulate the brain and human body. I do have control over my sexual appetite and organs, also my brain." "By the way, what would you have done had I tried to have sex with you?" "I really don't know, coming to think about it. I guess I would have given into you while in the process of hurt and anger." She replied.

Like I've said before, Doris was a very pretty girl, she was 5'9' beautifully built and clear in complexion, she was a brunette with very blue eyes. A man needed to have a lot of self-control not to force himself upon her, or to be enticed by her, you can honestly believe that. Because by this time I had almost lost my self-control, hard and tough as I was.

She told me about herself, and about her mother and stepfather. In return she asked me about my wife and children, and myself. She had quite an interesting life. She was well schooled academically and with life.

Her mother and stepfather had owned three department stores in Hanover, Germany. They had lived on the outskirts of Hanover in a beautiful home, which had belonged to them and paid for. As I pointed out before that Doris had problems. But I couldn't rightly put my finger on it. Well her problem was, as she rightful told me during our conversation on Sunday. She had come from a well-off family and was never short of money. But her friends, most of them were never in a financial position such as her. So they used to lean towards her and had abused the friendship. By leading her astray, and getting her hooked on drugs. Which she was made to buy to supply them and herself. Then while all that was going on her mother and stepfather got to find out about it. Then they tried to keep a tight surveillance on her and the friends, she said, but some how it was no use. "I just couldn't help myself." She said pitifully as she was smoking a cigarette, and at the same time taking a long puff of smoke from the cigarette. She was telling the story like it was yesterday. But it all began sometime back, when she was sixteen years of age. And as she stated she is twenty-three years old at present. Doris continued telling me the entire story. She said, "My mother then decided to send me to live

DANNY DANIELS AUTOBIOGRAPHY

in Berlin with my grandmother, so that I may leave the friends. But while I was in Berlin and trying to kick the habit of taking dope, which I couldn't by this time, I had met a boyfriend whose name was Carl. I had fallen madly in love with him, so he decided to use the situation I was in to his benefit, by putting me out on the streets to hustle money for him. Then the next thing I ended up doing was to leave my grandmother, to go live with him." I said, "But you had no need to end up hustling. You weren't short of money or were trying to have various things, which you've never had. Like in the case of a girl who came from a very poor family." She butted in by saying. "That's true my parents used to give me most things that I wanted. But he knew I wanted to go on a tour seeing different places, so he use that as an excuse. By saying if I had hustle for a month, we could have enough money to go, so that's why I decide to do it. I couldn't ask my parents to send me money to go on tour. They would think I was crazy. I wasn't even supposed to leave my grandmother. They had given me strict orders not to." "So what happened after that?" I asked her. She said, "After a month had arrived, I asked him if he was ready to start traveling." He said we hadn't enough money, and that we can't go until we got some more." So I told him, "In that case we are not going, but I am."

We cooked and ate, and returned to bed. Just speaking to each other, after love making. She was very loveable, and she was very good in love making so was I. Some how we both came from the same school, with just a few exceptions. As we lay in bed close to each other she asked. "What month were you born?" "November 1st, why did you asked?" she replied, "No one has ever treated me the way you did, or said the things you said to me. I am so glad I met you." "Your wife must be mad to have leave you." I said, "You are not the first one to have said that to me. Funny enough, quite a few women have used those remarks to me, when they come into my life, one after the other. But in the end they ended up doing the same as the others." She asked "Why do they?" I replied, "I wish I knew, I guess I usually go for the wrong type of women, the very pretty, and overall the glamorous ones." "That the only thing I can say." She said, "I knew you were a Scorpio, not many people understand you all." I replied, "You can say that again." She then laugh and give me a hug and squeeze. She laughs at the way I said it. I asked, "How do you make out now with the drug habit?" she said, "While I was in Barcelona, I manage to pick up some uppers, so I've been able to cut the hard stuff. Its alright, I can do without it now." I said to her. "I have to go to court next week February 12th 1968." Doris said "But your play opens on February 8th. What will you do?" I replied, "I will go to court at 9:30am and be back at the theatre." She said, "Your wife is taking you to court for desertion after she was the one who move out of this house. Also asking for maintenance for herself and three children. I can see you're not lucky with women. We do end up doing some crazy things. I guess it's our nature." "But you are not bitter against women, are you?" I replied, "Being bitter will never solved the problems." "No not bitter, I am weary and becoming skeptical of a woman. They can be the ruination of a man and themselves.

On the 12th of February, I attended court in Northampton, and my case for desertion was called. The charges read out, by the prosecutor, "Mr. Daniels you are being charged for desertion and maintenance of Mrs. Daniels' and your three children, are you innocent or guilty?" I replied, "I am not guilty sir, I have not lived in Northampton. I am still living in our matrimonial home in London. I did not desert my wife Jacqueline Daniels and our three children. I was summoned, at my home in London, my wife and her mother removed all of the furniture and the children out of the home, and brought them here in Northampton, Sir." The magistrate butted in by saying, "Hold on Mr. Daniels, say no more wait until I call this case.

By this time a week had passed, I was now home and looking forward to start rehearsing in a couple of days for the McBeth Play at the Roundhouse. A few of us had planned a party on Saturday and Sunday of that weekend. Yes, it was a two days ding-dong. The party had around one hundred persons, lots of food and drinks. Doris and I had a great time at the party. She was delighted, given a break from home to meet lots of people and socialize.

# 22

# The Final Week of
# Mc Beth Play

THIS IS THE FINAL WEEK of Mc Beth Play, the curtain will finally come down for good at the Wyvern Theatre. During that said week I had to return to the Northampton Magistrate Court to answer charges for Desertion and Maintenance for Jacqueline and our three children. The Magistrate saw the dept of my case where Jacqueline and her mother had planned to put a noose around my neck, and hang me. He was not a racial person, he was very intelligent indeed. In the sense of wheeling justice where justice belong. I was very lucky, or God was standing beside me during that case.

Its like I've said, the magistrate was not a prejudiced person, and instead he said once again to me, "Mr. Daniels don't worry, I will be the one who will be dealing with your case, so you can tell the court when you are ready for the case to be called. I wish you the best with your play going to London." I said to the Magistrate, "I thank you, your Honor."

The Roundhouse was built as a gallery during the occupation of the Romans in the olden days. It's a very large building. Its stand high up in the air with a high dome ceiling. Such a building is very difficult for an actor or actress to perform in. It takes a lot of experience and energy of the artist to give a wonderful performance. The size and structure is frightening, so I was looking forward to working there. It was wonderful for musical concerts.

I well recalled visiting the Roundhouse during the time of the Beatles and the Rolling Stones, where both of those two bands got started. Those were the wonderful days in London; it was a new era for us the young people. We used to say that, there is no place like London. Anyhow, an actor would need to tilt his head backwards and project the words towards the ceiling as he speaks, so the sound can hit the top and bounce back to the lower level. Doing that the audience can receive what the actor or actress had said. I was so pleased, and was looking forward into going to work at the Roundhouse. My voice was ideal for such a place. It was as if the place was tailor made for me. We started our rehearsal and a week had passed by.

This was the evening of the opening of the play. I came out from my home and walked across to the number three bus stop, which was not far from my home. As I was standing awaiting the bus to take me to the Roundhouse, I saw one of the most beautiful and elegant young women.

She strolled across the roads travelling from the Police Station and West Dulwich Train Station, and across Croxted road and to the bus stop where I was standing. I stood alone and she came and stood at the back of me.

"I've never seen you in these parts before. Do you live around here?" I asked her, she replied, "I worked and lived with a family, around the corner opposite the college." I then glanced across the road towards the back of my home. I then saw Doris looking through one of the kids' bedroom window and waving towards me, I then waved back to her. I said to the young lady, "Oh that's my girlfriend over there and pointed to Doris." I continued by introducing myself. "By the way, my name is Danny Daniels." She said, "Please to meet you, my name is Ingrid." In no time I picked up her foreign accent.

So I quickly asked, "Where about on the continent are you from?' She quickly replied to my question, and with a broad smile, all at the said time. "I am from Berlin, Germany." I then said, Germany, do have some gorgeous women and you are one of them." She said, "Thank you for the compliment." I said, "don't mention it, you've earned it." She then asked as the expression on her face changed. "Where is your girlfriend from?" I said, "Hanover, Germany, she hasn't been over here long, she sometimes get bored, especially when I am away, such as this time while touring with the play I am doing." She asked, " You're doing a play, what is the name of the play?" I said, "Black Mc Beth". By this time the bus arrived, and we both boarded the bus and off it went. We went up to the top of the London double-decker. She led the way to an empty seat and sat, I then sat next to her.

Ingrid was all excited as we continued our conversation. She said, "I would love to see that play, I heard on the radio, and on television about the play coming to London, at the Roundhouse." I quickly said to her, "I will arrange for you to see it." She said, "Oh, thank you, I've been seeing you on TV and a few films as well." "That's good." I said. "By the way, could you remember the house where Doris was by the window?" Ingrid said, "Sure." I said, "You can come to the house and you and Doris can get to know each other, I will tell Doris to expect you." Ingrid said, "I'm off on weekends, so I can come and spend the weekends." "That good." I said, "How far are you going?" She said, "The West-End." By this time we were at Piccadilly. Ingrid got up and said, "Bye, see you soon." I replied, "Take care." As my journey continued, I started to think about Ingrid, how beautiful she looks in every way when I cast my eyes upon her, while she was strolling across the road like an ostrich. She knew how to dress as well, matching the colour of her clothing. I continued to think of the friendship which can be developed between Ingrid and Doris. They both can be great company to each other.

The fact is, Doris will not be alone when I am not around, or home as well. My intention at the time of admiring and speaking to Ingrid, and learning that they both came from Germany, entered my mind that they could be company for each other. I did not have sexual fantasy for Ingrid, of course she could be a friend of mine as well.

By this time the number three bus had arrived to my destination, the Roundhouse Theatre. I headed to the theatre and got myself ready for the matinee show. I did two shows that afternoon and evening. Of course time had past and the end of the performance, I was tired. I quickly rushed and took off my makeup, and then showered. I left the theatre for home. But decided to travel back by train part of my journey, it's much faster that way. I then catch a bus at the Oval and Brixton Road to arrive home.

I finally got home and enter into the living room. Doris was not downstairs, so I shouted to Doris, "Hi what's happening, did you see me speaking to a girl at the bus stop?" Doris came and joined me in the living room, and replied "Yes, she came here and introduced herself. She said, "You told her to come and see me, and she did." "She seems like a nice person. Her name is Ingrid, she promised to come and spend the weekend with us." I said, "That will be nice, at least you will have a friend to speak with." Doris was looking very pleased with a smile on her face, and I was so pleased myself, seeing she had made friends.

Next day I made the same Journey to the round house and did my performance. After which I traveled back home by the sub-way and got off at the Oval. I then joined the number three bus on Brixton road to Dulwich.

While getting off of the bus I noticed my home in complete darkness. I opened the door and shouted, "Doris, are you in bed?" She then replied, "Come I have a surprise for you." I said to her, "I am coming." I went into the kitchen and put the kettle onto the stove, so as to make myself a cup of tea. I then started to wonder why was the place in darkness, and Doris was not downstairs waiting for me to get home like she normally does. It strikes me as being funny. I said to myself, maybe she is not feeling well. Making a cup of tea as soon as I enter the house was a habit of mine. Truly speaking, I would drink ten or twelve cups of tea everyday. I cannot stand the taste of water. It leaves a taste of steel or metal in my mouth. That came about a few years after stowing away and working in the coalmine. I finally made my tea and took it with me upstairs.

While going upstairs I heard a low sound of voices and laughter coming from one of the bedrooms. I strolled into the room, I quickly saw a woman's head pop up from under the top sheet, and Doris jumped out of the sheet and give a tug to pull it off the other woman. But the woman was quick to pull the sheet back over her head. By this time I realized that Doris was born naked, while killing herself with laughter, she tried to pull the sheet away from the woman, while saying. "Woman what's the matter with you? "Now, you think Danny never seen two women in bed?"

By this time the sheet was released by the other woman, I recognize it was Ingrid, covering below her belly bottom while speaking. "I don't know, if Danny would be mad at seeing the two of us in bed?" Doris said to Ingrid, "Come out from under the sheet, he's not going to bite you, stop being so shy." I said, "I have seen other women in bed before, don't worry about me." Doris then glanced at me and said, "If I don't mind, why should he, you don't mind, do you Danny?" I said, "I don't mind." Ingrid, "are you sure you're not mad at me and Doris?" I said, "That's right, I am very sure. Why should I be? You two were making love to each other." Doris said, "Yes and she was very good." While the entire conversation was taking place I was sitting at the end of the bed drinking my tea, and admiring Ingrid's beauty and the pair of beautiful breast as they stood up straight and firm. I then said to them, "Don't let me spoil the fun." Ingrid quickly said to

Doris, "so I was very good, eh." Doris said, "You bet, I am going to have my bath and mixed us a drink. Ingrid, why don't you let Danny scrub your back." Ingrid, "Would you like to scrub my back?" I then said, "Yes, I will scrub you all over, if you promise not to rape me in the bathroom." Ingrid said, "But I'm not promising not to do it outside of the bath." We both burst out into laughter, because of the way she said it, of course Doris was long gone taking her bath. Ingrid, "We both will shower together, yes?" I replied, "I've already showered at the theatre an hour ago, but I will give you a nice cologne bath and a shower rinse." Ingrid, "What's a cologne bath? I've never heard of it or had one." I said, "Have you had a bubble bath?" she answered, "yes," I said, "well its similar, you pour the cologne in the hot steaming bath. The steam brings the smells out of the bath, and spread the scent around the various rooms."

Doris asked as she entered the bedroom, "What you two have been up to, anything nice?" Ingrid said, "You're too nosey." She then got up from beside me, and strolled across to Doris from behind, as Doris was putting on her panties. Ingrid got a hold of Doris's pair of breast, and cup them into both of her hands, and nibbles on Doris's neck and shoulder. Ingrid started to wriggle her body up against Doris's from behind. By this time Doris became a bit relax so that Ingrid can do her thing. During the performance, I was stretched out on the bed looking at them. I began to wonder, how two women could be attracted sexually to each other. What allows them to do it, or to be that way? I was not against it. I started to question more and more. I said to myself, it's a trait, which some humans have. Two men have a similar sexual trait as well. A man needs another man to have sex with; it's a gland problem.

By this time Doris said, "Cool off Girl … let Danny take you in the bath and cool you down." Ingrid, let go of Doris and came to me. She got a hold of my hands and pulled me into the bathroom. Well I ended up bathing Ingrid. I then came out of the bathroom and got myself ready for bed, after getting a drink which Doris had prepared. In short we all had a couple of drinks before we went to bed.

After an hour or so, I put myself at one side of the bed. I let the two girls lie next to each other. But two minutes later, Doris said, "Let Danny come in the middle." Ingrid said, "Come darling you move over." Ingrid rolled across to where I was, at the end or the corner of the bed. I turned and put my arm across Ingrid's body and started to kiss her. While making love to her, she began to remove her panty and brassiere. We ended up having a sexual affair; at the end of it she jumped out of bed, and headed for the bathroom. I then turn onto Doris and we both went into action. Doris and I made love for at least one and a half hour, after which we got out of bed and took a shower together.

At the end of it all, I was so pleased with myself to have been able to lie in bed with two women at the same time, and to have sex with both of them, and pleased them both. Not to mention the fact, that I didn't had an "Orgasm," at the end of it all. Now that became possible, because women had taken the time to teach me in order to accomplish that. Well to be frank, after I was taught, I became a sex machine. Let's face it; a healthy human body is great, after that, sex is the greatest thing to a human being or an animal. Sex is the greatest stimulation to the human body. Other women had taught me not to just please myself during sex. So quite often, I would save my sperm because its fresh blood, so I save my blood. When a man can do that he knows he has good body control and restraint over his body. The night had passed and the three of us were satisfied with each other. I would say the night was nicely spent.

The following day was Sunday, and we cooked and ate, and mostly confined ourselves to the bed most of the day. Doris finally jumped out of bed and said, "I am going to straighten myself and put something on the fire.

You two love birds can knock yourselves out, Bye!" No sooner Doris disappeared downstairs, Ingrid started to make love to me. She began to get all sexually excited in the midst of our love making, suddenly came a knock on our bedroom door, then Doris' voice saying, "Danny, I am sorry to disturbed you, but you have a visitor, its Frank." I said to Doris, "Okay, tell him I'm coming." Doris then gives a loud laughter as she travelled down the stairs.

She must have heard groaning as she was coming up the stairs to us. Along with Ingrid statement as she was travelling down. Ingrid said, "Why did he had to come at this minute?" I replied, "I will soon find out. See you when you come downstairs… better luck next time." I jumped out the bed and went to the bathroom to get myself tidy. I later went downstairs to Frank, Doris was in the kitchen. As I arrived in the living room, Frank then said, "What's happening buddy boy, how is the play going?" I said, "The play is going fine." " Now tell me what's been happening work-wise since I have been away from London?' Frank said, "We had a couple of TV plays, nothing much going on."

Frank was a Black Actor, and a very good friend of mine. He was living half a mile away from me. He was happily married to an English girl. He was thirty-four years of age, 5-10 in height, and born in Jamaica. He would come by and check on me at least two or three times a week. I will do the same as well. That's how close we were. He was a very good actor as well, but as it were, we all didn't get enough work to give us a comfortable life. All black actors were living under that condition. The writers' did not write many parts for us blacks, like I've pointed out before. Scriptwriters when writing scripts regardless if it's a film, or TV film, or a play. They do not write many parts for blacks we just got a few now and then. Quite often it became frustrated for us by not getting enough work. Frank then said to me. "Quite a few times I would pass by and see lights in the house, I would then wonder if you were back home, so I would stop by." "I would think

Doris was here looking after the place." I said, "Yes she was here taking care of things." Doris by this time came out of the kitchen with two glasses of wine, while wearing a mini skirt and a low cut blouse, with no brassiere. She gave a glass of wine to Frank, then she came over to me, leaned over, kiss me on the side of my cheek, and then handed me the other glass of wine. Her breast was in full view. I then saw Franks' eyes pulping out of the sockets as he saw Doris' breast. I said to Doris, "thank you darling." Doris went back into the kitchen. Frank was sitting facing me, with his back toward the stairway.

Ingrid was coming down the stairs, she was wearing a French panty and brassiere, and also a see through dressing gown, she was strolling like an ostrich. She kept watching me all the way as she was travelling down and smiling, also winking at me. She went into the kitchen and joined Doris. I kept glancing at her and returning her smile. Frank said to me very quietly, "Where did you find that Bomb-Shell?" I asked, "Who do you mean?" Ingrid came out of the kitchen as Frank said, "I am speaking about Doris, Danny." I quickly evaded Frank question. "Ingrid, let me introduce a friend of mine to you." By this time Ingrid came and stood next to Frank and myself. I said, "Frank, this is Ingrid." Frank stood up and took Ingrid's hand, and gives her a hand shake as he greeted her. "I am so please to meet you." Frank then kisses her hand, then let go of it. Ingrid said, "Please to meet you Frank." Frank said to me, "where did you get these two lovely ladies?' Ingrid asked, "Would you care for some more wine?" I said, "Frank would you like another glass?" Frank said, "Sure." I said, "Yes Ingrid." She strolled into the kitchen. Frank then said to me. "Boy you do find the most beautiful and gorgeous women. Do you trapped them, tell me." I said, "They usually trapped me." Frank looked at me with despair. He then sat down, Ingrid and

Doris came to us with the wine. They handed a glass of wine to Frank and myself. The two girls sat down with their wine and joined us. Frank said, "You two are beautiful, are you sisters by any chance?" I said, "No, their not, just friends," Doris, "truly Frank". Ingrid butted in quickly and took over from Doris as she was speaking to Frank. Ingrid said, "We are Danny's new wives." Frank was a bit stunned, he then give a slight grunt, and then asked, "You two are his wives?' Ingrid said, does it sound funny to you?' Frank, "Well Yes…I." Ingrid butted in before Frank can continue his statement. Ingrid said, "Frank you never heard of two women sharing the same man or marrying to the same man." Frank said to me, "You sitting very quiet Mr. Daniels." I said, "Yes I am. The girls telling you as it is, so you deal with them. I am not getting into it." Ingrid said, "Frank, Danny lost one wife, so he's having two wives now. So if he lost one of us, he still has one." Doris said, "You understand it Frank?' Frank said, "Yes, I must try it sometime."

Ingrid said, "But the wives has to choose you Frank. Otherwise, you will find it difficult if you try to find the women in order to do it." "Most women will not go for it, most women want to possess their own man." "But the man will hide and have another woman secretly. Then when the wife finds out that he was cheating, it breaks the woman's heart." Doris said, "You ought to try it. Its becomes less complicated." "Come Ingrid lets go in the kitchen and get our husband something to eat. He must be starving." The girls got up and went in the kitchen. Ingrid shouts, "Excuse us Frank." Myself and Frank continued speaking for a long time. I later got up and took Franks' glass and went into the kitchen to get some more wine. Ingrid took the two wine glasses from me and ordered me out of the kitchen. Shortly after Ingrid came to us with the two glasses of wine and said to me, "you don't have a dog and you bark. Why didn't you call us to get you some more wine? You don't have two wives and still get up to serve yourself." I said, "Okay darling, I will remember that. "Frank and I laughed" Then Ingrid smiled, and went back to the kitchen.

Frank was getting all worked up by the way in which the girls were dressed. Because they both came out from the kitchen and joined us sitting on the carpet. While shifting and turning, twisting at times and changing their positions from time to time, trying to be comfortable. I could see that Frank couldn't keep his eyes from between their legs, while the girls were showing off their curves. I also came to realize that the girls were purposely teasing Frank but he did not know it. I knew and said to myself, "look at the way some men are. I could never look between a woman's legs." No way, because I get a feeling of embarrassment. I would want to turn away quickly. My eyes are like a camera lens. So I couldn't stop my eye line and focus. Frank was staying focus, and Ingrid and Doris kept teasing him. So I said, the girls were conscious of Frank taking a peep at their panties, and at the same time trying to see if he can see beyond that piece of clothing.

I was enjoying the histrionic of the two girls while they spoke to him. So to cut a long story short, our evening with Frank was nicely spent. It was getting late and Frank had decided to go home to his wife, and he bid us goodbye. The three of us later had our meals, and had a few more drinks, enjoy the television, and then went to bed. I was put once again between the two girls. I must say I had no choice in the situation. After which we had the entire night to ourselves undisturbed, and it was nicely spent in bed, so to speak. I would leave the rest to your imagination. We lived like that each weekend when Ingrid was off from work. But she would come by to see us and have a chat whenever she can. I also got some tickets for Ingrid and Doris to see the Black Mc Beth.

The two girls sat together and enjoyed the play. This took placed a week later after our wonderful weekend, and Frank visit.

Our relationship had lasted for five months. We would go the Clubs or the movies on Sundays because that was the only day I was off. Not to mention quite a few cast members partied as well. Ingrid later had to return to Berlin during the end of the fifth month, because of her father who took sick. Well I must say that the relationship was nice while it lasted. It is said, nothing stays the same forever. Doris and I were back to square one. Frank would come and visit us, as he normally does. While living with the two girls for the few months as husband and wives, I knew it would not last long it was only a passing fancy amongst the three of us. I will say it was the best thing that could have happened during that time, because I had lost my wife and three children. I was also going out of my mind up until Doris came into my life. Doris was a great savior to me.

I later appeared in court in Northampton, to defend myself against the charges of Desertion on two more occasions, in which case I asked the magistrate to put the case for a much later date. I intended to prove to my wife and her mother that I was not a fool. They were rich, and I was poor. But I had more sense than both of them. I decided to put the squeeze on them. I don't know if it was God who put that magistrate to try my case, or if God was standing besides me or what. But knowing what I knew now, it was God who appointed that magistrate. He was all cool and collective.

He knew from the offset that my wife and her mother were trying to rail-road me. I had a lawyer; I asked her permission to address the court myself. I then said, "Your Honour, I was brought here before you, here in Northampton, on desertion & maintenance support for my three children, also my wife. "your Honour, I have never lived in Northampton. I lived at my matrimonial home in London. My wife removed herself and our three children, her mother as the instigator. Her mother convinced her to leave me, and she will see to it, that my wife and children do not want for anything, and all I think about is poor people, not my family." The Magistrate quickly said to me, "Mr. Daniels stop! I will try this case myself to the end. Do not say anymore. I will let you get in touch with the court and inform the court when you are ready for trial." I said, "okay! Your Honor."

Time had passed and the Play Black Mc Beth came to end. Life was beginning to take a turn. I then went in search of a job. I was fortunate to find one, working as a Plasters Mate at West Minster Hospital, as the Hospital was being extended. A month later while working at the hospital, Doris informed me that she had telephoned her parents. Telling them where she was, and about me. Also how I had changed her, and I had gotten her off drugs, and how much she was madly in love with me.

She also told me, that she had mentioned to them about our plans to go to the USA, and to my home in Guiana for a visit. That we were short of money, and were working to acquire some more money. I did discuss my intention with Doris, about going to America, also Guiana sometime before, and she had liked the idea as well. Doris continued, my mother and stepfather was all excited on the telephone. They were so glad to hear from me. They also said that, they would send me some money." I then said, "It's nice of you to decide to get in touched with your parents. They seemed to be nice people, according to what you have told me." Doris, "Yes, they are."

My job at West Minster Hospital was coming to a close in a months' time, I was served notice. But one week after Doris had spoken to her parents, I ran into a bit of problem with Doris. I usually worked until 3:30pm in the afternoon, I went home early from work, Doris was not at home, only to find out that Doris went around the corner from were I was living, and West Dulwich Police Station. That location of course was where Ingrid used to work, facing Dulwich College. Doris came into the house wearing one of her "mini-mini", skirt. So I said, "Where have you been love?" Doris asked, "Have you been home long?" I replied, "I came home about half an hour ago, where have you been?" Doris said, I went around the corner hustling to get money. We need money Danny." I became cold and flip with fear as I respond, "Doris are you crazy! You did what? "You went three hundred yards around the corner from the station hustling, you want to put me in jail on pimping charges. I do not need that type of money or life." "Years ago when I had no choice was a different matter."

"Years ago I was the victim of circumstance, Doris! I am not a pimp, Doris! That was then. Now, do not let me catch you doing that again." Doris said, "Danny you know I love you." I received some money from home, and my parents' wants me to take you home so they can see you. The money we have cannot take us to Germany, Guiana, and America." I quickly said, "But Doris, I am working. Somehow we will get-bye." Doris said, "I am very sorry, I was not thinking, I am very, very sorry." I said, "Okay, let's forget it, if the police catch you doing that, they will deport you out of this country."

I later got in touched with the court asking for my case to be tried. I was given a date to appeared in front of the same Magistrate. He then called up my case on the Desertion, Maintenance and Custody of the three children. He then placed the ball in my court, so to speak. The Magistrate said, "Mr. Daniels, you were saying that you are still living in the matrimonial home in London? I said, "Yes your Honour," The Magistrate asked, "Now tell me when did you discovered that your wife and children were removed from the home?" I said, " Your worship, my wife's mother had planned a trip after she left South Africa to come and visit us in London, and then go to America. She sat down with my wife and I, and told us that when she returns from her American trip, she would take Jacky and I out to supper at an Indian Restaurant, and then to the Leister Square to see a play, a last minute treat before her return to Africa. I said, "That sounds fine". On my mother-in-law's return from the USA arrangements were made for our treat. I was at work, so when I got home, my mother-in-law met me at the door, she then said, "You are late, you will have to hurry. We also have a problem." "Jacky came home sick and she was sick, all over the train. So I told her to go upstairs and sleep it off. Don't wake her up when you go upstairs. I will leave her ticket so she can join us if she feels better, Okay?"

I went upstairs and saw my wife on the bed, flat on her stomach, with her face buried, into the pillow. I stood and look at her for a minute or so. Feeling sorry for her. I quickly got dressed and was all ready. I came down the steps and Mauve, my mother-in-law informed me that she would leave Jacky's ticket with the children. I then told the children to behave themselves and do not stay up too late. We then took off and catch the bus to London's West End. We went to the Indian Restaurant in Soho, and dined. After which we went to the theatre and started to view the play. During the intermission Mauve mentioned to me that she must run to the ladies, she got up and as she was about to go, when I asked her if she would like me to accompany her, she said, no, she will be alright. I must sit and enjoy the play, it's my treat."

The play started and was running for at least ten minutes, I became a bit worried. So I got up and went into the lobby. I saw one of the usherettes, and asked her to check the ladies to see if my mother-in-law had fainted in the toilet area, she left to go there since intermission. The usherettes went and searched the area, on her return. She said. "I am sorry Sir, but there is no one in the ladies." I told her thanks and I returned back to my seat and viewed the play to the end." "Now, Mr. Daniels, please tell me what happened when you got home from the Theatre". I said, "Your honor when I arrived home I saw all of the lights on, from the bus stop as I disembarked from the bus. No curtains at the windows. When I entered into the house, everything in the house was taken away.

Other than the master bedroom furniture, a Grundic tape set, a T.V. and an arm chair." The magistrate said, "You've mentioned that you would like some extra time to go filming in Brazil. Okay, get in touch with the court on your return." "Case closed".

Doris had presented me very highly to her parents. So therefore they invited me for a visit at their home in Hanover Germany. Doris and I had sat down and planned the trip to her home. She said we should be able to go to the USA and Guiana as well. She will get the money from her parents. By this time, Doris had received some more money, she decided to go ahead of me and I follow. She was packed in a couple of days. Doris was off to home; I was once again on my own. I continued working and saving my passage to follow Doris. Then one evening I heard a loud knock on the front door, it was around 6:30 pm.

I got up to answer the door, and to my surprised, as I opened the door, there stood two women, looking at the two of them they appear to be sisters, one I knew, but the other I didn't. The one who looked familiar, if I can remember correctly, her name was Gwen. She said, "Good evening Danny." I said, "Come on in, please excuse the house. "They came in and sat on the carpet. Gwen said, "Danny this is my sister, Basil's wife, Doris." I said, "I am so please to meet you Doris," how are you keeping Gwen? She said, "Fine!" Doris said, "I heard a lot about you." Where is the family? I then related the entire affair of the disappearance of the wife and children. Doris Daniel my sister-in-law said, "You have to get out of this house," I said, "yes I have to get out of this house, I have a German girlfriend and her parents invited me to go on a vacation in Hanover. Doris Daniels said, "Okay, you go to Hanover I will be going to Berlin, now take this number and telephone me in Berlin when you get to Hanover" "I will call your brother and tell him to book your passage from Germany for the USA. If Basil is scratching and groaning, 'you know him.' I will do it myself, when I return back to the States." I said, "I was trying to get enough money to visit the States and also Guiana." "My girlfriend planned to help me as well." Doris Daniels said, "I will purchase two tickets, do not worry about it Okay".

I replied, "Okay! And thank you very much." Gwen said, "You will be better off going to America, you will get more film work, because there are more Black films being produced in the States." Doris Quickly said, "That's correct, also it will be a new life for you." I said, "I think it will, sometimes one has to move on. I will come, its been twenty-five years living here in England, and I do not have much to show for it... its like the saying goes. "A cow gives you a gallon of milk, and then kicks the bucket over, all the milk is gone." Gwen and my sister-in-law stayed a while then left. The time had come for me to go to Hanover. Doris had telephoned me, and all arrangements were made. I booked my airfare, to depart from London to go to Hanover.

# 23

## *The City of Hanover*

WHEN THE PLANE TOUCHED DOWN at the airport in Hanover, I was met by Doris, her mother Flora, and Hans her stepfather. Doris came over and give me a hug and a kiss, she said, "This is my mother, Flora and my father Hans" I said, "I am so pleased to meet you both."

We shook each other hands. Hans then took my suitcase from me and said, "Come let's go this way. I am parked over here." Hans led the way and we followed. We soon reached a brand new Opel car." I had never seen an Opel car such as that one. After we drove away from the airport, through the city of Hanover, which was very beautiful, from the opposite side of the airport, and to the outskirts of the West Side, to their home. Their home was built to the ground like a semi-basement.

The upper ground floor of the house was street level. It was a beautiful designed house. Hans used his Genie, the garage door opener, and up came the door lifting itself, which rolled under the upper floor and the ceiling. We then drove into the garage, and we're in, the house. We exited from the car, and walked along the hallway. On both sides of the hallway was a set of closed doors. It was as if one was in a different world. The woodwork was Purple Heart and brightly polished. The floor was set in marble finish. By this time we were travelling up a short flight of stairs to the upper level of the house. Hans was leading the way with my suitcase. I was following him while carrying my black leather brief case.

We were followed by Doris mother, whom was carrying a lovely white puddle dog which was snow white and well groomed. We reached upstairs, which was gorgeously furnished. Hans opened a door and walked into the room and said, "This is your room Dan." He put my suitcase on the bed and said "Make yourself at home; come let me show you around the house." Flora said to Hans, "That's a good idea". Doris and I will go and fixed the dinner." We all went into various directions. Hans showed me all the various rooms in the house. The place was large and well spread out with a swimming pool at the back of the house, surrounded by a well-kept garden. The houses around the area were not close to each other, they were an acre away from each other. The soil of the land and surroundings were so beautiful. I said, "It's wonderful of you to have invited me into your home. The entire place is brilliant, one couldn't ask for more". "I could see you are a man of great taste and choice, I can see that your wife is a wonderful person as well. I will always remember you both, and this Place." Hans said, "Danny, I must thank you for the compliment. I can also see you are a man similar to me, I am glad Doris found someone such as you." He continued, "I do hope she can appreciate you, Doris mother and I love her. But she can be very difficult at times, we are worried about her." I quickly changed the subject by asking him, "Hans, I have never seen black soil before, is all the soil in Germany like this?" Hans said, "No, this area is called the Black Forest," I said, "I liked the way in which the pine trees are stretched out into the far distance." By this time Doris came out to us with a waiter with drinks and glasses, after she laid our table she sat down and joined us. Hans said, "Come let's have a drink Dan." Doris's mother later joined us. She said, "The meals are ready, so I will join in with a drink, you can tell me when you're all ready to eat." We sat and took a few drinks, after which we all ate our supper. We all spent the evening in a bit of conversation, and then we all retired to our various rooms. That was that, the following morning Hans called out to me. "Dan, are you up?" I replied, "Yes! Hans I am." Hans said, "Come and see me as soon as you can." I got out of bed and put on my dressing gown. I then went out to Hans' bedroom and knocked on the door. Flora came and opened it and said, "Hans it's Danny, he's coming." Hans came out to me and said, "Here's the key to the house, come lets go to the kitchen." Hans said, "Here we are, now you can make yourself at home whatever you need we keep in the cupboard." In it were all the seasonings and canned foods." The pots as you can see are over here," Hans continued their kitchen was like a fairy world, it was well designed and built to accommodate everything a kitchen needed. Even the seasonings were placed in alphabetical order in a line. All pots and pans were hanging and shining on the walls. The floor and counter top were well designed with Italian marble. I then said, "By the way Hans, I have to call my sister-in-law in Berlin, I will pay for the call." "Hans quickly replied, "Yes you can use the phone, you don't have to pay for the call or anything else in this home. You are free to use this home like your home, please do." I said, "Thanks you." We then went into the garden and sat for a few minutes, while the morning sun started to rise above the pine trees in the far distance. The sun was bold and bright it illuminated a soft glow of light around the sun. Making it a spectacular sight, it was the second time I had witnessed such a picture, once in Scotland and now. Hans said, 'Danny, I must be going, we have to run a couple of stores which we owned. So I will see you when we get back." As Hans went into the house I said, "Bye see you later" I later called my sister-in-law Doris, (my brother's wife) in Berlin and chatted about my going to New York, and Guiana. She asked how I was doing, and about other things in Hanover. I assured her everything was fine, I said, "I will call you later, bye." I then went to Doris room and knocked, but she wasn't there or any other place in the house. The time was 10:30am I then decided to take a shower, get dressed, and go and browse around the city. After a while I took off, sight seeing, I later sat at a bar where I took a few drinks, and made a couple of friends with two African students. After exchanging telephone numbers, I decided to return to Hans' residence.

# 24

## Towards End of
## My Stay in Hanover

I HEADED BACK HOME TO WHERE I was staying. By this time I had settled down in the home. Doris parents were very nice people indeed. The time I was there they made me felt comfortable, as if they had known me for years, not to mention the fact, her parents had entrusted me with their house keys. Both of them would leave home very early in the morning to go to their stores, they worked until 6.30pm. As I have mentioned earlier, Doris had left London a week before I arrived in Hanover, that was the time I lost control of her. It all started again, while Doris was in Hanover, she had promised me to quit her drug habits. She re-united with her old friends, at the Fisherman's Cove, hanging out, and getting back into the drug taking habit again. She felt so relaxed that she started back taking drugs because it was what she had missed.

One day I was in Doris room, when I noticed a few tablets stashed away between her bed, and a set of books, so I asked her what it was, after picking them up she quickly grabbed them from out of my hands, saying at same time, "its none of your business… and do not come into my room picking up what doesn't belong to you." I looked at Doris and said, "Okay! but tell me, what kind of tablets are those?" while I was waiting and looking at Doris straight into her eyes, I saw her eyes all glossy, as if she wants to sleep, her looks was different as if she was drunk, and was floating on air, she became all furious with me while she continued her expression, "You know what it is?" "Its drugs." I then asked, "When did you started back with this nonsense" she replied," two days after I got back home…. I went to see my old friends and we all had a nice time." I said "okay! Its your life, if that's what you want, its okay with me…" "But what about your parents?" "Do you think it's fair to them and me?" "What about if they found out with me in the middle of this." She simply said, "How can they find out, only if you told them."

I quickly got up and went down into the basement and fixed myself a strong drink of brandy and coke, as I sat relaxed, sprawled on a large sofa looking across a well stocked bar, after which I took a stroll to the back garden and sat down. There I began to think as to what I should do as I continued to sip my drink. I came up with an idea to get out of here, and to break off my relationship with Doris. I decided to go back into the house and get into my swimming trunks, for I needed to cool off some of the steam. There I saw Doris on the telephone speaking as I passed her all looking guilty, while trying to be calm. I then walked past her, got to my room, and put on my swimming trunks. About twenty minutes into the pool, Doris came and stood at the edge of the pool, all with her legs spread wide apart as if she was inviting me onto her, but I kept my gaze in the opposite direction. She said after realizing I was not interested, "I am going out, if you need anything to eat the icebox is there and the kitchen has everything." I returned to her room and saw Doris dressed in a blue jeans, and white sweater and a black knee high leather boots. Then she hurriedly tried to make her exit, she was furious because I found out she was still messing with the dope habit, so what was I to do? I stood my ground and played for time, Doris had planned since we were in London, to travel with me to South America and the States. She had ensured me that she could raise enough money from her parents for the trip, but I wasn't banking very much on that knowing the type of woman she was. So I anticipated the possibility of a letdown. I had decided to accept her and the family's invitation to visit Hanover on a vacation. Now I will have to play things my way, depending on Doris my brothers' wife, she had indicated to me that upon her leaving Europe, she will be booking myself and Doris passages to the United States and Guiana. My sister –in-law Doris, knew my situation, being separated from my wife and children, and also that Doris may just be a "Passing Fancy," if not she was prepared to take us both. I was making all necessary arrangements to be able to travel with Doris, my sister-in-law, who indicated to me, as being an actor (black) I will be able to get more work as my profession warranted, in the USA after getting a work permit.

But because of this dramatic turnaround, I must now look at all the possibilities of making my trip to the United States alone. By this time Doris parents had returned from work. They both asked me where was Doris after realizing she was not at home. I told them that Doris had left for the city of Hanover. They said, "Couldn't she take you to see the city?" But I assured them not to worry, Hans said, "We'll fix supper in a while, would you like to eat anything special." "Nothing special, I'll have what you eat." The mother quickly said "Hans you sit down and have a talk with Danny, I will do the cooking." I could see both of them were annoyed with Doris' behaviour. Hans said to me, "where do you want us to sit Danny? Out in the garden, in the house, or downstairs in the Bar?" I said, "lets sit outside, in the gardens". Hans said, "Okay, we'll sit outside." His wife, who was waiting patiently standing, said "you two sit down, and I will fix the drinks for you both." "What would you care to drink Danny?" I replied, "Brandy and coke" Hans said," I'll have a martini." she said to herself, "I'll take a little wine. I'll be back in a minute." I then asked, "How was your day at the store Hans?" He replied, "I had a very busy day… myself and wife, all of the salesmen were in today. We have to start ordering all our stuff for the winter season. Secondly we have a big summer sale coming up, today was go, go, go all the time." "Danny, how was Doris while she's been in London?" "How did you find her?" I quickly tried to cover up as I selected my words and answers which to give Hans, because I knew he was fishing and at the same time, I knew he was a clever man. Hans was one of those clever Germans', so was his wife. They were free from prejudice from the fact that they had invited me into their home, as a potential son-in-law. That much I had learnt from Doris, after she had spoken to them a few times while we were in London. So I told him she first seemed to have problems, and I thought that I had fixed it for her, but otherwise she was coping with everything. Doris was communicating by way of letters with her parents. All of her letters she will read, and then gave to me, so I can see exactly what was going on. Her parents were pleased to know that she was fine, and that she had met someone special, that she would like me to be her life partner, her husband. Also that my colour was not a problem with both parents, they were looking forward to me making their daughter happy. That was a big open question, at that point in time.

Hans expected me to be his son-in-law, and also to try to make Doris a better person. So much was expected of me. I said to Hans, "With all due respect, this is a well put question, which deserves a similar answer, but I will try to be frank and honest, but first- How was Doris, when she was living home with you all?" Hans replied," Danny, Doris basically is a nice girl, but sometimes she can be difficult. We have tried to give Doris all the education possible, a beautiful home as you can see, we have three stores, we have tried to make her happy, we also put Doris to run one of the stores, but instead she created problems with most of the workers, so we brought her to the store we manages, after a while problems between Doris and the staff surfaced, and she decided to call it quits.

Her next step was to become a diamond cutter, so we got her into the trade, she worked for two years... during all those time while working with her new found profession,

Doris was mixing with the wrong friends at a place called Fisherman Cave, in Hanover, then the drug taking started. It became worst, she didn't want to work or go back to school, so she can learn something , that can be beneficial to herself so we to sent her to Berlin, for her to stay with her grandmother, hoping she'll be away from her present friends, and all those undesirables she was mixing with." By this time his wife had returned with the drinks on a trolley. While serving us our drinks, Flora said, "Danny, why didn't you come the same time with Doris." I quickly asked her, "Why did you ask me that?" She sat down at the table and joined us as she continued, "Well I was thinking... when Doris came back from London, she was completely a changed person. I had never seen my daughter acting the way she did, for the first few days upon her return from London. She was always speaking about you. She couldn't wait to see you, how much she missed you. She was always telling us what a fine man she met, myself and Hans were happy for her.

After a week or so, Doris decided to go down to the city of Hanover. She kept going day after day.. So after a few days, we saw a sudden change in her looks, and behaviour pattern." I decided to pay keen attention to what was being said about Doris. Flora continued, "So I am of the opinion had both of you traveled together coming to Hanover, this behaviour of hers may not had occurred. Also with her getting back to her old friends." Hans butted in, "they are all a bunch of no good". "You ought to see them for yourself Danny, All the time they look as if they can do with a good bath and a hair cut. It's really a pity you didn't come over the same time with her, by this time we all were drinking while conversating. Flora said, "Let me run and check on the food," I'll be back, don't let me miss anything to my question."

Hans and I changed the topic, while we waited for his wife's return. After a while, Flora came and sat down. I turned to her and said, "Getting back to our conversation, Hans had earlier asked me, how did I find Doris while we were in London?" I replied "when I first met Doris, she seemed as though she was going through a state of uneasiness with herself, and her past experiences. She was confused and resentful. So while living with her, she would often speak to me of things she had done and was regrettable of them all. I was able to relate and understand her problems, then in so doing, I was able to snap her out of her old self, and put her on the right track, so to speak, at least I thought I did, during which time she gotten in touch with you folks, and she planned her trip home." Now I taught of the danger, in allowing her to travel ahead of me. After dismissing the idea of traveling back with her, I said to myself, she's a changed person. I now said to them both, "Somehow, I think Doris did not spend enough time away from her old acquaintances (so-called friends). Also, maybe she didn't spend enough time with me. I also told her of the possibilities of getting back to her old habits. She assured me that will not happen…. "I've learnt my lesson. As you can see what she told me was merely her opinion, unfortunately she's right back into it. I had to put some sort of trust in her, after all we were living together, and I couldn't be with her all the time, and I was busy doing a television play." Her mother said, "Danny, she told us that you are going to the States and also you will be going back to Guiana, the land of your birth." Because since you left, you've never returned." I replied, "Yes that is what we had planned to do." Both her parents quickly butted in all at the same time as if they had rehearsed it, they said, "Doris said that she would like to go with you on the trip." Hans stopped speaking allowing his wife to continue her saying, then he said, "tell him darling, what we all wants for Doris, Flora continued "I'll fix another drink," both myself and Hans said, "Thank you." We drank while Flora was about to get another drink Hans butted in by saying, "You go and see about the supper." "I'll fix the drinks." Upon Flora's return, Hans raised, his glass in a token gesture, while saying," cheers, "as his wife said, "We had told Doris that we will give her the money for the trip. We would like to give you Three Thousand Pounds, so that you all can have enough money to see you both on the way through the trip. We want you to take Doris away from here. We see that you will be good for her. She has never felt for no one the way she feels for you. We want her to be happy, she's the only child we've got, and we've worked hard so as to give her everything" I quickly butted in, and said "Hold it a minute... Three thousand pounds is a lot of money, secondly, what we are discussing is a very serious business. So let me say this, with all due respect, you both know I do feel and care a lot about your daughter," Hans butted in, "Danny, we knows that, while you were getting off the plane, and while you were walking through the embarkation section towards us, do you know what my wife said to her daughter and me? She said, now Doris that is a man. What a choice you've made. Hans, what do you think of him?" I said to my wife, "darling I agree with every word." "We immediately saw all the beautiful qualities you possess." "We both felt so proud of you, and then since you're here, we get to see and learn what a gentleman you are. We would like you to be our son-in-law, Doris told us about your past marriage and experiences. Danny all that you've been through in the past, they all add to the man you've become, so we know the type of man you are." I said, "Thanks for the compliments, but I will not sit here and say to you both, that its okay I'll take the three thousand pounds, and take Doris with me, because I am not that type of person. Most people would say yes, they will do it, then the next thing you'll know, is they'll take your money, after which they will dump Doris somewhere in the states."

"Well I just couldn't do such a thing like that which means I do not know how far she will go, neither both of you know how far she's gone with her old habits. But I do know this, I will not take Doris with me to Guiana while she's still on dope. I could never live that down with my folks or the public there. The Colony is a very small place, the mere fact that Doris is white, and I being black, everyone will be watching us to see the way we are conducting ourselves." "The same will apply in the U.S.A, but with one added fact … those there who wouldn't like to see a Negro man with a white woman, would only rejoice at the fact that Doris is a junkie. Knowing that, would only make life uncomfortable for both of us. So my friends, lets wait and see how Doris is shaping up, do not make any impromptu decision." Her mother said, "God knows how proud I am about you, I will always look upon you as my son-in-law, I want you to know and remember … that this home is also your home." Hans quickly said, "And that goes for me as well." He then patted me on my shoulder, as he said, "lets' drink to a good discussion." We all raised our glasses, and then we touched each other glass, and drank out our drinks. His wife asked for an excuse then off she went into the house to fix the food. Hans and I got up and took a stroll through the beautiful garden, he showed me around the place. He also pointed out the various houses nearby, explaining to me who was the occupants, plus how long they were living there, who came first, second, etc. All of the people in the surrounding areas were very rich indeed. All of the homes were built of the American Ranch style home, so was Hans's house. So while Hans and I was speaking in the garden Flora shouted, "Danny! Your sister-in-law, Doris is on the telephone. She wants to speak to you." I said, "Okay, Flora, I am coming." Hans and I return to the house. I then went to the telephone and spoke to my sister-in-law. She said, "I will be going home in the morning, is everything alright with you?" I replied, "Yes, but only book one ticket. When I get there I will tell you about Doris." She said, "Alright." I asked, "Did you have a nice three weeks vacation?" She said, "Yes it was wonderful. Okay I will let you go, take care." That was the end of our conversation.

Flora called Hans and I to supper. The three of us dined. Then we had a drink and retired to our various rooms after saying good night. I was lying in my bed between sleep and wake. Then suddenly I heard the sound of a car engine and a door of the car slammed closed. I quickly got out of the bed and rushed into the kitchen. I looked through the kitchen window. I saw three men Doris's age sitting in the car, while Doris lean her head into the car while speaking to one of the boys in the back seat.

The car was standing at a four corner road. But stop on the corner just next to the kitchen window. I quickly rushed back to my room, as Doris steps away from the car. I then check the clock in my room and it was 12:30p. m. I later feel asleep and on the following morning Hans and Flora was up, and I joined them. Doris was still asleep. Hans then said to me while we were having coffee. "Danny come to the store and let's have lunch. We will expect you by midday." I said, "Okay Hans." Flora said, "Well we must get going, and Doris is not up as yet. Bye Danny." And off they went.

As one can well see, that Doris is well away from her mother and father. She lay in bed while they were getting ready for work to help support her and she couldn't get up to say a word, and to see them off to work. In any case I went back to my bed and off I was back to sleep. Then I finally awoke at 10am. I did not intend to sleep that late in the morning, I finally got out of bed and strolled across to Doris bedroom, the door was half open and several voices can be heard in her room. I then pushed the door wide open, and to my surprised I saw the three young men, ages in their early thirties sitting in front of the coffee table, and on the table there was small heaps of white powdery stuff and small plastic bags next to the white stuff which was "cocaine" and they were bagging off the stuff into the plastic bags. I said, "What's happening in this house?" they all were very shock and nervous to see me. I continued, "Now pick up this shit from that table and get to hell out of this house, and don't come back here. Otherwise I will break your neck. Now hurry!" As they were rushing to get out of the room, they almost knock me over because of fear, and also trying to escape. I went into the kitchen. I peeped through the curtain of the kitchen window, and they got into the car and off they went. By that time Doris came into the kitchen fuming with raged. While shouting to me. "Who the hell you think you are, speaking to my friends like that?" I said, "Now you shut up. You are a bitch, bringing those half-wit and dope pushers in here." Doris quickly said, "Don't you speak to me like that. This is my home! and you can't come here, and speak to me and my friends like that! You are not in England!" By this time I became more into a rage than she was. I then gave her two slaps. She rushed out of the kitchen, and into her bedroom.

By this time it was getting late. So I got myself ready, so as to go to the store and meet Hans and Flora to have lunch. I finally left the house without speaking to Doris. I caught my bus and travelled to the city, and got off near the store. When I entered into the store, Hans and Flora were all ready, Hans said, "Flora, Danny is here."

Flora was in another room in the office. Flora came out into the front of the office and joined us while she sat in a chair and removed her working slippers, and put on her dress shoes, and said, "Danny is everything Okay, where is Doris?" I said, "she's home, locked up in her room when I left.

The three of us went to lunch, and the food was marvelous. We returned back to the office in the store. I spent the remainder of the afternoon with them.

We finally left the store for home arriving at 6:30pm, Doris was not at home. She came around 8:30pm while we were in the middle of eating supper. Doris joined us at supper finally. But later in the evening, Doris said to Hans and Flora, that I had slapped her. Hans asked, "Why did Danny hit you, you must had done something. What you did?" Flora asked, "Doris, tell us, what have you done to Danny?" they both asked Doris three or four times. And she did not utter a sound to the questions, she continued eating while Keeping a steady gazed on the food in the plate. By this time we three had finished eating, and Doris was left at the table. We retired into the lounge. Ten minutes later Doris joined us. "Tell us why Danny hit you, by slapping you." Hans questioned her, but there was no response. Flora chipped in, "Danny tell us what really happened?" I said, "Let Doris tell you." Doris still would not say a word. So I decided to explain to Hans and Flora about everything which occurred last night, when a car with three young men pulled up just outside the house. Doris and her friends slamming the door. Then the following morning with the same guys in her room bagging off the cocaine. By this time her mother and stepfather was very furious, her mother shouted, "Doris how can you do something like that, are you mad, and crazy, you want us to end up in jail?" Hans said, "Danny did not deal with you as he should. Also you took off on Danny, "What absurdity is this?" Get up and go to you room!" We later retired to our rooms after saying goodnight to each other.

A couple of days had passed. Then my brother Basil wife had called from New York, and told me that she had booked my ticket. A day later I went to the airline company and confirmed my ticket to travel. I discussed my departure with Hans and Flora. They said to me that they will take me to the Airport so as to catch my flight. Two days later was the time of my departure. So Hans and Flora accompanied me to the airport, and wished me a safe journey. I saw tears settled in both of their eyes.

# 25

## Brooklyn, New York

THE YEAR WAS 1972, A week before Guyana's Carifesta. I had traveled from Hanover Germany to Brooklyn, New York, via Guyana. My brother Basil Daniels and Doris Daniels had planned a trip for me to travel to Guyana after spending 24 hours in New York. Because Basil was going on vacation for two weeks in Guyana, they decided because I had left Guyana for 25 years, and had not returned since then, they planned that I would spend 24 hours and fly out to join my brother, and spend two weeks as well. Basil had flown to Guyana a day before I arrived in Brooklyn. Truly speaking when I arrived at Bains Bridge, Brooklyn, New York, I only had five U.S. dollars in my possession. My sister in-law received me with open arms at the airport, and into her home. Guyana was hosting the first Carifesta ever. I was given enough money to spend on the vacation. I arrived in Guyana in 1972. I saw some changes which took place during the 25 years I was away. The country I knew as a boy had change; it was heading down hill, by way of politics. Anyhow, I had a wonderful time seeing my children. I had a funny vision, when I looked upon the women in Guyana I did not see a beautiful woman. I did not see a woman who can attract me during my two weeks.

By this time, Basil, Sammy Walton and myself had return to Brooklyn. I settled in with my brother and his wife, three children and his wife's father. The same vision of not seeing a beautiful woman while in Brooklyn for a couple of weeks, before I started to see people the way they look. I later learn what causes me to have such vision of beauty.

It came about because I was living amongst white people, very rarely did I see a black woman or much black males as well. So my vision was accustom to the aquiline features which is what the Europeans race have. I became to realize my vision was centered on the European as a measurement of beauty, and the other looks of other people who does not have that 'aquiline' look was not very beautiful to an extent in my eyes. Isn't that a shamefull way in which the human eyes, which acts like a camera can, cause another human being to wrongfully discriminate against another? So I mention the above, because I feel I am not the only one who has experience such a human error. It is a terrible feeling. But I got rid of that feeling and experience very quickly, yes it was short lived.

I got a job through a close friend of Basil and Doris. The job was located in New Jersey, at Allen Packing as a porter. I worked there for six months, after which the company had closed down. I was very lucky, because I started a construction job with St Timothy Church Housing Project in the Bronx, New York. The job was demolishing the old buildings, and rebuilding new ones. At the said time, I was going through my English divorce from my wife, Jacqueline. Also going through the fact that I was separated from my three lovely children, and that the children was left open to be brain washed, by their mother, and grandmother, who did not like black people. I kept thinking that my children will be so brainwashed that they will grow to hate me, and themselves as being black, also the black race. The grandmother did not think highly of my race. Anyway what could I have done?

Nothing! I started to console myself that the children would grow-up to shun all the blind and ignorance ways of their mother and grandmother. Also the ex-step-grandfather Cliff, who had one time tried to rape the children mother in his car on the way to my home from the theater.

# 26

# Santa Monica California

I WAS WORKING AT ONE of the Chain of Stores located at Santa Monica, California, when one day my supervisor called me into the office, which was used as a Security Office. He said, "Give me your Badge and I.D., the gun and handcuffs. You are not working for this company any longer, because you falsify your Police Report." I asked him, "Whose Police Report are you referring to?" He said, "The guys who you arrested, and who went to three locations and steal various items." I replied, "But you told me that the case was finished and they Cop-A-Plea." He said, "But you falsify your report." I explained, "The report was not false, it was a clear report of some of the items that came from our stores from North Hollywood." The supervisor replied, "But you did not see them take the items from that store." I said, "That's true, but the items were priced with North Hollywood's marking gun, and it was our tags on the items, along with not having a receipt to show proof of purchase from any of the three stores. When I approached the suspects, after trailing them from the stores to the parking lot- with me was my Store Manager. I identified myself, after which I told the three suspects to accompany us back to the store, and let us clarify the matter. A search was conducted, where the items from the store were found in their possessions. So I can't understand what you are actually telling me now."

Ultimately what transpired was that I lost the case, and my job owing to the jealous supervisor, Neil. I could have brought a law-suit against him, but thought of it carefully not to, for if I did, I would have had too much prejudice against me. What I do know is that Neil was a Bastard who was very jealous of me, and which he felt that I was after his job, because of my aggressive style. From that point on I took life as it was presented to me. May God deal with Neil and the Judge, who presided over my case at Hollywood Labour Office. I felt a strong sense of despair, at the same time trying my best to stay focus.

My next job was with a man named Miller, who had a couple of Apartment Buildings, and would employ me from time to time to work as a painter, plumber or mason.

With no money after a while, my telephone was cut offed. My unemployment benefits were forfeited, which would have had amounted to ten thousand United States Dollars, along with extension from that period. I began to hit "Rock Bottom", no contract with my agents, no film nor television series. During which time I applied for Legal aid, (General Relief) I will not name the Company or the name of the man who built a chain set of stores, #1 to #189 around California State. The man had liked me a great deal, he heard of me from the head of his Security and his various Store Managers. I was highly appreciated for my work, and the saving of money by the firm which I brought about. The man also sent a message, through the Head of Security, asking me to write a book on my findings of his store. I wrote the Book which was called 'The Shoplifters', the man found out that I had worked twelve months without taking one day off from my job. He also found out that I was a movie Actor, and a Writer of movie scripts. That was why he requested that I must write the Book about his stores. The Book was written and submitted. It's a great book. The Book describe the various types of shoplifters, what makes a criminal, it also explained the losses which becomes an extra financial burden on the company, whose businesses were in various places up and down the United States. It brings about inflation in the Merchandising Arena. I decided not to publish the Book, 'The Shoplifters', because I was told by the Company's Lawyers, that the book would let the shoplifters become wiser. So I drop the idea of publication. The Company which at the time had become so large and prosperous, had decided to sell out to a much larger Company, and the man who had built the company to a large chain-line of stores resigned. So he was pushed aside with a bit of shares. Later some changes were made by the New Company owners. After those great changes took place, I continued working under the new management. But little did I know, I had a secret enemy, while working under him as one of my bosses. He was my enemy ever since before the company change hands by a sell-out. The Individual who became my enemy was jealous of me, because of my aggressive style our Chief Head of Security had very high regards for my working services in general.

That respect and knowledge of my services was known by the heads of the first company, and was relayed to the new management as well, putting me in line for a promotion by the new management. So this individual saw me as taking away his position which he held.

So he finally set me up, falsifying a police report of one of my cases and arrest. He stated that I had wrote a report which he had change, and got me dismissed, and I lost all of my benefits from the company, also my unemployment benefits as well.

During the lost of that Job, after working with the company for seven years. I worked as a detective and saved the company millions of dollars, and was well liked by those who were now retired. I was now in the hands that took over, and he the supervisor was in a position above me in the new company. I was not protected from my jealous boss. I was pushed into hardship and into the General Relief Program, after a Tribunal Court of the Unemployment System, and a prejudice court hearing. The Judge whose aim was focused on saving the company from their unemployment benefits program, which is money saved through the company,  when the worker work for that and becomes qualified to draw that company benefits. So by this time my enemy had convinced the Judge that I must not be paid those benefits. Because the company did not sell the items, which I had charged the suspects of stealing. The Judge stopped me from speaking, or presenting my claims that the items were sold by the company. Well it's a long story, the suspects were the persons who were supposed to have committed the crime. In this case, I referred to this "suspects" as the thieves. They did admit stealing the items from my location, also two other locations. That is called a "cop-out" when the person admits guilt. So I did not need to go to court to give evidence in the case.

A couple of weeks later that case, I saw my supervisor at one of our seminars. I then asked him, "how did that case go with the guys who stole from three locations which I caught?" He said to me, "The guys' cop-a-plea, that was a very good arrest you have made." I said to him "thank you."

# 27

# *My Repentance*

T HE YEAR WAS 1984 JUNE, I started to feel contrite or remorseful with myself for some of the things I had done. Also some of the other things which I had seen during my life time, which others had done as well.

So my spirit led me towards my Bible, which I seldom had the time to read. I picked up the Bible and started to turn the pages, one after the other in search of a prayer. So as to pray to "GOD". Truly speaking I had no knowledge of the prayer of which I was in search of at that said time. But I kept turning the pages of the bible back and forth. Then suddenly, I heard a loud Baritone Voice shouting at me, "Put down the Bible- Pray!" I quickly put aside the bible on the writing desk, and I said, "God, I do not believe in You! Why should I believe in You? I don't believe of Your existence!" Somehow, God knew that I was getting into a challenge with Him, ("God"). The reason for saying that is because He ("God") knew that I did not know the meaning of the word Repent, nor Repentance, I will not be repenting to Him in the way in which I intended, and not in the way of a prayer. Therefore He told me to Pray. Also, He knew that when He shouted to me to pray, I would not have prayed in the way I intended to speak to

Him. I would not find it in the Bible, which meant my speech to God is not from the Bible.

In the way I will be speaking to Him, I was about to get into a challenge with him. I did not know how to repent. So that is why God dealt with me in the way in which He did, so as to get me to repent.

God, shouted to me "Pray"! Now I will say this, "God knew my intention because he is God. He said, "Pray"! That I knew. Because my God Parents had taught me various prayers in the bible and how to pray. God also knew that I intended to speak to Him from my conscious soul, as I intended. I was then permitted by God to clear my conscious soul to Him, in the way I knew best, and that will be accepted as my repentance to Him. I began to question God, "If You exist, why, do You allow all those things which I have seen such as, instability, hunger of people around the world, children bare feet without food or clothing, gruesome killings, stealing, and homeless people?" "God, you have taken me practically around this earth, so that I may see and learn of the things above which I've mentioned. The wrong things which I have seen from time to time, they have made me very confused, and placed doubts into my mind about You, and of Your Existence as God." "After which I found myself drifting away from You, God. So that today, I found myself sitting in a chair in front of my writing desk, not kneel while speaking to You in a challenging manner." I then continued, "But God if You do exist, You should know why I do not believe in You and your existence; But somewhere in my mind or soul, or heart, I do believe that You exist. I want You to bring me back to You."

"God, but the only way You can bring me back to You is if You, please give to me the health and strength, and walk beside me, do give me great wisdom, open gates and doors of Hollywood, so that I can get a couple of movies to make enough money to write myAutobiography, develop a farm, so as to cut prices of food so that poor mother and

children who may need a second chicken leg to eat will
be able to get, and to keep them away from malnutrition.
To build a home, a shelter over my head as I am getting
older. Fulfill my dreams, which I came here to do as an
Actor, to make enough money for these things, So once
again God, I am asking You to bring me back to You. If
You do that for me, I will know of Your existence, and I
will follow You to the end of the earth. If I should tell
anyone about what You have done for me, and they do
not want to believe me, they can go to hell."

Lots of men will give women a child or children, and
then leave the mother with the burden of the children,
like my mother. Many a-days my sisters and brothers,
including myself, could hardly sit down to eat a proper
meal with our mother after I had joined them,  after I
ran away from my Godparents, "The Moores"  God, we
were poor as poor can be, up to that point of leaving
the Moores' at the age of 16, I had never worn a pair of
leather shoes God. My parents were not the only ones
living under those conditions in my home, and country
British Guiana.

# 28

## *Requests and Results*

THIS CHAPTER DEALS WITH THE results of the repentance which I had repented to "God." It started in June 1985. But before the changes came, life had remained just about the same, with just a little change which took me a little downhill, so to speak. I saw my finances what little there was, had all dwindled into nothing. I was living on Legal Aid from the American Government. But that was not enough for me to live on, and to move about Hollywood in search of work as an Actor. I quickly had to approach "Screen Actors Guild," Aid Department, so as to get help. The rent of my apartment was owing, not enough food to eat. I must thank "Screen Actors Guild" for the little help which was given to me. Now speaking about work as an Actor, that came very far apart, like I've mention before. I was only getting a few T.V. parts, and no Films. As you know, Actors money came mostly by working in a film, or in a regular TV series.

I would go five days a week in search of a job outside of my profession. And I was unable to get a job, because of the job application from which had to be filled out, as follows: "Please state your profession or trade, state your five or more jobs each year, also the reason for leaving each job. Now, from that point, when I stated that I am an Artiste, it becomes a no, no, because of my profession. I will be refused the job.

So, I could not find a job because I was an actor. I would be told "I am sorry, but we cannot hire you, because when you get a job as an actor you will leave this one here. We need someone who will work long. The money you will get as an actor, you will not stay here."

Because of the job problem as an actor in Hollywood, my livelihood became shattered for a few years. It was not until later after I had repented that my life started to change-uphill. The Legal Aid which was given to me from the US Government was not given freely, it's called "General Relief" and one had to work in a Government Institution so as to receive the monthly money to help to pay one's food and rent. The money didn't cover soap powder, or items such as luxury, etc.

# 29

## The Fulfillment

O N OR ABOUT OCTOBER 21, 1985, my agent Lil Cumber telephoned me and said, "Danny, I received a phone call from Lynn Davis Production, she would like to see you concerning a film by the name of "Thunder Run", it sounds like a good film. Now, your appointment is 1:00pm, at 725 Lakefield Road in West Lake Village, California."

I felt so good listening to my agent informing me about the above film appointment. I began to think to myself, "A Film, this is great. I must get this film. I've been waiting a very long time to get my first Film in Hollywood. This I must get."

I then started to prepare myself for the interview, and at the same time I started thinking about my approach during my interview with Lynn Davis. It came to my attention, that some years ago while working in England, a producer by the name of Ted Kotchief, said to me while I was home with him having a drink one early evening, as he was putting together the casting of a film by the name of "Two Gentleman Sharing." Ted said to me, "Danny you must try and remember this, you must never, never, cold read when you are called to an interview to read. First, be familiar with the script or the text. Danny, you are a character actor, you're not a straight actor." I never fully understood the difference before Ted had told me.

But I will tell you this, I never cold read after Ted had told me. An actor or an actress should learn and know his or her craft. I used to go to various TV and film interviews and cold read. I would attend, let's say ten interviews, and may-be, I would only get one or maybe two the most, out of those 10 interviews. A generically character, those which constitute a Genus, now, I did not know that I was born as a Genus, and that was why I became an Actor.

So I decided to go and face Lynn Davis and refused to cold read. Well I did so, refused, and said, "I am so sorry but I do not cold read a script." Lynn said to me, "Okay, take the script home and read it, I will be calling your agent, to fix another appointment." She did so two days later, and I went and read for the part. I got the film, it was a supporting role. So that was my first Film in Hollywood.

Three months later my agent was given a call for me to attend another interview. This time the film Company was named "RENEGADE Films, Inc.," located at 8033 Sun Set Blvd. West Hollywood CA, 90046. I attended the interview. The name of the Film was called, 'RETRIBUTION'. It was a co-starring role, 5th position, shared card main titles.- The card is the movie screen. I got the film the moment I walked in the room after speaking to the producer and director. By this time I started to see some changes in my life after getting this second film, the year of the above film was January 15, 1986.

# 30

## *The Lamp*

THEN LATER MY AGENT LIL Cumber received a telephone call from Houston Texas in 1986 requesting my availability to work in a film. The telephone call was made by a new and upcoming producer. His name was Warren H. Chaney, the name of the film was called, "The Lamp", and this film was my third film. Warren spoke to Lil Cumber and myself on a three way conversation on the telephone from Houston, Texas. That was a top starring role, single card, to play the part of a curator, by the name of Theo Bressling. I would be one of two curators' working in the Museum of Natural History, in Houston, Texas.

So I was told to go to Los Angeles Airport the following morning, and pick up my airline ticket, after giving my name to the airline clerk. I did as I was told. I finally got my ticket and boarded the aircraft, while sitting and waiting for the plane to take off into the air, I started to have a recollection on my life during the past nine months.

I came to realize that I was now travelling to do my third film. More so, I was getting a film every three months. I said to myself, things were looking up, my life was changing for the better, and I was so pleased with myself. I became very happy. I hadn't felt so fulfilled and happy in all my life. By this time the aircraft started to taxi along the tarmac. I've always requested a window seat whenever I'm on an aircraft, so I would sit and look out into the clouds. The aircraft finally lifted off and set its course.

Then approximately 30 minutes later as I was sitting staring into the clouds, I heard a deep baritone voice shouting in my ears, as if the person was sitting next to me. But no one was sitting beside me, the seat was empty. The voice said, "Danny! Let me tell you, your first film "Thunder Run" supporting role. Your second film "Retribution", co-starring role. You are now flying to do your third film, "The Lamp," top starring roll. I will further translate for you, "Thunder Run" and erased all "Retribution", hence comes light, "The Lamp." Now that was the voice of "God," it was his voice which bellows a loud sound into my ears and body, then my brain. Truly speaking while God was in the process of translating the above words to me, my entire body, soul and spirit became lifeless, as God took full control of me at that time.

When I became fully conscious as to what was going on and what was said to me. I became so scared, that I wanted to break open the window of the aircraft next to where I was sitting. But I did not do it because God was still in control. But by this time I was about to arrive at the Houston Airport.

On my arrival I was met by the Producers' wife, Mrs. Deborah Winters. She took me to the studio where they were filming. Deborah then introduced me to the Producer, Mr. Warren Chaney, who had cast me to play the part by the part of, a curator, in the said movie. It was a wonderful character. Mr. Warren had greeted me and asked me about my flight on the plane. I told him it was fine. Mr. Warren called one of the female workers, and told her to bring us a copy of the movie script. During the arrival of the young lady and script, Warren said to me, "Danny hold a bit, I will take you to your hotel." I said, "Okay, Mr. Chaney."

After Warren was given the movie script, he said to me, "here is a copy of the script Danny." He then shouted across the floor of the film set-up, "Bill, please bring Mr. Daniels a chair over this way." Warren pointed to a near-bye corner as Bill brought a chair across to where we were standing. Mrs. Chaney, Warren's wife, was still using her maiden name as an actress. She was still standing next to her husband and myself, while he attended to me, as Bill places the chair into the near-bye corner, as Warren pointed to the corner, off Bill went after Warren thanked him. Warren then said to me, "Danny sit there for a while; we'll be closing off after we get this shot in, I won't be long." I said, "go ahead Mr. Chaney." Then off Mr. and Mrs. Chaney went to a far corner of the Film Set. I sat into the chair which was provided for me, and started to read my script. After an hour and a half, the shooting of that segment of that scene was completed for Saturday. Mr. Chaney came over to me and said, "Danny, come let's go, I'll take you to your Hotel. By the way, have you ever visited Texas?"

I said, "No, this is my first time, Houston seems like a nice city." By this time, Warren and I came out of the studio into the Office area, and he introduced me to the Director of his film, and a few other people of the production. Then off we went into a Limousine, and drove to the Hotel. We reached the Hotel, half an hour later after travelling on one of the beautiful freeway which runs along a section of Houston City. We went into the Hotel, and I was booked in, and was introduced. The keys to my section of the room were handed to me. Mr. Chaney then said to me, "tomorrow you will be picked up, and then you will join me and wife for breakfast." "The driver will come and get you at 9:00am, and bring you to us." We'll be seeing you then.' I said, "have a good evening, and I'll be seeing you." They both went their ways. I was then accompanied to my hotel room by a Bell Boy. Well, I was very much into the movie script, during the journey to the hotel while Mr. and Mrs. Chaney chat a bit on the way. Warren Chaney had told me while we were waiting outside of the studio for his wife to come and join us, he said to me, "you'll be starting work on Monday, the call-sheet will be out later and be brought to your Hotel." I replied, "Fine." I finally settled down into my hotel room, which was very nice indeed. Truly speaking our accommodation as actors and actresses were always provided with the best in mind, I must say. Sunday morning I got up bright and early after reading the movie script, 'The Lamp.' I stayed in my hotel room and read the script almost completely until 2:30am Sunday morning. I was awakened at 5:55am, I was very pleased with the treatment of the script, which Mr. Warren Chaney had written, and called it 'The Lamp'. Also I was very pleased with the Character by the name of 'Dr. Theo Bressling' who is a distinguished looking Black Scientist, and also having the honour to be chosen, to play the part.

Also my call-sheet was brought to me at my hotel room. But the ironic part of my work which had been set out in the call-sheet for Monday film shooting had been changed later Sunday afternoon. Now, the changes which were made away from my call-sheet were totally ironic. Because the new scene which I was told about around 4pm on Sunday, and had to read and crammed, so it can be committed to the brain. It was six pages of dialogue, with one or two interruptions on each of the six pages. The remainder of the dialogue was my part of each of the six pages. It is a known fact that most Actors and Actresses can only cram three pages of a movie script, similar of each of my six pages. The three pages took 24 hours to be crammed. That Sunday morning I had breakfast with my producer Mr. Warren Chaney, his wife and a few members of the cast. I started to work on the Monday evening as was planned for me to start work in the Museum of Natural History in Houston Texas. The six pages of dialogue was shot during the entire Monday evening. The filming was done throughout the various corridors, by tracking shots with very few stops, as one of the actresses who came to see the two Museum's Curators, Dr. Albert Wallace and Dr. Theo Bressling, an older scientist. Well that scene went great indeed, without any mistakes. The entire shooting of the film went great. It was a splendid cast of actors and actresses. By this time I was working three weeks on the film, and all was going fine. Then suddenly came a big surprise. I went to bed as usual. It was a Monday night to be exact. During the night I started to dream. Please read this section slowly and carefully. Now here I will explain carefully. I went to bed and fell asleep as usual, during my sleep I started to dream. This is the first of three dreams, which will occur one after the other starting from the Monday night in the hotel room. I dreamt about weed and cocaine. I will take you back a bit. Now, three weeks before I got this film 'The Lamp' a friend in New York told a friend of his to check me out. The guy got in touched with me after leaving my friend in New York. Now, when this guy arrived here, he got himself a room at a Motel on Western Ave. he then telephoned me, and introduced himself. He said, "Mr. Daniels, my name is George from New York, a friend of Walter Page. He told me to speak to you about the shop."

He told me the name of the motel and his room number. I said, "Okay, I will come and check you out." I finally got to the motel and rang his room bell. Mr. George from New York came to the door and let me in. We shook hands, and then George pointed to a chair for me to sit in. As he sat in another chair facing me, we spoke a while. Then half and hour later while speaking to me he took out the Bambu cigarette paper and continue to roll a joint of weed, mixed with cocaine. He then pointed the cigarette to me. I quickly refused to take it. George then placed the cigarette between his lips, and then flicks a light onto the cigarette. And began to smoke, by this time George had taken 6 to 7 puffs of the cigarette, and then suddenly a quick change came over me and I said to George. 'Give me a pull.' George passes the joint to me, I then took three puffs. After a few seconds I began to taste bitterness in my mouth. Then the inner side of my jaws started to get numb. I quickly handed back the cigarette to George. I did not like it one bit. I had decided not to smoke that again. I had smoked weed, but never felt drunk, or hallucinated or otherwise. So my first dream during the Monday night was based on the Cocaine and Marijuana. I was then awakened by the Almighty, shouting in a loud baritone voice to me, "Wake up! Wake up!' You had a dream. Think! Think!" I then sat up in the bed and glanced at my travelling clock, which sits on the bedside table next to my bed. The time on the clock was reading 5:55am. I lay my head down while closing my eyes on the bed head board and relax. The voice once again said, "don't ever let me catch you smoking that stuff again." It was the voice I always described, which I'm familiar with; it is a loud baritone voice. It is the voice of God, whenever He deals with me, by way of speech to me. I then opened my eyes, and began to think about what I have heard, at the said time. I became a bit confused and scared. Now the above is the first dream. I went to work the Tuesday, and continued my filming, I said nothing to anyone about my dream, but then on Tuesday night, I went to bed as usual. Then came my second dream. This dream was about a friend by the name of Stanley Trotman, him and myself being friends for about thirty odd years starting in London, England, since 1951. During those rough days, I cared for this friend, I paid his rent, and bought him food, and I also took him out to clubs and dance halls in London, after picking him up in my car, I would put a few Pounds into his pocket from time to time while visiting his home, or whenever I saw him. He was not working in those days, many blacks couldn't have a job in London, simply because they were Black.

Stanley Trotman migrated to the United States during the year 1969, a few years before I went to America. On his arrival in the United States he lived with my brother,

DANNY DANIELS AUTOBIOGRAPHY

Basil Daniels, his wife and children. He stayed with Basil for a couple of weeks. Stanley's wife came to America a short while before him. Stanley was very close to myself, my wife Jackie, and our three children in London. Stanley had arranged with his wife that she'll go first, and then he will joined her over there in the States. For years Stanley would associate with the boys back in London, but were never really appreciated by them. I was the one who tolerated him, because he was shy, and after all he is a human being. He couldn't get a girlfriend in years, and whenever he did, it will not be long before the girl dumps him. He had a jealous tendency, along with a bit of deceitfulness. I overlooked those qualities, which he had, for I saw in him other qualities that drew me to him. Let me say this, Stanley and his wife had bought a house in London three years or so, after he finally got a job with Ford Motor Company whom he worked with for three years, as a comfortable married man with his own home. His wife encouraged him into selling the house after the mortgage kept piling up. That was when he came to me explaining his position. I had just finishing doing a TV play, and was about to be paid, at the said time I was owing 'child support', for one of my sons whose mother was thoroughly against me because I ceased to be with her, because of her lifestyle and her ways. She took me to court for 'Child Maintenance', which was owing. That was a common practice of her, because I was married with three children, and she did not like the idea of me being with another woman. Like I've said, the money for child support was there to pay. But I discussed it with my wife Jackie, about Stanley who was on the verge of loosing his house. The money for child support, and also other bills that I'm suppose to meet with within our home. I said to my wife Jackie, "I am not going to give Kathleen the money, she has money, she is not short of money like we do, she is just spiteful. I am thinking of going to jail for the money, should they arrest me, which will be the best thing to do. Then that way I will be able to shake her off from her Black Mail." I finally decided to give Stanley the money and I went to prison. Now I can assure you that, that was a grand move. For that prison term was my last, I have never given her a dime in fourteen years, and she never took out another summons for me. So back to Stanley Trotman, being in New York, and then travelling up to long Beach, California to join his wife. Apparently when Stanley arrived at the apartment where his wife was staying, he knocked on the apartment door and a Black African male, 7 feet tall, an American Citizen, opened the door. The man asked Stanley who he wanted, he quickly told the man who he was, and he was there to see his wife, the burly 7 footer said to Stanley, "listen to me don't you come knocking on this f......ing door. Get your ass out of this building." Stanley's wife in the mean time was standing slightly behind King Kong. The man then chased Stanley out of the building, which he hurriedly complied with. In this second dream, it all started during a dream on Tuesday night. I walked up a sky scraper by the way of the ramp to the roof of the building. It was a flat roof top with a Penthouse on top. The building had no steps or stairs to travel up to the top. One had to travel by the way of a ramp walk- way. The building was thirty floors in height. There was an elevator in the building. But the elevator do not take people upwards, it only travel from the top with passengers, stopping on floors when it is requested to do so. I did not walk up to the top of the skyscraper alone, instead I was accompanied by two friends. A girlfriend of mine and the other friend who knew I was in the city filming. He was the one who told the dope dealer that I was in Town, and that he must bring me to him, who lives in the penthouse of the building, and who I hadn't seen in quite some years, and was now living in Houston, Texas.

After the three of us had finally reached the top, I looked over the side of the building onto the streets below. The building was at the corner of a four section junction. While looking onto the streets below, I saw a car travelling from East towards West, but ended up turning left at the corner of the building which I was standing on, above looking down. While looking below at the car as it turned the corner, I saw Mr. Stanley Trotman sitting in the front seat of the car next to a woman who was driving the car. While looking at Trotman in the car. I heard the deep Baritone voice saying to me "He is not your friend!' 'Leave him alone." My friends and I continued to walk towards the Penthouse, the boy knocked on the door. A voice shouted, "Who is it?" over an intercom. Then, the boy who is with us shouted, 'its Small Boy.' The door lock kept a loud noise as a bolt shoots out of its position. Small Boy pushed the door open, he then usher us into the house. I saw Big Tommy, the Dope Dealer. He shouted across the room, while being in his bed, "Hi, Danny Boy, nice to see you. It has been a long time." I then said, "it's quite a long time, a long time, Big Tommy." The apartment was well furnished and secured, when one cast their eyes around the large spacious room. By this time Big Tommy sat up in the bed, where he was, I quickly went over to him and shook hands with him, he then said to me "make yourself at home, have a seat." I then went to my girlfriend and sat next to her, as Small Boy moved to sit in a chair next to the one I was about to sit in. By this time Small Boy then sat on a sofa facing me and the girl. Big Tommy said to Small Boy, "give them a drink, Small Boy, and bring me one as well, also get one yourself." Small Boy stood up as he asked, "what would you all like to drink." I said, 'A Beer, if you have Beer." My girlfriend said, "I'll have the same." Then off Small Boy went to serve the drinks around, while Big Tommy and I engage in a conversation. I said to Tommy, "This is my girlfriend, her name is Laverne." Big Tommy said, "I am so pleased to meet you, Laverne." Big Tommy raised his glass into the air as we toasted. Big Tommy said, "Welcome to Texas, our wonderful City of Houston." I then said, "Cheers, So I can see, you are still on the hustle." Small Boy quickly said, "what else can we do here, not much work for us Black People here, after all the oil fields closed down. But we do not sell the White Lady." Big Tommy then said, "Danny that White Lady is a killer to mankind. But somehow people confuse the issue with Marijuana, or weed as we know it. 'Marijuana is a medication to many sicknesses. The world will discover its full use later." Small Boy by this time was in the process of building a joint of marijuana. Small Boy then try to pass me the joint, and I refused it. He said, "Don't you smoke anymore?" I said, "yes, sometimes, but not the coke." Small Boy then tries to pass it to Laverne. She quickly said, "Pass me." He then began to smoke on his own. But then later on Laverne said, "Pass it to me, I will have a couple of puffs." Laverne then started to smoke. I then said, "Tommy I will be cutting out my Boy. I will see you another time." But funny enough, when Laverne had a change of heart, so to speak, she refused the joint but later decided to smoke it, after her refusal. I gave her a look of disgracefulness.

Immediately the loud Baritone voice awakens me from my sleep, "wake up, you had a dream, Think! Think!' 'I sat up and look at the bedside clock, and the time was five minutes to six. I then lean the back of my head against the head board of the bed. After which I closed my eyes. The entire flash went through my brain. I then woke up from a sort of spiritual sleep or trance, not lasting too long. It's a sick surge to describe. Now after given dreams during my sleep each night. The Almighty would then awaken me each morning at five minutes to six. This dream took placed on Tuesday night. But the dream itself tells me of what I will hear in the morning after I was awaken by the loud baritone voice, shouting at me while I was asleep. I sat up and look at the clock, the time was five minutes to six. I then relax myself, as I lay the back of my head against the head board of the bed. My third dream on Wednesday night speaking started with the said voice talking to me, "you always wanted a wife, and children. I did not give birth to you like an ordinary man, to have a wife. I gave birth to you for a specific reason, but you, always wanted a wife and children. But that is what you wanted." I quickly open my eyes out of the spiritual trance which 'God' had put me into as I lean my head and close my eyes. Then I rest my head backwards on to the head board of the bed. I did mention that description before. But I did not mention the spiritual realm during the course while God deals with someone. When He (God) delivers the key to one of his Spiritual Genius. One becomes lifeless, and starts to cower, by the sound of the voice, and the words in a sentence. A couple of minutes later after opening my eyes, I began to think about the three children and their mothers, and my separation from them. Also other children and their mothers, as to why I am not with one mother or child. I said, "God, why did you remove me from twelve children, and nine mothers?" I then started to cry, shedding heavy tears. I got out of the bed, and got some paper and pen. I then started to write my daughters; Deborah, Yvonne and son Richard, telling them of my dreams, I will go into a more detailed description of the children later in another chapter.

# 31

# *My Discussion with Chaney*

NOW ON THURSDAY MORNING AFTER writing the letters to the three children. I got myself ready for filming. I arrived at the studio early, by this time I was a bit worried and confused by the dreams, and the time five minutes to six, and then the sound of the same voice calling me up each morning, and afterwards giving me a lecture into the does and don'ts. I did not have a full understanding as to what was taking place. I called Warren Chaney as soon as he walked on to the film set, as the set were busy preparing for work. I quickly said, "Mr. Chaney, I would like to have a word with you." He then replied, "Okay, Danny, I will be with you in ten minutes." He then went and spoke to the film director.

Mr. Warren Chaney returned and sat next to me. We were in a nice little corner away from everyone. While the entire film set were busy with the final touches for shooting. Warren said, "what's the matter Danny?" I said, "I am scared Warren." Warren quickly became on the defensive, probably thinking it was about the Genie Lamp, I was working on, reading and translating the graphic on, The Lamp. He said, "Scared! What are you scared about? You scared about the Lamp?" I said, "No, it's not the Lamp or about the film, Warren. I have been having dreams every night, for the past three nights. Also voices wake me up, and then speak to me." Warren said, "Danny stop being scared. I want you think back as for as you can remember as a child. Tell me about your life in Guyana, England and also America and coming to do this Film."

I said, "I can remember when I was two years old." I told him of the two ghost experiences, about my grandmother before she died, and the thunder bolt experience, also about stowing away for fourteen days and nights, without food or water. I also discussed sections of my life in London and Scotland. I told him about my life in America and Hollywood as an artiste before and after repentance. Then into Texas, my three dreams in full.

Do not forget, I have mentioned bits and pieces of Warren Chaney. I will now mention a bit more of him. Warren was at U.C.L.A. (University of California, Los Angeles) he was a professor. I can also tell you that he's brilliant and highly spiritual. I must say it's in the Chaney family. Lon Chaney, the Genius, the man who stands in wax in the Wax Museum in Hollywood, is Warren's uncle, the root of Geniuses. Warren Chaney said, "you are a Genius, "a spiritual Genius." Now reader you will confirm the above statement later on.

Warren said to me, "Now Danny, listen to me, you were born in Guyana as one of Guyana's geniuses. You are an artistic genius, also a spiritual genius." I quickly said, "What are you talking about? How can I be a Genius and Poor?" Warren quickly smiled and said, "Danny, you are very naïve in the sense. What would you like to do in life?" I then replied, "Warren I would like to get a few movies, so that I can make enough money to build a lovely home, a shelter over my head, before I get too old. Also, have a large farm, so that I can feed mothers and children who do not have a father helping the mother to support the children, if the child needs a second chicken leg to eat. I can cut the prices of food, so as to stop malnutrition, then to continue writing my Auto-biography." Chaney said, "Have you ever heard of Rembrandt or Picasso, the great painters?' They had no money when they died, and they were geniuses. So one do not need to have money because of one being a Genius. The family quite often collects the money later if the Genius dies before the big money comes in, you don't know what is happening to you in the Hotel?" I quickly asked, "what is happening? Tell me." Warren said, "Danny you are receiving the key to your genius-ship. God is giving you the key. It all started on the aircraft while coming here. I will tell you this, God wants the book which you are writing, and He wants that Autobiography you are writing. The Book is the Bridge to the Bible. I want you to promise me that you will write the book, and finish it. Now if you stop, and get involved with other things and not that book. You will die a horrible death. Do you understand?" I said, "I do understand, I will not stop writing it." Warren then said, "Now stop acting, go home and pick up the pen and do you realized how much you will get in two years, after the book comes out? You will get two hundred million US Dollars. Also, you will win the Noble Peace Prize when the Book comes out. By this time some of the other actors had completed the first and second shot, and I was about to start work.

Warren and I separated, and we went towards our work. Well it's said, all good thing comes to an end. Time had passed, and by this time my period of working on the film came to a closed. And I was getting ready to travel back to Hollywood, California.

281

# 32

## *Houston to Los Angeles*

T HIS IS MY RETURN FLIGHT after working on the film
'The Lamp', in Houston Texas. I was so pleased
with myself while travelling to the Houston
Airport to catch my flight. I said to myself, "At last I finally
hit the top star billing, single card. After working about
forty films, playing supporting cameo parts." Well it was
a great accomplishment after leaving England and given
the chance to hit the top billing. So coming to America,
I had made a wonderful move. Also 'God' had moved
me away from England and later given me the key to my
Genius-ship while filming 'The Lamp,' in Houston, Texas.
My entire composure as a person had changed; it was as
if I was given a new lease on life. It's a wonderful feeling.
It is so hard to describe, words cannot be put together to
describe the feeling, it's more or less a spiritual realm. By
this time I had boarded the aircraft, sitting over the wing
of the plane, next to one of the aircraft windows. The
passengers were coming aboard and seating themselves.

Then ten minuets later as I was sitting comfortably in
my seat, a male Caucasian came and sat in the seat next to
me. I then said to the man, "Good morning.' He replied,
'Good morning!' Fifteen minutes later the air- craft taxied
down the tarmac, and took off. I then introduced myself
to the man, "My name is Danny Daniels." I stretched my

hands towards him and we shook hands. He told me his name, but I forgot it. After he told me his name, I said, "Do you live in Houston?" the man said, "No, I do not live here, I live in California I came here on a seminar, and you?" I replied, "I live in LA, as well. I came here to do a film." The man asked, "What sort of film were you doing?' I said, "It's a tale of terror, about a Genie killing people in the Museum of Natural History." The man then asked, "What's the name of the film?" I said, 'The lamp.' He said, "So you are an actor, that's good." I then asked, "What sort of work do you do?" He said, "I am a surgeon that's why I had to come here for a seminar." I said, "Doc, I had a terrible time while being here, I use to get a set of dreams during the nights in my hotel room, and then a loud baritone voice would shout and wake me up each morning, at five minutes to six, saying, 'Wake up! Wake up! You had a dream, Think! Think!" I would then glance at my bed-side clock, and the clock would point to five minutes to six. I would then lean the back of my head onto the bed, and then closed my eyes and relax myself. And then the voice would then speak, repeating the dream I had during the night. I then went to my producer and told him of my dreams, and the voice." He quickly asks, "what is the name of your producer?" I replied, "his name is Warren H. Chaney, he was a professor at U.C.L.A. Mr. Chaney started to question me about my past, starting from my early childhood. After which he concluded that I was born a genius, and I was receiving the keys to my genius-ship. He said, "Tell me some of the things that Mr. Chaney asked you to tell him about, from your childhood." I told him everything which Warren and I had discussed. He quickly said, "You remind me of two people." I quickly said to him without hesitation, I know the two people you're referring to." He became very amazed by my statement. He said, "you know the two people I am speaking about? "Tell me who they are." I said, "President Kennedy and Martin Luther King." He shouted, 'Oh my God! What is this, you are a genius, your producer was correct." I then started to question him, as I said, "Hi Doc, tell me this, do human beings have a spirit and a soul?" The funny part of those questions, I did not ask the question because I did not know or believe, I was asking him so as to be certain. Somehow, God was inspiring me to question him, so as to gain more knowledge on the subject. He then said to me, "Yes, we do have a spirit and a soul ... I will enlighten you. We not only have one soul, but two souls.

The two is an upper and a lower souls, the lower soul is what condensed bad memory. "Have you ever heard that when a woman is giving birth to a child, the pain in which she endures no man can endure such a pain?" Well that pain goes to the lower soul in order to be condensed. When that pain is condensed it is then forgotten, because of that process, the woman can go once again to have another child, or several other children.

Now in the case of a man the lower soul works the same way as of a woman, lets say a man is hammering a nail into a wood or a wall, and the hammer misses, hitting the nail head, and the force of the hammer strikes a finger of the man, that pain also goes to the man lower soul, in order to be condensed as well. The same applies if one or the other strikes a match to light a gas stove, and the fingers and match stick goes near to the flame when the stove is lit, then the said person gets burn. That pain goes immediately into the lower soul, and in no time the pain is gone into a slight pain. The severity of the pain disappears all together." He then said, 'Well in this way the three entities are located together, the spirit sits above the upper soul, and the lower is below the upper soul." I will explain my composure and my attention while, the man, the surgeon was speaking to me, it was as if I was in a spiritual realm, so as to understand and to remember, all which was said to me. It's like God was saying to me, "Now you remember what's being told to you, so that you may write it later when I need you to write it.

"I 'God' brought this man to you so as to enlighten you." It was shortly after that I quickly said to the surgeon, "I can tell you the way in which the three entities are in the human body'. The man said, "Tell me." I then told him. The man quickly shouted, "Mr. Daniels, write it the same way in your book, like you said it to me. No man or woman can doubt you when you say it in your book.

When I go home, I will tell my wife that I had the pleasure to sit next to you, who just received the keys to his genius-ship."   I then said, "Well your wife will doubt you and laugh at you". The man said, "You are right, she will." We both burst out in to laughter. A while later we arrived at Los Angeles Airport, and we came off the plane. We then went our separate ways, and I did not ask the surgeon his name once again.

I should have written it down so as to put it into the book. It's a shame. I am sorry, but I do know when the book is published, and perhaps read by him or his wife for that matter, she will know that her husband was not lying to her about me.

# 33

## Who Am I?

THIS CHAPTER WILL EXPLAIN IN depth as to who I am. You must therefore read and follow my instructions and line carefully, because God gave it to me. While writing this section of my autobiography, "Book" here in Guyana in a village by the name of Yarrow Kabara. Yarrow being the name of a fish, and Kabara being the name of a snake.

When I started to write the chapter "My Birth and Birth Place", as I wrote the year 1927 and then started to write the address where my mother was living during the time of my birth, God took full control of me and suddenly started to give me divine influence, or stimulated me by inspiration. This inspiring influence was a voice within my body that said, "Remove the first two numbers of the year you were born, and add or total the two back numbers and see what the two back numbers total. "The year is 1927, it comes to nine, and three times three is nine."

God then inspired me further, He said, "your mother was living at 66 Leopold Street, now add the two sixes, it is twelve, its four threes' amongst the 66. I continued one after the other as the Almighty kept giving me one inspiration after the other to document these numbers.

I was told to check my army number; so I got up and search for my army discharge. The number is 14-3-13 and to my surprise after checking the paper and totaling the numbers it came to thirty. He said, "Remove the three from the zero, the remainder is three."

Later after dealing with the army numbers. God asked me, "Where were you living when you stowed away to go to Scotland?" It was 63 Cross Street. The Almighty then directed me to check my British National Insurance number which was given to me when I arrived in Scotland after stowing away. The numbers are as follows, LT930135B these numbers also signify the threes' as well. He then said now check your American citizenship certificate number, its all threes'.

The Almighty told me to examine the amount of mothers who bore my twelve children, nine mothers. Examine the way in which your twelve children were born to those nine women. There were two boys and one girl, then there were two girls and one boy, and later two boys followed by one girl, then there were two girls and one boy.

Those are the facts of the children and mothers who bore them. But, let me tell you this, my first three children who were born in British Guiana when I was at the tender age of eighteen. All three of the mothers committed fornication while they were three months' pregnant. I just could not understand it at the time, but it was later brought to my attention by the Almighty. I will explain that knowledge in the chapter "The key to my genius-ship." My foster brother Henry Griffith, who apparently was overseas to fight in the war during World War Two came home a few months after V.E. Day. I was at Takama Battle School, training and building the Battle School, when Griffith returned. My girlfriend was living at 63 Cross Street, and was 3 months pregnant with my child. Her pregnancy was hardly showing because of her built. Griffith did not know that she was expecting a child. He made a pass at her, and she played into his hands, and they had three sexual encounters. On the fourth approach she told him of our engagement and her pregnancy, which caused him to withdraw. When I returned from Takama, Griffith told me of the affair, and I broke off my relationship with her.

I started an affair with another girlfriend and that too was the same as the first, this time with a friend of mine. Also a third girlfriend did the same as the previous two, while she was three months pregnant. My first child's mother name was Tina, she admitted to the affair with Griffith. The second child's mother was Ruby, she and my friend Pilgrim had an affair and it was he who brought my attention to it. The third girlfriend's name was Leila, and she committed fornication with a boy by the name of Seaworthy. This affair took place while I was stowing away and was in Scotland. But, I will say this, while getting these inspirations from the Almighty; It lasted throughout for as long as three hours without stopping. It was a very frightening ordeal receiving these inspirations one after the other, and seeing the numbers after totalling them, it would add up and stand out as threes'. Then, to be able to go and find each paper immediately, and dealing with the numbers in the various papers. Not to mention the fact that most of the papers were safely kept for years, while moving from place to place in various countries. The Almighty said, "Examine the house number which I brought you into and you are now living." The numbers are 234 that is nine when it is totalled. Now this house and land belonged to one of my aunts. I knew nothing of it. I was never in contact with my aunt while being abroad for forty years, or while she was constructing the house on the land. So that again is very puzzling indeed. Is it not God's work? Well it is! God do work in strange ways. I then started to tremble with fear at this point; I was then directed once again by the Almighty. "Check the spelling of the name of the village which I brought you in to live." The name was pointed out before, but I will repeat it. The name is Yarrow Kabara. The two names have six letters in each name. That is twelve or each of the six is two threes which ever way one deal with sixes, is all threes. Finally while being scared and trembling. I quickly put down the pen and push the writing pad to one side. I got up and went across the road to a small shop in the village, in order to buy a couple shots of rum and Coca Cola. But when I got to the shop it was closed for the evening. I wanted the rum and coke to steady my nerves. So I went back into the house and continued to write again. The inspiration continued once again. This section of my direction, "You are to go and find your first wife's birth certificate, or the marriage certificate, and check the letters in the spelling of her name." I did as I was told. The names are as follows Jacqueline Elizabeth Duthon Peters. Now count the letters in the various names, after removing the first name, Jacqueline, totalling them.

I will now close this chapter with this last inspiration, the Almighty said to me as follows, "Your last son amounted to thirteen children, his name is Dan Dani Daniels. He was born June 12, 1989. June is the sixth month of the year and that has two threes' also. Now I found this entire chapter very alarming, as I kept going one after the other with God's guidance, by the way, I was being inspired into the direction to search for each piece of paper and then to examine the various numbers, which each document had consisted of the three's. To describe it precisely it was very frightening at the time. But I continued while being so scared. The spiritual guidance kept me going to overcome my fear. Jacqueline Elizabeth has nine and ten letters in each of the two names, and the last two names, are Duthon Peters has six letters in each of the last two names, like I have pointed out before its enough to make one scared indeed, and she gave me the last three children, so to make twelve children. Also to have been able to go and find each piece of document (paper) after all those years, not knowing that one day I will be writing this Book. God knew that one day he would want me to sit down and write it. Therefore he made me keep these papers safely, and later giving me this entire spiritual guidance I am closing this chapter the way in which God motivates a person. It is called 'inspiration.'

# 34

# *Nature and God*

WHAT IS NATURE? IT IS the essential character of all things. It is the ultimate. To be born or to die is part of nature's will and law or rule, also, to even exist.

Nature is referred to as being "Mother Nature." We do not refer to God as being "Mother God," in context of the two. The belief of nature being the mother is highly correct. Now, since the above saying and acceptance of nature as being the mother, then God wanted the records to be straight. It is nature who gives birth to God, and not the other way around. Nature's domain exists way above heaven, the universe and earth. Nature removed God from Her domain, and placed God into heaven, and then gave God an abundance of power which nature possesses. God was given a spiritual gift above all spirits. He was also given his heavenly spiritual scientific knowledge. That gift from Nature to God cannot be matched by anyone or anything other than nature. So in actual fact nature lends itself to God, and give God all which nature sees that God will need to assist the mother of control, and to build and to maintain the standards of mother and son. Yes, God is the son of nature. That gift from nature makes God what He is, to create and to control the heaven, the universe and the earth.

God, as we know, is a spirit, and a spirit has no blood, no bones or flesh like the human's beings or animals. A spirit has a transient life which means it can appear and disappear. It is a shadow. It is air, it appears as a silhouette, one cannot hold onto it.

I must say this before I go further. Most of the world's population does not believe in spirits, yet some of them who do not believe in spirits, they tell themselves that they believe in God. Now that is so ironic, to believe in God and not a ghost, or spirit. If you do not believe in spirits or ghosts, you cannot believe in God. All existence in heaven are spirits, all human life has a spirit in the human body. God communicated with us human beings by way of our human spirit.

Nature has an opposite disposition to God. Nature is kind and cruel. Now those two tendencies are an awareness of Nature, the mother of God. Nature is kind to us humans and to all other life forms. Nature produced the earth we live on, and earth is important to us. But yet, at the same time, earth can be cruel to us as well. So nature gives birth to God, so that God can control the cruel elements of nature when she becomes destructive. Nature made God into a being.

Opposed to Nature, God is kind and merciful, full of forbearance and compassion. Nature made God that way so that he will be able to control nature's cruel tendencies. Also, to work in unison to make things what they are. As we know it in the Bible.

While God was setting the standards in heaven, Nature was giving birth to the universe and earth. So that God can take over the other planets, and put them into working order, as we know them today. That implementation took nature and God billions and billions of years to build. While God was constructing heaven and his manual the "Holy Bible" and his angels, Nature was also busy as well. Some of his angels were also giving him a helping hand as he give them various tasks, as he see is needed from time to time.

By this time earth was formed by nature. The cosmic egg had exploded and finally given birth to earth. That again, took billions and billions of years for the gases to escape and the earth's crust to be formed. During all this time God was still at work in heaven compiling the does and don'ts in the Bible so that we on earth will be given his revelation when life on earth began. The universe was formed and heaven before that. When nature and God finally completed the earth's formation they placed life on it, such as plants to produce food, animals and human life.

By that time God had already created his disciples including Lucifer the "devil." Lucifer and his followers were in the process of giving God a rough time in heaven. Lucifer was very antagonistic, and incited his followers against God. The antagonism became worst and worst. God began to have second thoughts when he created Lucifer, and to see the problems that Lucifer was causing in heaven. God came to realize that one of his main disciples were giving him a lot of problems, and was also leading others to follow him as well. God also saw other problems that can arise in his creation of the human race.

The documentation of the Holy Bible was still being worked on by God it was not completed. God saw a bigger problem in creating human beings, and giving them a freedom of choice to choose between good and evil. God did not want to create robots in making all humans the same like robots are made. He was implementing a balance. He knew that his mother, nature, gave his creation a balance. So he wanted to give us human beings a balance as well, to choose good or bad, do not forget it was Lucifer who made God have second thoughts, because of Lucifer and his followers.

God is no fool, he can think quickly. He is capable of remedying or counteracting an evil or wrong. God saw the situation as being crucial. He knew he had made a mistake by giving birth to Lucifer and his followers. He also felt that he made a mistake in giving human beings a freedom of choice, between evil and good. God saw that the free will of humans will caused conflict, by his creation. He knew that human beings will vary, like Lucifer and some of the others he created in heaven.

So he decided to remove Lucifer from heaven and put him on earth with his followers. The time had come for Lucifer and his followers to be removed. God then said to Lucifer. "I will give you your own domain, earth. There you shall serve me. I will have control over you and you shall serve me well." God saw Lucifer as being wicked. He saw mankind as well being wicked by the freedom of choice he gave them. God knew that all mankind would not choose the better of the two between good and evil.

So Lucifer was put on earth to test us humans so that God can see the good from the bad, and be able to deal with each of us as against our evil doings, as according to the Bible.

Let me say this before I go any further. Heaven do not have any long lasting problems. No problem can penetrate heaven. It is pure, holy and highly spiritual. The problem in heaven had only existed during the period while Lucifer was in heaven. That was the first and last of problems in heaven. Nature and God had developed heaven to be free from problems.

Nature and God knew that the problem areas would be the universe and earth when they were created. When God transferred Lucifer from heaven to earth, Lucifer duties from God were as follows; he is to test each and every one of us human beings by using all of his wicked traits, which he so possessed. In so doing God will see each and every human beings' faults and weaknesses in order that he, God, may deal with all human beings who are great sinners, all who lived outside of the laws and rules of the bible.

So the problem in the universe was remedied by giving birth to God, who would then find all solutions to eliminate whatever problems should exist. The only problem, which existed, is the problems on earth, and God is in control of the earth's problems, and billions of human beings who are unaware of the earth's problems are being taken care of by God. Why do billions of people not see the world's problems? Because they are not paying close attention to the Bible, and translating it correctly. God can, and He does, alter all of nature's destruction to the human race. God can also alter human destruction as well. But do not forget we have been given a free will, the Bible tells us that. So it is the human race that has to alter the course of the destruction, which was brought about by some human beings unto other humans. God is giving us long latitude before he draws the line and stops our destructive nature. It is also said in the Bible, "Nothing stays the same forever!" and that is a fact. Read the Book of Revelation in the Holy Bible and you will see the statement that nothing, stays the same forever.

The Holy Spirit is God, he will communicate with the human being by way of the human spirit, in the human body. That will make the human spirit strong; therefore, the human being will be strong and become protected from Lucifer. So it is important to keep focusing towards God constantly. If one does not keep focusing on God, then Lucifer will infiltrate his wicked spirit into the human and push the human unprotected and weak spirit aside, and control the human being. Lucifer will direct his spirit into doing whatever he wants, he can make you steal, commit murder and commit suicide. Lucifer will guide his spirit into leading you to do whatever he wants.

Do not underestimate Lucifer; he is tricky, cunning, deceitful and very tempting. He is smart. Lucifer's spirit appears in all sizes and shapes. His wicked duties varies vastly, so like I've said, that human spirit of ours need to be protected.

The Holy Spirit is God's spirit. God communicates with human beings by the two spirits, the Human spirit and His spirit. That is what makes the human spirit strong and protected, and at the said time one must keep focus constantly to God, otherwise Lucifer will gain the upper hand and direct his spirit unto you, so as to make you weak, and to do what he needs to be done. That infiltration of Lucifer's spirit into the human spirit will force the weak human spirit aside and take over the human body. The spirit of Lucifer will then create havoc, yes, great destruction and devastation as that resulting from Lucifer's spirit gaining possession of the human body. The Human being will fall prey to the wicked spirit.

The spiritual existence in heaven is highly sophisticated, it has a higher form of spirit than the spirit on earth, and they see and dwell amongst each other. They are the servants and the messengers of God. They are God's Disciples. Those heavenly spirits from time to time, were sent down from heaven to earth to help God's Prophets like - John, Joshua, Judah, David, Solomon, Saul, Daniel, Ezekiel, Moses, Abraham, Joseph, etc, Jesus, the Son of God. They were also known to us as geniuses, but when God planted all the above on earth, they do not have a transient life; they are given a human life with a special spirit, which has a close relationship with God.

When nature created earth, God placed human beings on it along with other things. He gave each of us a human spirit in our body in order to communicate with each and everyone of us from time to time. He also gave us a free will to do good or evil. It was up to us to choose between right and wrong. Yet it was a choice left to us. Later, as the human animal developed along with other animals, God knew that His creation of human beings was unique when comparing it to animal life. Yes, we are animals (superior).

Returning to developing the human race. God also sent His disciples from heaven. They came one after another and they were teachers. Those disciples, each of them was given a section of God's manual, the Holy Bible.

Those disciples were sent to teach, educate and reveal the written revelation of God's will to humanity. What was God's written will? Was it not the manual, the Bible? Of course, it was the Bible. That Bible was being written before earth was created. The universe was being created as well while the bible was being written. It was heaven, which was created at first. God lives in heaven, not on earth or the universe or the sea. After earth had settled down and life was established on earth, by the time God had completed the bible. He then dispatched His disciples' one after the other with various sections of the Bible onto earth to enlighten His children (human beings) from time to  time those disciples were not ordinary human beings; they were highly spiritual. God gave them those orders to do His work. A disciple is highly protected against Lucifer and his wicked spirits.

Let me say this, to understand the Bible and God's word one must first think about the thousand of years dating backwards, thousands of years before Christians or before the Old Testament, which was written mostly by the Jews in Hebrew, and a few short passages in Arabic. Now before the Old Testament, thousand of years during the cruel days of earth and the birth of the human race, the Bible was not revealed to earth by God's disciples. So we should focus from the early period when the revelation was sent to earth. Now the word revelation means to reveal or the disclosure of something not previously known or realized. That was God's disclosure or manifestation to man and His will to mankind. The 'will' means a gift from someone written on paper. Now the word "testament" means "covenant", or agreement. So the Old Testament is the covenant God made with the human race about their salvation. The meaning of salvation is "a saving or being saved from danger, evil, difficulty, destruction." Or, one can say, a spiritual rescue from the consequences of sin. How many of the world's population have ever read the Bible? How many of the world's population who know how to read and write? Well It's only a quarter of the world's population are able to read and write properly.

Then more people became capable of reading, and translating the bible, and practice the guidance of God's Bible. It will be better for all mankind. We will be able to see, and to understand, that all mandkind are brothers and sisters in the eyes of God and in God's true will to man. We are all God's children since that is so from the beginning time. It means that, all of God's children are produced as the first born of male and female human being. This first gift to mankind, had complications. God knew that his creation which had been designed by him to continue, Will multiply themselves to cause human problems.

God then knew by giving man this free will, man can or will abuse the rules, the laws in his book of "God's Law," the Bible. So God let it be known the first existence of the human race came about by Nature and God. Therefore we are all brothers and sisters under the first creation. The first creation will not bring about detriment and degeneracy. Because the first creation is widely spread by his creation. But the second creation of plan on earth will be a closer creation by man himself under man creation on earth. And this given will to man to multiply himself can cause destruction and degeneracy if mankind does not follow his command closely.

So God found a solution. The solution must be obeyed. Each birth will come about by a male and a female, and those pairs will be known as husbands and wives. They will also be known as mothers and fathers. The children of each pair will be known as brothers and sisters. That closeness of birth and production must not co-habit with each other. Other wise destruction and degeneracy will take its course in bringing about destruction to the human race. Therefore a record must be made and kept of all birth. So man implemented a record keeping of the births of the human race, "A birth" Record of all those birth under the above human production. During the early creating of the human race. There was no such thing as paper, or ink. It was the early primitive times. The messengers of God the almighty did not come to earth in the days of cave man. That is correct. Cave man knew nothing about "The Holy Bible," or revelation. It was not until God the Almighty sent his servants one after the other by the way of Human Being, with a special spirit in those human body. So as to give them spiritual guidance, such as revelation and inspiration. God's Bible follows after.

Now the above are know as the second brothers and sisters or the earthly production of brothers and sisters, the Bible has it when translated properly. So read your bible carefully. The human race was given proficiency at birth by God. Man's proficiency at birth lies in the Holy Bible." So if man do not read and follow the bible; he will never be able to function with true proficiency. The Bible is the greatest book that was written. There is no other book that can come close to it. The Bible has all the rules and laws pertaining to all functions of things, which created by man and God. It is God who gives man the will to create on earth so that man will have a perfect existence for himself. With the help of Nature and God.

This chapter can be looked upon as being the bridge to the Bible. So at times when I refer to sections which is in the Bible, and advised the reader to go to the bible. It's because, its' only a bridge to the bible, and the bible will take the reader further in depth of God's, do's and don'ts. I do not have to give you the reader, all of God do and the don'ts. It's all being written before by other messengers of God the Almighty.

# 35

## The Big Bang Theory

T HE ABOVE THEORY IS A Cosmic Egg, which was formed in the universe like other planets. It took thousand of years to form, and to travel while it was going through the motion of its maturity, and it kept travelling from the, higher hemisphere to the lower hemisphere which is known as earth's hemisphere, and earth gravity. So as to reached its final destination in order to give birth to earth. When it reached the earth gravity, by that time the cosmic egg was fully matured, it then came to a stop. Then it burst open, giving a big bang. It was loud, and then came the black smoke, which was gas, and other matters, which came out of the Cosmic Egg. All elements began to separate itself from the thick blanket of gas, which looked like smoke as it began to ascend into the cloud.

The above process continued for thousands of years. The black gas covered the entire earth's hemisphere. The area seemed like night. The moon or sun could not be penetrated through that dense gas. The formation of the gas and matter (elements) had formed a round ball in the earth gravity area where earth was to be formed. The rain continued to fall and started to form a belt, a circle around the gas and the elements and matter. Then after most of the gas had disappeared in the higher hemisphere. Mother Nature had continued to take her course in doing her job, time had passed and the rainwater which had formed a circle around the elements and the remaining gas, as a great amount of gas had gone. The rainwater, which was also trapped in its earth gravity area, had started to collect dust, which sent down by nature into the water in order to mix with some of the elements. So as to form mud, in order to turn to rock.

But before the rock was formed, the thick form of mud accumulated had engulfed the amount of gas and all of the various elements in the center of the mud in order to cook, and to (bake) until it was the correct time nature would bring about its changes in its process. While the cooking and baking continued, rock started to form. The rainwater started to give rise and later started to become the sea. Please do not forget what I had stated as being the time span of this formation, from (Cosmic Egg) to the (Earth Formation). The period was millions of years… not seven days like it's written in several (Bible or Bibles).

As the rock continued to form and changed from mud to rock. Then the rain became the sea. Then finally the mud disappeared and established the inferno. (The inferno) is a surface, a big ball of fire in the center of the earth's crust, which kept expanding as years went by. That is why we get volcano, which makes a vent, in the earth's crust through which molten rock (lava) rock fragments, gases ashes, are ejected from the earth's interior. A volcano is active while eruption takes place in the (inferno) but a volcano becomes dormant during a long period of inactivity when all activity has finally eased in the inferno chamber. The fire in that chamber never goes out or stops burning.

The big bang theory is the evolution, the starting of the Earths' formation. Not knowing about it, it's like eating an apple and not knowing what produce it or where it came from, but we just eat it. God wants us to know of the above theory, "Earth Formation." Because we will then be able to understand the Bible more, and therefore understand our existence and purpose in life, and the earth on which we live in, and walk upon. Because the above theory is before the bible as pointed out before. Also to learn right from wrong, as in the Bible.

Man has changed God's Bible and many things, which were sent down from heaven to earth by God, to his messengers' one after the other. The changes were made by many rulers so as to divert and deceived the under privilege and less learned ones, from God's law and rules. So the people who were ruled by those, who made the changes of the bibles, will be able to rule by subjection.

We shall return to the earth formation. By this time streams had formed as land started to grow, and spread from the water around the mud and rock, as it kept growing and spreading. The sea was expanding as well and becoming deeper and deeper. The earth's crust continued to grow out from between the water, which was the sea formation.

Then that major piece of land had grown to form a continent. That first land will be known, as the continent of Africa. That piece of land and the continent was to become the greatest piece of land, above all other lands. Nature and God had designed it to be the most important land in the "Earth World." Let no man, woman, or child, think or say different.

The African continent is where life of trees, animals, and Human Beings started. The exact area of the Garden of Eden was Ethiopia near to "Djibouti." This is why Ethiopia is mentioned in God's Bible, because of the importance of the area.

Like I've stated above. It's the land of the beginning of life! Respect it as being so, Mother Nature and God wants the entire world to know it. No where else life started! Let me say this now. I am not a preacher such as those who stand in a church preaching sermons or preaching the Bible, I do not consider myself as one of those. Now if I were to be one of those, I would have been ordained by the almighty to do that.

Now I consider myself as an Artist and a Spiritual Genius and a Writer. Because of the life in which I have lived before writing this Book, and while I am writing this Book. I also consider myself as a messenger of God in this 21st Century. So I try to write the best way I am capable of, for a third grade school dropout. I am proud of saying, "Dropout."

Let us understand the section where I've mentioned about the inferno being in the center of the Earth's Crust. It did not erupt to the earth's surface until the earth was fully formed and extending itself into various continents.

This chapter must be considered as being the Bridge to the Holy Bible. Before bibles came to earth, or before any of God messenger's came to earth as well, or the start of "Genesis." It's not been written like a bible or bibles. It's a brief account of the earth formation and the beginning of our earth. It's a crossover to the bible. It's called the Bridge to the Bible. By this time Stone age begun, because of the formation of rock growing, and spreading to form other continents. The Gas was still ascending into the clouds.

After which the ice age came to cool off the earth's surface. The ice age did not last for a long period, because of the geographical area, such as the "Equator." Where "Mother Nature" had chosen to start the advancement of all living things. Africa is the center point of the earth's crust. Also the hottest part of the earth/world. While the black smoke of gas was lifting into the air, the area was covered with thick dense black gas before it was all cleared up. Then the sun penetrated what little remaining gas was left.

The sun brought brightness. That was called Day. The land was still void and empty and peaceful. When the sun travels below the top of Earth, darkness starts to trail the sun. Then the early darkness is called the "Evening," then the full darkness comes "Night" one day is completed. This is a very important message, and description from God to me. So that I can pass it on to you in our Earth's World.

The Universe is an area, where all of the various planets are situated. Heaven is situated well above the universe. Heaven is a mighty Christian World. It's a world of spirits. The Angels, God, Mother Nature, and Jesus, all live and Dwelled in that Area, and the life there is completely different to our life here on earth.

All existing life is immortal and has a transcend life. They do not die, they live forever. The angels are not given a freedom of choices, such as we on earth were given. They also have a job to perform. If they were given a freedom like us to work or not to work at any given time, the earth would come to a stand still. Why? Because they have to attend to the various planets. The workings of planets are done by God and Angels, also Mother Nature. So what I am saying and describing. It is God who is inspiring me to say it in my writing of it all. God has pointed out that during the transformation of the cosmic egg, he God and Mother Nature was in Heaven, the Cosmic Egg was traveling to Earth's Gravity so as to give birth to earth, Mother Nature was in heaven, God pointed all which needs to be done can be done from Heaven, by them both. God also point out by saying to me, "I am not visible to anything which I have given life to. I make contact with my voice, dreams, also by inspiration." Those are three ways, when someone is inspired it's done by spiritual contact. "That is why I have given you my children, a spirit in your body from my spirit to your spirit, I'll be able to make contact, if you focus to me."

# 36

# The Beginning

I N THE BEGINNING MOTHER NATURE created the Heavens and the Earth. Now Earth was formed and empty. Darkness was lifted and the deep of darkness was now gone, and the spirits of "Nature and God" was hovering over the Garden. This was the time for Mother Nature to present the garden to Her son, God. This was the greatest of all creation unto our present time known to the human race. This is the transfer from Mother to Son "God." God was pleased to see what Mother Nature had blessed Him with. God knew it was time for Him to take over His duty from His Mother. He knew the land was ready to bring forth life on the soil.

Mother Nature then said to God. My son this is Your Land, now blessed Your land from East to West and from, North to South. Plant the seeds of all, which I have given onto You. I have created you with great wisdom.

I have created the heaven, the universe and now the Earth. Stand above the three of them all, which is of my creations. I am the ultimate, my son; you are now the ultimate as I created you. I my son was created with faults, but cannot remedy my faults. But I created you to remedy your faults or mistakes, and mine as well.

My son, I am kind with all which I have created, but I am not humble. That is why I created you with great kindness and humbleness. You have mercy, forbearance, and compassion. I do not have those qualities. As your mother, I named you, "God," Which means "Good." All needs to be done, is to remove one letter from the center of the word "Good," leaving you with three letters, the name that I gave you, "God" is good. Mother Nature continued to speak to God. "Now dress your garden, sows the seed of life, plants of all kind so as to feed all living things. The animals and birds shall have food from the plants which seed you have sown." Your seed of life is a Bacteria Element to produce life; it can also take life and cause death. There is good and bad bacteria. It's like good and evil. The good bacteria are like you with your name "God," from the Word "Good." The Evil side of Bacteria is the Evil side of your mother, you are to control it. God then started to create life in the Garden of Eden. Then came vegetation on that soil, plants, grass, trees of a vast variety, food to eat, fruits. Then a vast variety of animals, birds, fishes, snakes, etc. All of those things came into the Garden of Eden before human life was created. All living life (things), came about by various bacteria. That is how God produced life on earth. Plants have its' own bacteria, human and animals have their own bacteria as well. That was in the first creation by nature. The above was in the first creation of all living things. A foundation is of no value unless a building is built upon it. A building is impossible unless there is a foundation.

So the Old Testament and New Testament are essential to each other, so in actual fact the creation of earth's formation is important to the bible history. So that we can understand where we are and who we are in the world we're living in. So, we can have a better way of life and respect each other.

The Garden of Eden like I've stated before is "Africa," let no man say its not or was not, or have doubts about that. Africa is in the "Tremendous heat Zone," it is known as the Torrid Zone, the area of the earths' surface between the tropic of Cancer and the tropic of Capricorn, and divided by the equator. This area is where life was created at first by God. The Black African race was the first Human life to have born on this Earth Planet. Mother Nature continues to speak to her son, "God my son, you have created Lucifer, now he is you opponent, He was created for a very high position here in Heaven. You made Lucifer the seal of perfection, full of wisdom and perfect in Beauty. You have now decided to put him in the Garden of Eden." That is why I have created You to deal with My failings, and the cruel elements of My creation. You also have the ability to remedy all mistakes that you may make, and I have made as well. You my son I know will implement ways so as to have full control. This section of the Garden of Eden I cannot compromise to do God's work and wishes. He inspired me not to do so therefore I will not. God pointed to me that millions of people of my race will feel ashamed to accept the valid and true point which I am about to make. Its not a fact that we black people should be ashamed of. It's just one of those things which God had to do with the Life and destiny of the Human race. Millions of people may not have been aware of, or have taken into consideration.

I have pointed out that Africa is the Garden of Eden, and it was the first birthplace of the Human Race. The African race was the first to have been born on God's earth as I've pointed out before several times. God then blessed everything in the garden, which Mother Nature and He God had created in His garden, and was given a life; everything was blessed one after the other, in the garden. God then selected a male and female, and then named them, Adam and Eve. The two people, Adam and Eve were Black Africans. The two were chosen by God as a special pair. Messengers from God did not come down from heaven to earth. So as to bring God's manual, "The Holy Bible." God's rules and laws were still in heaven, and were not fully written and completed. Lucifer was a torment and was causing diversion around the Almighty. That was why the bible was late into arriving on earth. With the do and don'ts. God did not intend to create an opposition, When He decided to create Lucifer. God was creating an assistant to help him. Lucifer was to be God right hand man. A very high position in heaven.

Thus says The Lord God "You were the seal of perfection, and in Beauty, you were perfect in your ways from the day you were created, till iniquity was found in you." Lucifer had known almost everything about what God had written in His Bible. Which the Human Race was guided by and had to follow. Also the fact that God had decided to give the human race a freedom of choice, so as to choose. So Lucifer was well ahead of knowing God's plan. But he did not know God's entire plan. Also that God can remedy mistakes by the wink of an eye. Nature had given God lots of wisdom. Lucifer did not have half of God's wisdom, but Lucifer thought he did, and was of the impression that he was on the same level as God. God did give us freedom of will. Animals can eat each other, also the fish in the sea can eat each other. Human beings will kill each other as well because of that free will given to all living things. God also said to Lucifer, "You are a great deceiver and a scum, along with those whom you impress and lead them to follow. You and those who think you are the greatest in heaven disrupt the holiness here. I shall remove you and put you in your own world, and there you shall serve me well until "Dooms Day". God removed Lucifer's spirit from heaven and sent him down in the garden. The spirits of God disciples or messengers was not on earth before Lucifer. So Lucifer was sent by the way of spirit to join Adam and Eve, also the others in the Garden. By this time he had decided to corrupt the life in the garden, by starting with Eve. Now don't forget God the Almighty had given every animal, especially the Human Animal the greatest gift of all gifts. It's the Gift of stimulation. I will take you to another which gives you a further meaning of "Stimulation," Lucifer decided to attack God and all mankind, "By going after Eve, and the others in the Garden of Eden, and using the greatest gift given to man and woman, 'Sex.' That is the greatest stimulation, which was given by God to the human race, and other animal life. So lets' set the record straight once and for all. God wants it to be done. Eve did not eat an apple. It was fools who said that in the bible. Trying to be modest. Now getting back to corrupting the garden by using sex, the greatest stimulation. Which will produce mankind. Lets' take the AIDS Virus as one example. I can give you many examples. But I will not, the Book have to finish quickly, God wants me to finish it quickly. The reason why God stated marriage before sex, it was because of documentation and record keeping amongst the Birth of the human race. So as to stop degeneracy amongst the birth of people, otherwise the human race will deteriorate. That was God's way to stop degeneracy, of brother going with sister, father and mothers going with their own children, etc. Lucifer knew all of the above things while he was in heaven. So finally Lucifer decided to seduce Eve, and used sex as his main tool. Lucifer seduces Eve into having sex with him, outside of marriage. He entice Eve while chasing her all around the Garden and around the various trees. Until Eve became tired and was out of breath. She then gave into Lucifer after she fell onto the ground. After Lucifer completed his act. Eve later went to Adam and persuaded Adam into having sex with her. Adam was actually seduced by Eve because he was totally against it. But Eve did not give up; she kept on and on and broke down his defense by getting through to the weaker side of man with the help of Lucifer. Then she finally broke him down. Like a man breaking down a wild horse. A woman can easily do that to the opposite sex. An example, "like Samson and Delilah." By this time Lucifer became like a mad man, ranting and raving while running about in a circle and grunting sexually as he dance about.

By this time some of the animal joined in with their sexual performances. God had become disgusted with the sight below him. It was a sight for sore-eyes. While God was giving me the inspiration to write the above. I myself became disgusted with what the human race can do in the eyes of God. So I do know the way in which God had felt. But one thing I can say, it was not everyone who took part with Lucifer and his followers, God showed me that while writing the above. At the end of the seven days, and seven nights peace and calm came into the Garden of Eden. The thunder and lightening, and everything else came to a dead stop. A cursed was already fallen upon the first piece of land. Time had passed by, no rain, no thunder, no lightening, came upon the earth's surface. God said to me, "get up and go into your bedroom, and look upon the wall where your calendar is kept, and check the month, the day, the year," I did as I was told. I knew it was not the "Devil" who was dealing with me, but it was "God." The reason I know it was not the devil, Satan. Because while dealing with God and writing this book, God has given me a special knowledge, and feeling and awareness when he focuses on to me. So I've learned the difference between the two of them. Do not forget. I am a "Spiritual Genius," and to be of such, one will be given a special gift by God so as to do His job. I will get back to the guidance. We the human race on earth must try to understand that millions of us do have weak spirits, and because of that we do not focus to the outer realm which is where Jesus, and God the Father along with the angels are. Now the other workers of God are known as God's Disciples. Satan then capitalized on our weak spirit and wangle and dangles us against each other. Also along with the "Dead" which was cast back on to Earth by God so as to redeem themselves. Therefore as one can see and understand it is not an easy task which God has in fighting Satan. We have to assist

God in fighting Satan, by leaning and always focusing to Jesus and God. We add our spirits to the spirit of Satan, and that which gives Him more and more strength.

The start of Genesis, and the beginning of God's messengers who will bring the word and guidance to mankind on Earth no matter where the earth's crust may start and end. We are to share the earth's minerals amongst nations of the Human race. The minerals belong to each and everyone. No one man has the Godly right to stake any claims on the earth minerals, nature and God produce it for all of the animal life, and human life. It must be shared willingly and equally and not unjustly. We are to respect each other no matter of colour or race. No man or woman should own more soil, lake, river, water to drink, or things from out of the earth's crust more than another. We are to share the gifts from God. Pick up your bible and read it. You can bring about changes before the "Armageddon" otherwise the world shall perish. We in the World today do not understand that we are presently living in the start of the "Armageddon." The devil has been gathering nations to fight against each other. They are spirits of the Devil, which go out to Rulers, and Kings on earth, gathering people for Satan, to go into battle against each other, the meeting ground of the battle of the Armageddon, that is to come. But He will liberate his land and the chosen people. Read and follow your Bible carefully, towards Armageddon. "Then I shall remove the cursed," say's the Lord. I will discuss earth further. Satan had corrupted earth immensely from the time his spirit was sent down from heaven into the Garden of Eden, "Africa." He caused the black race to suffer by the way of great sacrilege under the hands of "God." Earth was designed to be the "Second Heaven" and not the earth as we called it or accept it to be. Heaven is the first, and the second was to be link-up with the first. God had designed it where we would have been able to travel spiritually from one place to the other, and live in Harmony. Also these are more facts; "God" wants me to bring them to your attention. The earth was intended to be the "Second Heaven," this was decided by God before Satan; "Lucifer" the Devil spirit was sent down from heaven. During the existence of the second world if it had come about. Also it was God's decision so that we on earth would live to the age such as Adam, 930 years and Noah, 950 years before they died.

Because of mankind disobedience at the time, God said, "I will not allow people to live long like Adam and Noah." From now on mankind will not be allowed to live more that 120 years." Because God saw that some of his creation was faulty, and not going the way He, God had intended for the world and earth to be. So He said, "From the time of me creating Lucifer to this present time, I am sorry that I ever made them, and put them on the Earth." He said, "I will wipe out these people I have created, and also the animals and the birds, because I am sorry that I ever made any of them." Now, God created a son who is known as Jesus to take the place of Lucifer after he was sent to earth. God described Lucifer which is 'Satan,' in God's word as "The Prince of this World." The world which God was referring to at that time was Heaven, where God and Lucifer were at the time, not Earth. God said, "Not earth below, Heaven the first, and only the first Heaven. So us here on our earth can see and understand that Satan was 'the Arch-Angel', 'The Prince of Heaven.' Such a position which God had placed Lucifer was a high one, the top of all other Angels.

Now, let me go a bit further with this example. Just imagine that a man has a factory. He is the boss and owner of the factory, That is God. The Boss decided to employ a man as his foreman. He says to the Foreman, "You, I make foreman, because I trust you. Whenever I am here, you'll be the foreman, when I'm not here you will be the boss.

You will see everything in order, and my business keeps going smooth. I trust you, and Love you." After a while, the boss found out that the foreman was getting over-ambitious- first, he started causing dissident among the workers, and the boss in the factory. The foreman started to tell the workers that the boss was only using them, and that He the boss was getting everything and they were getting next to nothing getting "chicken feed.' In a short time the boss found out that the foreman was conspiring with some of the workers to start a rebellion against Him. So what the boss did was simple, He fired the foreman and all of his followers. This is what happened; Lucifer did that while he was in Heaven. God had so loved Lucifer, that he put him in charge of certain things in Heaven. Lucifer was exonerated from Heaven. Jesus was not just close to God, but God chose Him as His son, who was sent by His Father from Heaven to Earth. His mission was to preach the Gospels, and to be offered as a sacrifice for the redemption of mankind sins. Jesus blood was spilled by others, and it was not Him (Jesus) who shed his own blood.

The Jews was so fortunate to have Jesus so close, but instead of listening and obeying his teaching, they condemned Him. God wants the world to wake up, and pay heed to take notice, as to what is happening all over the world, 'the Earth'. The destruction which Satan has brought upon us ever since he came to earth. God said. "See it before it's too late." "For too late shall be the cry."

This Section of God's inspiration to me was very frightening at the time. The "Almighty" was in actuality telling me of the Tremendous Powers and influences the Devil Satan have on this Planet Earth.

I must have had a difficult time with God as He explained to me that I must tell the world of Lucifer's Great Powers and his deceitful ways. Let me tell you it is quite obvious that if the Black Race was the first on Planet Earth, and by casting Lucifer from his Heaven above into the Garden of Eden, who could he be, not a Black man and a Black Spirit at the time. I can tell you the reader it was not easy for me , for a long time I was very fearful of what I was instructed to say to the world. "That Lucifer was Black man." What would most Black people do to me for saying that, would amount to slaughter (of me). At first I bluntly refused God's wishes, when He (God) shouted at me, "I command you; you are to do as I command!" "And let there be no compromise!" Once again reader try to understand and see that Lucifer's Powers are so extreme that he can appear in the form of someone or something good, and deceive the ordinary and average person.

Lean on me while reading your Bible and you will be saved from the bottom of the Pit on Dooms Day.

# 37

# *Spirit and Soul*

LET ME DEFINE A SPIRIT and soul. These two entities are not the same. The spirit and soul are totally entirely different from each other. They each have their own purpose and duties. There are various types of spirits. I have already discussed about "The Holy Spirit" but I will refer to the heavenly spirit at times while dealing with spirits. A "Jumbie" as it's called here in Guyana, a ghost, a demon, and a spiritual life. That life is known as a transient life. That life is very weird, it's air, wind, images, it moves swiftly and it stays no one place for a long period. It is regarded as separate from matter. The heavenly spirit is completely different to all other spirits. The life in heaven is a high Christian life. Among spirits they are immortal spirits dwelling amongst each other. They perform their duties by spiritual contract. God is the leader of all heavenly spirits. The duties of God is vast, God has three worlds to control, Heaven, the universe and earth. Let me point out that nature stands behind God. Whatever God and his disciple's need, nature will provide Him with. Nature also issues God a will as well.

Now getting back to spirits, when a person dies, they became a spirit being, so we on earth have never consider what becomes of all those spirits? Well it is simple; the spirit goes through a chain reaction, controlled by God and the devil.

Spirits are good and bad. The spirits on earth are as follows, the human spirit, this is a very important spirit above all other earthly spirits. That human spirit is assigned to all human beings at birth, not before. A baby in the mother's womb would not be assigned a spirit; it will be protected by the mother's spirit. But upon its birth God will assign a spirit to that child. The spirit may be a reincarnation of one of the child's past generation or close relative willing His spirits to man. That is God's cycle in God would also will some spirits to the devil. When the spirit is cast back to hell on earth. The hell section on earth is controlled by the same spirits like to serve the Devil and not God. Do not forget we have a free will of choice. A person may choose to steal and not work, that is because of your free will. So choosing to steal would be your personal choice. But if you go by God's statement, "By the sweat of thy brow you shall eat bread," which is translated, you shall eat by working and sweating.

The spirits controlled by the devil is made to communicate with the living with the help of a third party, a medium.

The life principle, especially in mankind, is regarded as inheritance of the breath "or as infused" by a deity, same as the soul (sense 1) 2. The thinking, motivation, feeling part of man, often as distinguished from the human body, mind, and intelligence. 3. Lives, will consciousness, though and so on, regarded as separate from matter. 4. A supernatural being, especially one thought of as hunting or possessing a person or house.

The human soul, let us not be misguided the human body has two souls, its upper soul and its lower soul. The upper soul sits above the lower soul and the lower soul is there to condense bad memory. The spirit sits on top of the upper soul. Like a bird in a birdcage, the soul is an entity, which is regarded as being the immortal or spiritual part of the person. There in an old saying and it's a fact, it is said that a male could not bear the pain which a woman endures while giving birth to a child. The severity of pain or bad incidents, which can cause a person to be fearful or go mad, is lodged in the lower soul. Sometimes the Almighty will store incidents in the lower soul, until he is ready to resurrect them. Had it not been for the lower soul the female would not attempt to go through the physical action to conceive a second child. The pain of the first child is condensed when it enters the lower soul. Another example, if a person is in the process of hammering a nail and the hammer misses the nail while holding the nail and strikes the finger or hand. That pain rushes to the lower soul and is quickly condensed and the person can pick up a second nail and continue his hammering. The same applies to striking a match to light a fire and being burnt in the process. A second attempt will be made to light the fire.

The upper soul, which is closest to and is under the human spirit, serves as a distinct center and a spiritual protection of the two souls, and its memory contents. One must bear in mind that the human spirit do leave the human body in order to travel during one's sleep at night and day. The human spirit will only remove from the two souls during sleep. The human body cuts off section of the body during this time. The human body during sleep, the brain closes off itself from the spirit and the two souls. It is then, and only then, that the spirit can leave and wander. While the spirit is away from the human soul and body, the soul and brain becomes disconnected. The brain will not function correctly without the spirit being in its place, sitting above the souls. The human needs the spirit to be where it belongs and to have that spiritual connection so as to function the way it should.

The spirit is then protected closely by the Almighty so as not to be interfered with by Lucifer, while it is roaming and picking up data to take back to the human while the human is asleep. The data will then be transmitted to the human brain while the brain is asleep. The data will then become a dream while the brain is still at rest or asleep. During the transmission of the data the spirit will sit above the upper soul and the processing of the data will be selected and separated by God and the spirit. The data subject that is not good for the human, will then be separated and be directed to the lower soul, and the remainder will then be transmitted to the brain as a dream by God and spirit. That is why it is said or believed that when one has a dream but cannot remember that dream fully do not force yourself to remember your dream or a part of that dream.

The absence of the dream or part of the full dream comes about by the separation of the condensing process by the souls. God and the human spirit will be the ones who will make the final choice of what will be transmitted to souls and brain as a dream. Bad subjects and images, which is taken back to the human, if not filtered and separated, will derange that human brain; God may not desire that at the time.

For example, you may have a dream of falling from great heights, but one would never complete the falling and hit the ground. That impact of hitting the ground will awaken the brain with great fear and shock. The person will then awake by the fear of the impact of landing on the ground.

Lucifer is the most evil of spirits. It is Lucifer who controls all evil spirits on earth. The evil spirits are the ones, which are not rested and are the spirit which God has cast back onto the earth after going to heaven the third time.

I will refer to the Bible when Jesus said to Nicodemus, "Except a man to be born again he cannot see the Kingdom of God." John 3.3 Now people are asking the same question today that Nicodemus asked, "How can a man be born again when he is old?" What is it? What does it mean? But Jesus said to him again, "Marvel not that I said unto thee. Ye must be born again." John 3:7.

Jesus and John, quotation is a fact. This is another quote, the new birth, what effect has it on the person that receives it? "Therefore, if any man be in Christ, he is a new creature, old things have passed away, behold, all things have become new" II Cor. 5:17. To be born again as it was stated in one of God's ruling, we are given three births by God in order to redeem from sins committed. This is the way God has it to be. When all babies are born the human spirit is implanted into a child at birth. At the end of one's first life, when that person dies, that spirit goes to the Almighty to answer for his or her sins committed while was on earth. That is known as to, "face redemption".

The second birth is then given so as to redeem the first sins (to deliver from sins and its penalties, as by a sacrifice made for the sinner) that is the meaning of redeem.

Its penalties for the sins committed during the life of the spirit and human being on earth. The casting back of second time of that spirit on earth will pass on to a member or an ancestor of the first spirit and human being. This second spirit can help to change the sentence from being legacy amongst the ancestor or ancestors. It applies just like I've pointed out before.

The third birth applies the same as the second birth to redeem. If redemption is not exercised furring the third birth, then the spirit will be removed from the cycle. The spirit will then be sent back on earth to become haunted and to wander. This haunted spirit becomes an evil spirit, an evil ghost. The spirit was evil during its existence on earth. The spirit becomes Lucifer's servant.

www.ingramcontent.com/pod-product-compliance
Lightning Source LLC
Chambersburg PA
CBHW020846090426
42736CB00008B/258